Beckett and D

Continuum Literary Studies Series
Also available in the series:

Beckett and Decay

Kathryn White

continuum

Continuum International Publishing Group

The Tower Building   80 Maiden Lane, Suite 704

11 York Road   New York

London SE1 7NX   NY 10038

www.continuumbooks.com

British Library Cataloguing-in-Publication Data
A catalogue record for this book is available from the British Library.

ISBN: PB: 978-1-4411-1512-6

Library of Congress Cataloging-in-Publication Data
A catalog record for this book is available from the Library of Congress.

Typeset by Newgen Imaging Systems Pvt Ltd, Chennai, India
Printed and bound in Great Britain by MPG Biddles Ltd, King's Lynn, Norfolk

For Mum and Dad – with love

Contents

Acknowledgements

I wish to thank Gerald Macklin for his enormous support and invaluable help during my research for this book. The many wonderful conversations that we had about Beckett's work inspired many of the points raised in this study.

I am grateful to James Knowlson who answered questions regarding Beckett's 'Sounds', 'Still 3' and *Breath*. I wish to acknowledge Julian A. Garforth, whose help in locating sources was greatly appreciated, and Calder Publications who helped to provide clarification on numerous points. Special thanks go to the library staff at the University of Ulster, and to the staff of the Beckett archive at Reading.

Acknowledgements are due to the publishers Faber and Faber Ltd for their permission to print extracts from Beckett's *The Complete Dramatic Works* (1990), and also to Grove/Atlantic, Inc. for permission to use extracts from: *How It Is* by Samuel Beckett. Copyright © 1964 by Grove Press, Inc. Used by permission of Grove/Atlantic, Inc. *Happy Days* by Samuel Beckett. Copyright © 1961 by Grove Press, Inc. Used by permission of Grove/Atlantic, Inc. *Endgame and Act Without Words* by Samuel Beckett. Copyright © 1958 by Grove Press, Inc. Used by permission of Grove/Atlantic, Inc. *Poems, Short Fiction, Criticism, Vol IV of The Grove Centenary Edition* by Samuel Beckett. Copyright © 2006 by the Estate of Samuel Beckett. Used by permission of Grove/Atlantic, Inc. *Watt* by Samuel Beckett. Copyright © 1953 by Samuel Beckett. Used by permission of Grove/Atlantic, Inc. *Murphy* by Samuel Beckett. Copyright © 1957 by Grove Press, Inc. Used by permission of Grove/Atlantic, Inc. *Disjecta* by Samuel Beckett. Copyright © 1984 by Grove Press, Inc. Used by permission of Grove/Atlantic, Inc. *Collected Shorter Plays* by Samuel Beckett. Copyright © 1984 by Samuel Beckett. Used by permission of Grove/Atlantic, Inc. *Waiting for Godot* by Samuel Beckett. Copyright © 1954 by Grove Press, Inc. Copyright © renewed 1984 by Samuel Beckett. Used by permission of Grove/Atlantic, Inc. *Complete Short Prose* by Samuel Beckett. Copyright © 1995 by the Estate of Samuel Beckett. Used by permission of Grove/Atlantic, Inc. *Three Novels* by Samuel Beckett. Copyright © 1955, 1956, 1958 by Grove Press, Inc. Used by permission of Grove/Atlantic, Inc. *Nohow On* by Samuel Beckett: *Company* Copyright © 1980 by Samuel Beckett. *Ill Seen Ill Said* Copyright © 1981 by Samuel Beckett. *Worstward Ho* Copyright © 1983 by Samuel Beckett. Used by permission of Grove/Atlantic, Inc.

Excerpts from Samuel Beckett's letters of 6 September 1959 and 19 November 1963 to Alan Schneider © The Estate of Samuel Beckett reproduced by kind permission of the Estate of Samuel Beckett c/o Rosica Colin Limited, London.

Extracts from the Authorized Version of the Bible (The King James Bible), the rights in which are vested in the Crown, are reproduced by permission of the Crown's Patentee, Cambridge University Press.

Finally, I am most grateful for the encouragement of my family, friends and colleagues, without which this book may not have been realized.

Introduction

who may tell the tale
of the old man?
weigh absence in a scale?
mete want with a span?
the sum assess
of the world's woes?
nothingness
in words enclose?

Tailpiece

The subject of decay is paramount in Beckett's work, and it manifests itself in various ways through theme and artistic form. The word *decay* is often used by critics in general reference to Beckett's thematic emphasis and philosophical outlook. However, this subject has not been widely explored from the premise that it is the fundamental core of Beckett's work, dominating the work thematically, linguistically and artistically. Of course, it must be noted that this exploration of the theme of decay in Beckett's work is by no means a study in negativity in relation to Beckett's prose or drama. This study is not a prejudicial examination of the Beckett canon, as the theme of decay, paradoxically, facilitates an investigation into the richness of Beckett's artistic and linguistic style.

Often people, who are not completely understanding of Beckett's oeuvre, work from the presupposition that he is a depressing writer, whose bleak outlook on the world offers audiences and readers a negativity which holds little appeal in some (literary) circles. It is true that Beckett is not a writer who celebrates life and language. He is, however, a writer who confronts the realities of existence through a language that he himself deems to be ultimately ineffectual. And, as will be illustrated throughout this study, Beckett's language is, in fact, a language of poetic beauty and linguistic innovation. Hence, the theme of decay is illustrated through a language that is aesthetically beautiful; and it is here that the paradox lies.

Beckett's world of desolation and despair can be difficult to confront because it does encapsulate 'how it is' to be alive. However, to describe his work as depressing is to fail to appreciate the truthfulness of his message, the moving quality of his words and, of course, the comic element in his work, which is found in both the drama and fiction. Beckett confronts the futility of existence and the tragedy of the human condition, areas which have received much critical attention; however, his corpus of work must surely be seen as a manual for coping with life, as we come to acknowledge the reality of the words from *Endgame* that 'The end is in the beginning and yet you go on' (Beckett 1990: 126). As Knowlson says, Beckett conveys 'a view of life which sees birth as intimately connected with suffering and death and which sees life as a painful road to be trod' (1997: 2). And Beckett illustrates the strength of 'spirit' which keeps us treading that painful road. Therefore, despite the degeneration which dominates the Beckettian world, the characters continue onwards because they have no alternative but to go on.

Everything in Beckett's world appears to be in decline and this erosion affects the characters physically and emotionally. Hence, we see characters in dustbins and urns; images of torsos; heads and mouths trapped in environments which are, similarly, subject to sterility and deterioration. However, this study also investigates Beckett's representation of the mind, and how it functions in a world that is subject to decay, trapped within a body that is essentially perishing. And finally, it explores Beckett's use of language and his ability to represent degeneration through words, which are themselves flawed.

Beckett illustrates the chaos of existence and so he had to adopt a style of writing which would adequately convey the shapelessness of life. Hence, he had to give 'form' to formlessness through a language which, itself, appeared to have no form, but which was meticulously crafted. Speaking with Tom F. Driver, Beckett 'said':

> What I am saying does not mean that there will henceforth be no form in art. It only means that there will be new form, and that this form will be of such a type that it admits the chaos and does not try to say that the chaos is really something else. The form and the chaos remain separate. The latter is not reduced to the former. That is why the form itself becomes a preoccupation, because it exists as a problem separate from the material it accommodates. To find a form that accommodates the mess, that is the task of the artist now. (Driver (1961) quoted here from Graver and Federman (1979: 219))[1]

The artist creates 'form' where none exists, as art is the only consolation achievable from an otherwise derelict world. The chaos and mess, to which Beckett refers, are the terms used to describe the absurdity of existence and the failure of man. Beckett was well aware of the realities of life, that in life there exists only death, and from the moment of birth we are essentially 'Dying on' (Beckett 1990: 426). Knowlson speaks of Beckett's 'early fascination with the mineral, with things dying and decaying, with petrification' (1997: 29). He states that Beckett 'linked this interest with Sigmund Freud's view that human beings have a prebirth nostalgia to return to the mineral state' (Knowlson 1997: 29).

This obsession with decay, which manifested itself in Beckett's early life, would stay with him, dominating his work from the beginning until the end, and prompting him to find a form that would 'accommodate the mess'. This study therefore explores the importance of both theme and form in Beckett's work, and it shall be considered whether Beckett will, in future generations, be remembered for his representation of existence or his innovations in language.

The study is divided into three Parts. Part I explores Beckett's representation of physical decay, Part II examines mental erosion and spiritual attrition, and finally Part III investigates linguistic and artistic contraction. This three-part structure allows intensive examination of the major components in Beckett's work, from the premise that they are linked and dominated by the theme of decay. Both the drama and the prose work are examined in each chapter (with the exception of 10 and 11) in order to ascertain a clear indication of how Beckett incorporates similar themes in both mediums. The examination of both prose and drama facilitates a more comprehensive study of the theme of decay, and allows a clear interpretation of Beckett's writing within the confines of each chapter heading.

Part I, entitled *Physical Decay*, focuses primarily on the human condition, examining how the body is pre-disposed to failure from the moment of birth. Beckett presents the body as a hindrance, an inadequate machine which will ultimately break down. To be physical is to suffer, and Beckett illustrates the pain of existence, denying us the possibility that death may provide a release. This part also explores how Beckett's landscapes exemplify the degeneration of his characters.

Chapter 1 introduces Beckett's preoccupation with the failings of the physical body, and examines how Beckett's characters are limited because they are physical beings. Perfection does not exist in the Beckettian world and, hence, we acknowledge how each of the characters suffers because of the inadequacy of the human body. This chapter examines how Beckett presents the body as being subject to degeneration, and how from the moment of birth we, essentially, begin to decline. We are all *de facto* handicapped, it is a universal truth, and Beckett illustrates the imperfections of the human body and its limitations, and portrays his wonderment at the human capacity for going on, despite the great physical adversity that we face. Molloy says that, 'To decompose is to live too' (Beckett 1994: 25), and Beckett illustrates this decomposition, portraying the body as physical wreckage.

Beckett's representation of the aged is a horrific study of the implications of growing old, as he presents the gradual atrophy of the body caused by the passing of time. Hence the second chapter investigates Beckett's representation of the aged from a corporeal perspective, examining how Beckett illustrates the ageing body, and investigating how the characters deal with the condition of being old; characters such as Maddy Rooney, whose advance in years and lack of physical strength prompt her to declare – 'Oh let me just flop down flat on the road like a big fat jelly out of a bowl and never move again!' (Beckett 1990: 174). Beckett presents the twilight years as horrific, as the diminution of the life force is coupled with isolation and past regrets. We witness how the body and mind are often at odds, as the body is failing but the mind is still active, very much aware of the physical changes that are taking place, and unable to prevent degeneration.

Chapter 3 turns away from Beckett's depiction of the body, and investigates his landscapes as a reflection of our corporeal disintegration. The landscapes may be described as apocalyptic, as the natural world is presented in a state of degeneration and corrosion takes precedence over vitality. This part engages with issues such as Beckett's preoccupation with monochromatic scenes, the lack of colour, which dominates his world, and the sterility, and fragility of the environment. It examines why everything in the Beckettian world appears subject to decline, and illustrates how the environment provides confirmation of the degeneration of the characters, with the external erosion emulating their inner decay. Beckett's characters appear to linger somewhere between life and death, illustrating the fragility of life, and conveying the reality that we are all scarcely alive. Chapter 4 investigates Beckett's representation of death, and questions whether death provides termination. Life appears temporary, but death is not always a fleeting experience, and so Beckett forces us to re-conceptualize death, suggesting that even though the body may die, we cannot be sure if the consciousness discontinues. This chapter examines Beckett's depiction of death as a process, and illustrates how, and why, Beckett conveys death as a physical and mental experience, with bodily death and mental death not necessarily being simultaneous. It, therefore, serves as a bridging chapter, as it engages with mental processes, raising questions that are investigated further in the following part.

Part II, *Mental Decline and Spiritual Attrition*, explores Beckett's representation of the mind and how, similar to the body, it too is prone to deterioration. Beckett illustrates the Cartesian dualism of body and mind throughout his work, and hence this part focuses fundamentally on the workings of the mind, investigating the implications of memory, for example. Here we investigate mental weariness, examining how the inability to comprehend life often results in tiredness of mind. Insanity is also explored, illustrating how Beckett re-conceptualizes mental disorders. Part II also investigates 'the ebbing spirit', examining the 'spiritual' element of existence, as opposed to the physical and mental components.

In Beckett's work memory appears to serve as a negative influence, as the characters cannot escape the past, nor alleviate the pain associated with it.

Characters often idealize memories and, at times, feel compelled to invent memories in an attempt, perhaps, to eradicate the pain of past experience, and thus reduce the suffering of present existence. Chapter 5 explores the concept of voluntary and involuntary memory, examining why Beckett refrains from idealizing memory, forcing one to conceive of it as being a negative influence within the mind, as it is connected to suffering and psychological anguish.

The sixth chapter is an examination of mental weariness. It investigates how the effects of time on the mind, coupled with the harshness of existence, produces mental fatigue in characters who are plagued with isolation and cannot prevent rumination. Beckett illustrates that old age is, perhaps, not defined by the number of years lived, but is, instead, determined by one's mental condition. The inability to stop thinking ultimately results in the mental weariness that is experienced by many of the characters. This chapter explores how tiredness of mind can produce a negative impact on the body, causing premature ageing and feelings of dejection which may ultimately facilitate mental breakdown. Hence Chapter 7 engages with the issues of insanity and mental disorders which are prevalent in Beckett's work. Conventional definitions of insanity no longer apply, as Beckett offers an inversion of the general perception of madness, illustrating that sanity and insanity are not polar opposites and that madness is not, necessarily, a negative state of mind.

Chapter 8 moves away from the mind and looks closely at spiritual attrition and decline. Beckett's characters possess an inner strength which keeps them continuing in spite of the arduousness of the journey. This chapter investigates how the weariness of living eventually erodes the spirit, examining how the characters function once the will to live has left them. The futility of existence and a lack of hope forces the spirit to decline gradually, until the disillusionment with life eventually causes the spirit to die and one collapses under the monotony of living. This chapter also engages with the possibility that bodily death and mental death must be joined with spiritual death if one is to achieve complete termination, assuming that complete termination can, indeed, be achieved.

Part III, entitled *Death of the Word*, examines Beckett's form and style of writing, and explores the idea that 'decay' is to be found in the language itself, as we recognize that words are pre-disposed to failure. It appears that Beckett endeavours to write language out of existence in an attempt to locate silence. This part focuses on Beckett's shorter works, examining how he endeavoured to find a 'form' for formlessness. We witness how Beckett takes language to its extremes, forcing it to acknowledge its own futility. And we see how he, with the use of neologisms and linguistic inventiveness, succeeds in creating new genres, which attempt to express silence. This final part examines the poetic beauty of Beckett's 'dying' words.

Chapter 9 looks at Beckett's desire to write words out of existence, as he recognized the impossibility of successful artistic expression, as words, similar to everything in life, are prone to failure. It is used to establish theories and pose questions on the subject of linguistic and artistic contraction, theories that are investigated further in the following chapters, and aims to identify the concept of the 'decay of language'.

Chapter 10 builds on the previous chapter, examining how form is as fundamental as content. This chapter is structured differently from earlier chapters, as it focuses solely on the shorter drama, investigating how the involvement of non-linguistic elements, such as music, serves to challenge language, forcing it to acknowledge its own ineptitude. Beckett's 'dramaticules' convey a linguistic crisis, as they illustrate the difficulty of expression and the degenerative nature of the word. We witness how everything becomes pared down, as Beckett endeavours to create new forms of drama that are essentially meta-linguistic and illustrate the arduousness of the creative process. And the following chapter examines the linguistic and artistic contraction found in the shorter prose fiction, investigating how conventional narrative is discarded in favour of a new style of writing, which Beckett describes as the 'literature of the unword' (Beckett 1983: 173). These are experimental fictions designed to capture the formlessness of experience and in these shorter texts we witness an increasing poeticization of the language which appears to be a direct result of the reductionism. The shorter prose fictions illustrate the degenerative nature of language, as with 'worsening words' (Beckett 1999a: 29), Beckett endeavours to write words out of existence. The final chapter looks at Beckett's preoccupation with voices, ghosts and silence. It examines the themes of isolation and loss, investigating the probability that we are all in fact alone, and explores Beckett's determination to depict the void and attain silence. This world of 'shades' illustrates Beckett's increasing resolve to escape the burden of language, as everything appears subject to decay and we witness the tragedy and death of language itself. We witness how Beckett captures the evanescence of life and language, and consider whether the supreme aesthetic moment is attained in the expression of 'nothing'.

As this study engages with issues such as Beckett's depiction of the physical, his approach to mental conditions, and his innovations in language and form, which are all dominated by the theme of decay, we recognize the aspiration of the writer who attempted to 'fail better' by illustrating the degenerative nature of life and language simultaneously.

Part I

Physical Decay

Chapter 1

The Body Infirm

The end is in the beginning and yet you go on.

Endgame

Physical handicaps, diseases and affliction are prevalent throughout Beckett's work, and his characters frequently endure some form of physical impediment. It is necessary to examine these afflictions, as they provide a stepping-stone into other areas of physical and mental decay. The afflictions which will be analysed in this section should be viewed as limitations that affect the characters' physical being, making their lives more difficult to endure and their struggle onwards more painful. Beckett magnifies the infirmities that affect us all; hence, this amplification of physical malaise enables us to relate to the characters, as we recognize that their pain is an illustrated intensification of our own suffering. Beckett's representation of the reality of the human condition, found in the drama and the prose fictions, forces us to acknowledge the inadequacy of the physical body and recognize its inevitable failure.

Published in French in 1952, *Waiting for Godot*, which Beckett classified as a tragi-comedy, is a useful starting point from which to examine the implications of being physically infirm, and the profound influence these afflictions have on the characters' lives. Our initial reaction to Act One would be to state that, although the characters do have minor ailments, their conditions are not severe enough to describe them as being physically disabled. However, as one delves more deeply into the problems that the characters suffer from, one quickly becomes aware that these 'minor' ailments undoubtedly hinder their day-to-day existence. For Beckett, to have physical being at all is to be in a sense handicapped, as one is trapped in the physical machine that is the body. Hence, the Cartesian dualism is highlighted, as the body is in fact a degenerating vehicle that houses the, all too often, imperfect mind.

It is evident that Estragon suffers from sore feet, and when we first see him he is endeavouring to remove his boot, in an attempt to provide relief from the pain and misery that he endures everyday from this affliction. Although many people would not describe his condition as serious, it is necessary to

view it in the proper context. Perhaps to someone else the problem of having painful feet would not be a great inconvenience, but we must remember
that Estragon is a wanderer, like so many of Beckett's characters. Therefore
his condition limits his movements, and he rarely finds relief, as his journey
appears never-ending. Godot never comes, therefore Estragon never reaches
a safe place where he can rest and recuperate, and without rest his problem
can never heal.

Similarly Vladimir is also plagued with an irritating condition; the exact
nature of his ailment is never actually specified, but we are certain that his
problems are bladder related. Perhaps he suffers from some prostate problem.
Therefore, due to his affliction, he experiences pain when passing urine; as a
result he must refrain from laughing in an attempt to limit the number of times
that he must run off to relieve himself. Beckett's description of the play as a
tragi-comedy is clearly illustrated here, due to the fact that if Vladimir experiences pleasure and proceeds to laugh, his pleasure will ultimately lead to an
encounter with pain. Vladimir, therefore, essentially must refrain from feelings
of happiness or joy in an attempt to cope with his urinary problem. This urinary problem consequently has the same effect on Vladimir's life, as Estragon's
problem has on his, in that it essentially dominates his life and shapes his
entire existence physically, mentally and indeed emotionally. It is obvious that
Vladimir and Estragon are no longer in the first flush of youth. The fatal dic-
tatorship of Time is bringing physical decay upon them and they are in fact
powerless to prevent their own degeneration. It is therefore evident that a physical problem, no matter how insignificant can influence one's mental state and,
therefore, does become a handicap both physically and psychologically.

The second act evidently consists of what may be described as 'conventional'
handicaps, due to the fact that Pozzo is now blind and Lucky has gone dumb.
Evidently this physical deterioration is shrouded in mystery because we are left
uncertain about the time difference between the two acts. Pozzo has become
abject and dependent, assuming the more submissive role played by Lucky in
the previous act, and calling to mind the patient/carer coupling that is evident throughout Beckett's work. Although time appears ambiguous in this play,
Beckett does state that this is the following day, and we are therefore left won-
dering how these characters could have gone blind and dumb overnight; we are
offered no explanation of the exact cause of their afflictions, and the characters themselves appear unaware of the fact that the previous day they could see
and speak. However, it is through this drastic decay of the faculties that Beckett
is able to highlight the shortness of life, and the burden of being physical. Birth
and death are simultaneous in Beckett's world, with only enough time available
to experience the suffering. Pozzo illustrates this point as he states:

one day he went dumb, one day I went blind, one day we'll go deaf, one day
we were born, one day we shall die, the same day, the same second, is that not

enough for you? [*Calmer.*] They give birth astride of a grave, the light gleams an instant, then it's night once more. (Beckett 1990: 83)

With the passage of time, our plight inevitably deteriorates, and Pozzo is keen to stress the fleeting nature of our physical existence. Beckett's work suggests that it is abnormal to be alive, as birth essentially equals death. At the moment of birth we basically become defective in one way or another, as no one is born perfect, not in this world or in Beckett's. If we call to mind the biblical idea of being born into sin, it is evident that the human being after birth is effectively tarnished, in both biblical and Beckett terms:

> A recurring theme in Beckett's works is the suggestion that the source of man's troubles lies in his being born, and the very fact of his birth means that he must atone for this birth and that he must cope with his existence, both on physical and mental planes. (Cormier and Pallister 1979: 1–2)

And the Bible, from which Beckett often draws, is littered with images of, among others, blindness, lameness and deafness; hence it conveys representations of the imperfections of the human body. However, in biblical terms we can be saved from our defectiveness, but in the Beckettian world there is no salvation and no release from our suffering. If we are born only to return to the grave immediately, then life, which is only an instant, one fleeting moment, does not allow time for youth. Perhaps this is why Beckett nearly always presents his characters as aged, due to the fact that from the moment of birth we begin the ageing process and start to deteriorate, and youth is such a fleeting experience that it is over before we can acknowledge it.

Eva Metman, in her essay 'Reflections on Samuel Beckett's Plays', describes Pozzo's blindness and Lucky's dumbness as 'not really a change but rather a becoming manifest of what was there before: his inability to meet others' (Esslin 1965: 123). This synopsis is accurate, as it does illustrate the characters' reluctance to interact fully with others or indeed with each other. However, it is also possible to suggest that degeneration is an inevitable consequence of physical being, implying that the degenerative gene is present from the moment of conception and the passing of time results in its manifestation. If Pozzo's blindness and Lucky's dumbness had occurred over a period of time, the effect would have been less dramatic, but because their afflictions come within a '24-hour' period, Beckett successfully reminds us about the brevity of life and the unreliability of the body. These afflictions illustrate that this day, Pozzo and Lucky have decayed a little further and are effectively one day closer to the grave, where Lucky will become blind and Pozzo will go dumb. Thus Beckett is endeavouring to illustrate the process of physical decline, its mysteriousness and its inevitability.

It is important to remember, however, that these afflictions do not prevent the characters from going on. Pozzo's blindness essentially provides relief for

Lucky as Pozzo becomes more submissive, and Lucky perhaps finds amelioration in his dumbness due to the fact that he is no longer able to perform. It is
possible to suggest therefore, that physical hardships provide a form of comfort
for these characters, as they can take 'refuge' in their afflictions. These adversities may give them hope, with the knowledge that the body is declining; therefore it is possible they go on, not as an attempt to survive, but as a need to reach
the next day, where perhaps they will encounter more limitations, and consequently be reassured that they are one step closer to the grave and nearer the
end of their suffering. John Calder says that Beckett 'states quite clearly that the
reason for our existence might simply be to allow pain to exist' (2001: 10). To
be alive in Beckett's world is to be physical and to be physical in Beckett's world
is to be damned, and *Endgame* personifies the defective physical condition.

  Endgame, first performed in French in 1957, proceeds one step further
than *Waiting for Godot*, and perhaps Hamm personifies the Godot that never
arrives; if so, Vladimir and Estragon would be advised to go on waiting and
pray that their 'saviour' never finds them. The afflictions portrayed in this play
are clearly more serious, and the experience of transition from the exterior
world of Godot to the interior world of Hamm, illustrates the encroaching
and claustrophobic atmosphere that these characters must endure, as they
further degenerate in a world that appears almost hopeless. Beckett sets out
to represent all the discomforts, the miseries, the indignity and the tragic
absurdity of physical being. There is a presiding sense of doom and physical
decline here, and it appears as if the end of the world is near, or as if very little
life remains after some form of holocaust.

  When we first meet Hamm he is covered with an old sheet, perhaps better
described as a shroud, denoting the idea that he exists somewhere between life
and death: a state of limbo in which he and the other characters are among
the last survivors. Hamm, similar to many of Beckett's characters, is confined
to a chair, and although not a conventional wheelchair, as it is described as an
armchair on castors, it does prevent him from being totally incapacitated, and
therefore serves the purpose of affording him some mobility. Hamm, however,
does not only have the affliction of paralysis, he is also blind, consequently pro-
jecting his already bleak world into complete and absolute darkness, thereby
distancing him further from the other characters and spiritual regeneration.
He therefore inhabits the darkness in which he condemned Mother Pegg to
die. Consequently the opening line, 'Finished, it's finished, nearly finished,
it must be nearly finished' (Beckett 1990: 93), illustrates the plight that these
characters face. However, to view it as prognostic is to be surely disappointed.
This is after all only the beginning of the play and a world in which Beckett
does not permit the luxury of finishing.

  We are again presented with the blind master and his servant, with the role
of the servant this time being played by Clov. It is clear by now that no one is
beyond the reach of some form of limitation (as so often with Beckett the whole

situation is conceived of in terms of physical negatives), and Clov is plagued by the condition of not being able to sit down. This bizarre condition is interesting, as it appears to further highlight Hamm's impediment of not being able to stand up. The limitations of each character almost appear to complement each other, in that if the two afflictions were to merge, we may find in the middle some form of tolerance, and perhaps 'normality', resulting in Hamm possibly feeling slightly envious of Clov's adversity and indeed vice versa.

The Beckettian protagonist resents the wretched physical existence that has been thrust upon him. However, despite the obvious physical handicaps, the determination to continue is very much apparent, and Hamm immediately acknowledges this point as he states, in response to his previous declaration that there can be no misery worse than his own, 'And yet I hesitate, I hesitate to . . . to end' (ibid.). This hesitation to end life, which many characters feel, perhaps suggests that their suffering is not intolerable and that they do reap some 'reward' from the monotony of living; however, to view it in this context is possibly to be misguided. Beckett's characters are reluctant to finish living, despite the suffering they endure, because for them death is not an assurance of termination, and the next world may be more unbearable than the one in which they already exist, as *Play* clearly illustrates. Beckett observes with quizzical wonderment the human capacity for going on despite the great physical adversity that we face. There is no explanation for our condition and indeed no redemption from it.

Nagg and Nell are physically maimed too, as they are no longer in possession of their legs, and they are also afflicted by the deterioration of their hearing and vision. Beckett's reasons for placing them in dustbins appears rather ambiguous and many would perhaps suggest that Beckett views the decayed physical condition as being worthless. Indeed, Beckett views physical being as valueless, due to the fact that from the moment of birth we are programmed to degenerate. It is evident that these characters are incarcerated; they are imprisoned by their own physical condition coupled with the bins that also confine them. The Nagg/Nell partnership is representative of how we are physically reduced by time. From the vigour of youth through to the slowing down of middle age and on to the indignity of old age, our physical story is one of decay, decline and degeneration. Each stage of life represents a stage of deterioration, and Nagg and Nell perhaps represent the most advanced phase, as the grotesqueness of their appearance forces us to acknowledge the futility of the human condition, and the unattractiveness of the aged physical form. Through them Beckett successfully captures the comic/tragic nature of life and drama. However, it is evident that as Beckett's work progresses, humour is gradually discarded prompting the theme of tragic despair to become paramount.

Hamm is clearly pessimistic. He fears birth, children, growth and regeneration, as he recognizes the suffering that plagues existence. Although Clov suggests that nature no longer exists, denoting the idea that time itself has ceased, Hamm responds with – 'But we breathe, we change! We lose our hair, our teeth! Our bloom! Our ideals!' (Beckett 1990: 97). Physical degeneration is evident from this statement, but it also conveys a sense of internal dejection. Spiritual decay, which is analysed in Chapter 8, is obviously not outwardly apparent; however, through time it does have a profound effect on one's physical decline. It has been suggested that the room depicted in this play represents the inside of a skull, with the two windows consequently denoting the eyes.[1] If this theory is accepted, the play appears to become even more claustrophobic and the drama may be described as representing the drama of the mind. Therefore it is possible to suggest that the physical and mental components of decay ambiguously merge in *Endgame*.

Hamm may be described as being relatively sadistic, due to the fact that he appears to take satisfaction in the knowledge that others also endure suffering. Like many of Beckett's characters, Hamm is a storyteller, reiterating tales of pain and misery. These stories may be an attempt to pass the time, but they may also provide relief; by dwelling on a fictitious person's despair, the suffering of oneself may be momentarily alleviated. However, Beckett's characters often tell stories about individuals who are the personification of themselves, and therefore they may not, in reality, achieve amelioration through their narrative. Hamm's blindness corresponds to the metaphorical blindness that many Beckett characters endure, as they often appear lost, endeavouring always to find their way in a world devoid of meaning.

It is interesting that the medication Hamm takes in the morning to revive himself, and in the evening as a sedation, thereby providing relief from the pain he endures, is slowly running out. Like the desolate landscape outside his room, described as 'the . . . other hell' (Beckett 1990: 104), everything is decaying. Hamm resents Nagg and Nell for bringing him into this world, and essentially blames them for his suffering, describing his father as an 'Accursed progenitor!' (Beckett 1990: 96). If procreation is therefore a mortal error, due to the fact that one is effectively condemning this new life to a state of suffering, then perhaps this is why sexual relations are nearly always presented as being almost seedy in Beckett's work. Sex cannot be viewed as an act of love, because it would not be a loving act to bring a child into such desolation. The body is therefore not associated with pleasure in Beckett's work but much more readily with pain. Life becomes the affliction, which the physical body must endure, and to be on earth is to be condemned. Hamm emphasizes this point as he says to Clov, 'Use your head, can't you, use your head, you're on earth, there's no cure for that!' (Beckett 1990: 125). The problem is not in dying, but in how to reach death, and these characters endeavour to find their way in this world where the journey becomes the prime objective, and not the theory behind the reasons for being.

The sighting of the small boy at the end perhaps provides hope that life has not fully ended in the desolate environment which surrounds Hamm's home.

However, it also brings despair to think that the journey has not yet finished and the suffering will not yet cease. In this world of degradation and decay, which is rife with physical handicaps, the possibility of regeneration does not provide hope, but rather produces a feeling of dejection, in the knowledge that life will continue, and death will remain elusive.

Beckett's early novel *Molloy*, (published 1951), which constitutes the first section of the 'trilogy',[2] provides an alternative mental reaction to physical being. Similar to many of Beckett's characters, Molloy may be described as a wanderer, and although the journey he undertakes to find his mother may, on the surface, appear relatively simple, the complexities of his quest soon become apparent. Memory plays a significant role in this text; however, Molloy cannot be described as an omniscient narrator, and due to the ambiguous nature of his memory, we find ourselves entering a world which appears almost devoid of meaning. From the beginning it is evident that Molloy has severely deteriorated. He begins his narrative possessing no teeth, enormous knees, one stiff leg and asthma, plus other weak points that he chooses not to mention; and as his journey progresses so too does the degeneration. This novel dramatically illustrates the process of decay, as the human body essentially breaks down before us and is reduced to a physical state which is almost unrecognizable: a human existing but not a recognizable human 'being'. Once again the parents are blamed for the child's woes, and Molloy remembers his mother as 'her who brought me into the world, through the hole in her arse if my memory is correct. First taste of the shit' (Beckett 1994: 16). Again we are reminded that, in this world, life is not a gift to be cherished but a condemnation to be endured.

Although decay is prominent throughout this text, it is evident that the characters' perception of their own degeneration offers an alternative viewpoint to the decomposition of the physical being. 'To decompose is to live too' (Beckett 1994: 25) claims Molloy, suggesting that the process of decay is not to be viewed as a nearing of the end, but rather as a reminder that we are still alive.[3] Beckett therefore implies that while we suffer, we at least know we exist, and while we exist we are doomed to suffer. As stated previously, this novel portrays a journey, a journey which in reality may never have existed, except as a figment of Molloy's overactive imagination. A quest, which takes place purely within one's mind, contemplating facts which in reality do not constitute what is real, may be symptomatic of a mental form of decay, a theme which will be developed later. However, it is interesting that the novel begins in Molloy's mother's room, which undoubtedly has connotations of the womb. It may be suggested that Molloy's desire to find his mother may, in theory, be an unconscious yearning to journey back to the womb, a place which provides protection and a refuge from suffering. Or perhaps this is another instance of the desire to end, to reach a state of non-consciousness. Perhaps an invisible umbilical cord runs throughout this text, forever connecting Molloy to his mother and indeed, Molloy to Moran. But by going back to the womb, Molloy may be risking rebirth and regeneration, a 'deliverance' that Beckett's characters would not wish for. Conversely, it may be viewed as a form of death, of being 'delivered' from existence into non-being.

As the narrative progresses, Molloy's physical infirmities become more prevalent and the deterioration more rapid:

> For just as I had difficulty in sitting on a chair, or in an arm-chair, because of my stiff leg you understand, so I had none in sitting on the ground, because of my stiff leg and my stiffening leg, for it was about this time that my good leg, good in the sense that it was not stiff, began to stiffen. (Beckett 1994: 71)

Problems with feet and legs are widespread in Beckett's work, and perhaps this stiffening of the good leg is a blessing in disguise for Molloy, due to the fact that it takes the focus off the bad leg, thereby alleviating the intense pain, which he feels in one leg, by effectively affording him another pain on which to concentrate. It is evident that as the good leg stiffens, the already stiff leg begins to shorten, and Molloy states, 'But when one shortens, and the other not, then you begin to be worried' (Beckett 1994: 76). This declaration implies that these impediments are not an encumbrance to Molloy and suggests that he actually desires further adversities, thereby calling into question the implications of decay itself. Kenner describes Molloy's journey as 'the degeneration of body into physical wreckage' (1973: 95). This description is indeed appropriate, as the deterioration of the physical being is clearly presented through the representation of Molloy in his final stages. By the end of his narrative Molloy is crawling, almost childlike, endeavouring to continue his journey despite his physical incapability. He says, 'I pulled myself forward, with an effort of the wrists. For my wrists were still quite strong, fortunately, in spite of my decrepitude, though all swollen and racked by a kind of chronic arthritis probably' (Beckett 1994: 89). This image of Molloy crawling through the forest evidently inspired Beckett, as he again returned to the idea in his novel *How It Is*, where the forest is replaced by a sea of mud and the crawling becomes all the more difficult, as the protagonist wrestles with the arduousness of the human condition, endeavouring to breathe amidst the mud of existence. Molloy's childlike form complements the idea of a journey back to the womb, and as he lies motionless in the ditch, it is evident that his quest is nearly complete.

However, as Molloy's narrative draws to an end, Moran's rhetoric clearly begins. Similar to his predecessor, Moran also embarks upon a journey in an attempt to establish the exact location of Molloy. Therefore, although the text is divided into two sections, the parallels that begin to emerge between the two parts make the ambiguous quality of the novel more apparent, and the unity of the narrative more complete. Molloy suggests that 'perfection is not of this world' (Beckett 1994: 90), and his affirmation is proven through Moran's account of his own expedition. Similar to Molloy, Moran begins his narrative suffering from swollen painful knees, with morphine tablets proving to be his favourite sedative. Medication plays a major role in Beckett's work and we are reminded of Hamm's tonics and sedatives, which he uses to alleviate the pain of existence. Beckett illustrates that no one is beyond the reach of some form of impediment, and so Moran's son is burdened with having 'naturally very bad teeth' (Beckett 1994: 104). To be born with bad teeth is an image that appears almost grotesque; babies are obviously born without teeth, therefore to be born already possessing decayed teeth is an image that Beckett may use to illustrate the leap from birth to old age in one instant. Beckett himself suffered from oral and dental problems,[4] and we question whether dental decay is perhaps a metaphor for wider human physical decline.

It is clear that no explanation is offered regarding Moran's search for Molloy, and Moran himself appears unclear about who exactly he is looking for. However, it is evident that as his journey progresses so too does his degeneration. Similar to Molloy, Moran's perception of physical affliction is by no means conventional, and he too almost desires to encounter further suffering. In a speech that offers a paradoxical viewpoint on the implications of decay, Moran states:

> And it would not surprise me if the great classical paralyses were to offer analogous and perhaps even still more unspeakable satisfactions. To be literally incapable of motion at last, that must be something! My mind swoons when I think of it. And mute into the bargain! And perhaps as deaf as a post! And who knows as blind as a bat! And as likely as not your memory a blank! And just enough brain intact to allow you to exult! And to dread death like a regeneration. (Beckett 1994: 140–141)

This speech clearly illustrates physical decay and its advantages; for Moran to be in this stage of physical wreckage would be for him, paradoxically, cathartic, and a condition that he would aspire to. However, similar to all of Beckett's characters, Moran fears to cross the thin boundary between physical disintegration and death, because in death his condition may be no longer 'tolerable'. Death would be a form of regeneration, as it would provide release from the physical body and the afflictions that pertain to it. Due to the fact that Moran welcomes physical adversity it becomes apparent why he dreads mortality. Dan Rooney also highlights this idea of physical decay and its advantageous nature as he states, 'The loss of my sight was a great fillip. If I could go deaf and dumb I think I might pant on to be a hundred' (Beckett 1990: 192).

Moran is clearly not burdened with the severity of afflictions which affect Molloy; however, the similarities between the two men are too extensive to be ignored. As Moran's journey progresses he appears to assume the characteristics of Molloy himself, and it may be suggested that his quest to find Molloy harbours the prime objective of essentially 'becoming' Molloy: 'Physically speaking it seemed to me I was now becoming rapidly unrecognisable' (Beckett 1994: 170). Although Moran never actually finds Molloy, it may be suggested that he discovers him internally; his search is therefore complete, as he intrinsically discovers himself. If we are to view both chapters as one complete narrative and change the sequence around, it is possible to suggest that Moran may represent an early Molloy, resting on the precipice of degeneration. If this theory is sound then it is evident that we are again dealing with Beckett's preoccupation with how the individual changes through time. And if Molloy and Moran are to be viewed as one and the same, it is evident that Beckett has inverted the conventional image by presenting us with the older persona, followed by the younger.

Molloy's obsession with stone sucking is interesting; the complexity of this routine, and the methodical nature of his habit, obviously offers Molloy some form of comfort and pleasure. Of course, the stones themselves will not evade degeneration, as the sucking process will ultimately cause them to erode. Psychoanalysts believe that during early development, which is described as the early oral phase, one encounters the stage of sucking and enjoyment, essentially a drinking of the mother. The later oral phase is characterized by biting; this corresponds to a new complexity of the child's relation to the mother through the development of teeth. The first element is therefore benign, with the latter being described as more aggressive.[5] Consequently, it may be suggested that although Moran could possibly represent an early Molloy physically, it is Moran who appears more aggressive. Moran therefore inhabits the later oral phase, while Molloy, due to his sucking tendencies, remains in the benign stage; therefore the image of old and young is once again inverted. Due to the fact that Molloy is advanced in years, although still inhabiting the early oral phase, it may be suggested that he represents the old person who reverts to his childhood. Beckett is enabled therefore to illustrate youth and ageing in one instant and highlight the brevity of life. Through their physical impediments, this novel illustrates that for these characters, decay can paradoxically be a form of regeneration. To be totally incapacitated would, for Moran, be a cathartic experience. However, to actually die and be reborn into this world, or into the next, is something these characters evidently dread, as death is not an assurance of termination. Although Beckett portrays degeneration in a dramatic form within this text, he clearly illustrates the evolutionary process of the self and the individual's mechanism for coping with physical decline.

Moran's health at the end of his narrative is approximately the same as Molloy's, when Molloy begins his own quest, thus giving the novel a cyclical quality and a unity, which despite its ambiguities makes this text undoubtedly complete. Molloy states that 'it is forbidden to give up and even to stop an instant' (Beckett 1994: 81). The never-ending journey must therefore continue, and despite their physical degeneration these characters evade death, ultimately existing on a plateau, which may be best described as a 'finality without end' (Beckett 1994: 112).

However, the ambiguous quality of *Molloy* does not compare to Beckett's earlier novel *Watt*, which he wrote during the war years. This narrative should not be viewed as a conventional story, but rather as an experience or set of emotions through which Beckett illustrates the unreality of reality. The novel examines a form of insanity or mental disorder through the representation of the protagonist; however, it also provides insight into Beckett's portrayal of physical affliction within his early work. Perhaps best described as the diary of a schizophrenic, *Watt*'s lack of continuity should not be viewed as its damning feature, but ultimately as its saving grace. The impact that this novel has upon the reader is evidently profound and often difficult to describe; however, it undoubtedly leaves one feeling deeply affected, despite the fact that he/she may not be able to define exactly 'what' the novel is about. And similar to a lot of Beckett's work, it is evident that physical infirmities are prevalent, especially within the representation of the Lynch family.

In *Watt* there is a cornucopia of evidence to substantiate the theory that for Beckett the body is a constant source of discomfort, pain and indignity. Watt himself is described as having poor healing skin, symptomatic perhaps of a blood disorder, with the result that he possesses running sores in various parts of his body. Unlike Molloy he has no trouble with his knees, except that they do not bend while walking, and therefore he is the first of Beckett's characters to move with a 'funambulistic stagger' (Beckett 1976: 29). Tetty evidently is not sure if Watt is a man or a woman and perhaps this androgynous quality prompts Mr Hackett to mistake him for a 'roll of tarpaulin' (Beckett 1976: 14). The inconvenience of the physical state is highlighted in this text, as the break down of the human body erodes the erroneous ideal of the body beautiful. And the pain, which is equated with every day living, is dramatized through the synopsis of Watt's footwear:

> In this boot, a twelve, and in this shoe, a ten, Watt, whose size was eleven, suffered, if not agony, at least pain, with his feet, of which each would willingly have changed places with the other, if only for a moment. (Beckett 1976: 218)

The body is a constant source of discomfort and we basically do our best each day to placate the pain we experience. Watt, similar to Estragon, suffers immensely each day due to the ill-fitting nature of his footwear; and again we see the problems associated with the physical structure, as even clothing it can ultimately lead to discomfort. Right from Beckett's early work we see that most characters endure some form of affliction and Beckett is clearly conveying his belief that to be physical is to suffer. However what is interesting is that, as the work progresses, not only do the physical impediments continue, but we actually see the body fundamentally disintegrate until we are left with just body parts; for example Mouth in *Not I*, the heads in *Play*, Winnie in *Happy Days*. The recognizable human frame becomes reduced to such a point that it ultimately becomes redundant, and it is here that Beckett turns his attentions to the workings of the mind.

Watt undoubtedly suffers both physically and mentally, and the following episode, detailing Watt's encounter with the brambles, equates him with Christ:

> Then he turned, with the intention very likely of going back the way he had come, and I saw his face, and the rest of his front. His face was bloody, his hand also, and thorns were in his scalp. (His resemblance, at that moment, to the Christ believed by Bosch, then hanging in Trafalgar Square, was so striking, that I remarked it.) (Beckett 1976: 157)

As Mary Bryden confirms, 'though the subject under scrutiny uncannily mirrors the detail of the Christ-ordeal, he himself is not Christ: he merely resembles a Bosch-like portrait of Christ' (Pilling and Bryden 1992: 52). Estragon also equates himself with Christ; he affirms, 'All my life I've compared myself to him' (Beckett 1990: 51). Beckett is undoubtedly drawing parallels with Christ to highlight the intensity of our suffering on earth. And this suffering is perhaps best illustrated through the portrayal of the Lynch family. Beckett uses 11 pages in total to give an account of the afflictions pertaining to this family; and through his use of extremities, he effectively illustrates the ineffectuality of the physical being. Blindness, paralysis, and weaknesses in the head and chest, are only a few of the adversities affecting the Lynch family. This skit on Irish rural life, which is evident also in *All That Fall*, is characteristic of the assumption that, despite the severity of one's illness, the next person's disease will be notably worse. Beckett's representation of physical disability, combined with his use of black humour, again conveys the tragic/comic nature of the work:

> There was Tom Lynch, widower, aged eighty-five years, confined to his bed with constant undiagnosed pains in the caecum, and his three surviving boys Joe, aged sixty-five years, a rheumatic cripple, and Jim, aged sixty-four years, a hunchbacked inebriate, and Bill, widower, aged sixty-three years, greatly hampered in his movements by the loss of both legs as the result of a slip, followed by a fall, and his only surviving daughter May Sharpe, widow, aged sixty-two years, in full possession of all her faculties with the exception of that of vision. (Beckett 1976: 98)

This description of the Lynch family continues for approximately ten pages. And Beckett's predilection for medical terminology and for technical anatomical words is very much evident. However, it is Beckett's construction of sentences, which makes this episode so effective and prevents it from becoming a monotonous account of illnesses found exclusively in a medical dictionary. The body is portrayed as being mechanical, a functioning organ, which ultimately becomes a hindrance. This is illustrated through the account of Liz née Sharpe, who is described as being more dead than alive, as the result of having 19 children over a period of 20 years. Again the body is portrayed as being analogous to a machine, as Liz née Sharpe produces babies as quickly as is physically possible, appearing similar to a production line. Interestingly, Tetty sums up her experience of childbirth as being 'one of riddance' (Beckett 1976: 13), suggesting that the creation of new life is an affliction both for the mother and the child and should consequently be avoided. Although an extreme representation of physical infirmities, this episode essentially conveys the reality of the physical condition. We can clearly see the numerous problems that can affect the body and recognize how susceptible the physical frame is to illness. A mass of bones, flesh and organs, the body is essentially programmed to decay and there is no escaping this reality; all Beckett does is illustrate this truth.

Physical disorder is a pulse, which runs throughout *Watt* and indeed all of Beckett's work. However, it is evident that Beckett's representation of the physical being illustrates that we are doomed from the beginning and 'decomposing' is a process that we must all endure. Perhaps this is why Murphy endeavours to live only within his mind, to escape the suffering of the physical reality. However, as we progress further into Beckett's work, it becomes evident that the mind itself cannot escape the process of degeneration, and similar to the body, it too becomes afflicted, as the advance of decay takes precedence over the possibility of remaining mentally articulate. Decay evidently has many guises, and although one may escape the burden of physical impediments, it becomes clear as we move into the following chapter, that the process of ageing harbours degeneration, as there is no escape from 'that double-headed monster of damnation and salvation – Time' (Beckett 1965: 11).

Chapter 2

Old Age
The Dictatorship of Time

Who may tell the tale of the old man?

Tailpiece

Old age is essentially the condition that awaits us all. Unless removed from existence by accidental death, illness or suicide, we are assured that, despite physical prowess during youth, our advancement in years will ultimately condemn us to mental deterioration and physical breakdown. It is the only reality that exists before death. Beckett's representation of the aged is a horrific study of the implications of growing old and the undesirability of reaching those twilight years, when all we have to look forward to is bad health, isolation and the overwhelming need to reach the grave. Youth in Beckett's world is rarely portrayed, perhaps because we spend the greater part of our existence in the confines of bodily breakdown.

'A late evening in the future' (Beckett 1990: 215), is the setting for Beckett's drama *Krapp's Last Tape* in which we are presented with a weary old man and his tape recorder. This play, written in early 1958, although deceptively simple, illustrates the severity of ageing in an atmosphere where isolation takes precedence, and memories serve to reinforce the horror of the present. The confrontation of man's various selves provides a dramatic outlet from which to examine the progression of a life and attempt to comprehend the complexities of growing old. And the juxtaposition of the old man on stage, with the voice of an earlier self, highlights the deteriorating influence imposed by the passing of time and the inability to curtail the process of ageing. We wonder if Krapp would prefer to age on and die, or recover his lost youth.

The title of this drama portrays a sense of finality, and we presume that Krapp's present recording will constitute his final memoir. However, the word 'last' may be antithetical and therefore may not suggest finality, but instead a continuance, thereby creating a sense of prolongation and a denial that the end is near. The 69-year-old we see before us perhaps recognizes the limitations of his age and acknowledges the reality that his physical frame may not endure another year, thereby appearing resolute in his acceptance that his present recording may ultimately be his final effort. The age 69 is significant, as Beckett was acutely aware that the Bible allots us three score years and ten, suggesting therefore that Krapp is rapidly approaching death.[1] A 'late evening in the future', although appearing ambiguous, is perhaps representative of the progression for all human beings, as only in the future will we confront our latter selves imprisoned by the burden of old age, and unable to recognize the characteristics of a former self. The protagonist's name portrays the worthlessness of his life and perhaps alludes to the futility of universal existence. Knowlson affirms:

> the harsh sounding name of 'Krapp' with unpleasant excremental associations that lead its owner and the watching audience back to a decaying, disgusting, yet still demanding body with which Krapp has tried in vain to come to terms all his life. (Knowlson and Pilling 1979: 81)

Krapp, at a point of physical and intellectual decline, is condemned to an isolated existence within his den, where darkness and light appear representative of the contrasting nature of the succession of selves, and may also imply the Cartesian separation of body and mind.[2] In an interview with Tom Driver, Beckett said, 'If there were only darkness, all would be clear. It is because there is not only darkness but also light that our situation becomes inexplicable'.[3] Driver (1961) quoted here from Graver and Federman (1979: 220). There are certainly factors in this drama that appear beyond explanation. Dr Szafron, a member of *The Stay Young Research Corporation*, in 1969 claimed that 'age could not be equated directly with decline' (Felstein 1973: 11). We may therefore assume that other factors have contributed to Krapp's degenerative state. One may indeed argue that Krapp appears old before his time, due to the fact that 69 is not a tremendously advanced age, and yet Beckett chooses to describe him as a 'wearish old man' (Beckett 1990: 215).

Beckett provides many physical indicators of old age, including Krapp's white face, which may be attributed to anaemia, suggesting a poor diet resulting perhaps from his solitary life. The disordered grey hair, laborious walk and difficulty in hearing suggest an individual who may be described as a physical mess, resulting from the uncontrollable breakdown of the body; describing Krapp as hard of hearing is undoubtedly ironic as this is a play that dramatizes the art of listening. The rusty black trousers which are too short, the rusty black sleeveless waistcoat that complements the grimy white shirt, and the dirty white boots portray an image of dishevelment, and are indicative of an individual who no longer takes pride in his appearance, viewing the preservation of the self as inconsequential within a body subject to the degradation of old age. It may be suggested that Krapp's physical appearance illustrates the diminution of his life force, as the outward appearance perhaps reflects the inner decline. The tatty garments are therefore representative of a body that is equally in a state of disrepair and disintegration. There is, of course, no hope of reversal and so one must continue onwards, enduring each solitary day, and striving for the completion of one's life journey. And, although Krapp cannot in reality return to the past whence he came, he can in theory, with the use of the tape recorder, relive those memories which are perhaps best left undisturbed. The tape recorder creates the illusion that time is reversible, that we can go back as well as forward. Kenner describes *Krapp's Last Tape* as a 'last bitter parody of those vases celebrated in *Proust* where the lost past is sealed away' (Fletcher 2000: 136). Cronin suggests that 'The Beckett man has usually no past except, since he has been born, a mother or mother memory' (1997: 380). This is of course true for many Beckett characters; however, in this drama the past is prevalent and very much accessible. One questions the desirability of being able to access moments in time, which ultimately transport us from the reality of the present and can only temporarily provide relief from the individual that we have become, and the life in which we now exist. These tapes provide escapism for Krapp and yet they also reinforce the horror of his current situation, as the voices from the dark provide the only source of company. There is a very real sense of the human tragedy, as the drama illustrates that our few moments of happiness are ultimately transient and cannot be recaptured.

As Krapp makes his selection of box three, spool five, he relishes the word 'Spooool!' (Beckett 1990: 216), repeating it many times with a child-like tonality. Here Beckett illustrates the cyclical quality of life, demonstrating that the old individual often reverts back to childish tendencies. The mind and the body are therefore at odds, as the mind may adopt a youthful approach, while the body perhaps declines to function with youthful vigour. The memories that are recorded on box three, spool five, including his mother's death, the 'vision' and 'farewell to love', serve to reinforce the black and white imagery that is so prevalent throughout this drama. These memories are illustrations of incidents in which dark and light are mingled, reminding one of the Manichean theory: a dichotomy of spirit and flesh associated with light and dark, and perhaps representative of the Cartesian separation of body and mind; a separation which is very much apparent in this drama, as the mind has essentially been preserved, while the body has been condemned to deterioration. We may therefore suggest that the effects of old age have condemned Krapp physically, but not mentally; and yet this argument would prove erroneous. No one can deny that Krapp's memories are preserved and will withstand the deteriorating influence of the passing of time, as they are captured on tape. However, it must be noted that memory and memories cannot be equated, and although one's memories may remain intact, it is to be expected that old age denies one's memory the opportunity to function efficiently. Beckett illustrates Krapp's defective memory, demonstrating his inability to recall past events, such as the black ball and the not so memorable equinox, thereby suggesting that incidents which may appear important in earlier life, tend to lose their significance as one grows old. It is the tragedy of everything becoming the victim of oblivion; the past can seem like a receding dream which eventually fades utterly.

With his hand cupping his ear, Krapp leans towards the machine, almost embracing it, in order to hear the words that it will emit, and hence, the irony of the situation becomes evident. The ageing process cannot be avoided and, despite our reluctance to acknowledge that we essentially have no control over our bodies, old age confirms the horror of physical breakdown. As Krapp's hearing is currently defective, we may presume that it will eventually fail completely, and despite the preservation of memories, these tapes will prove obsolete, as no longer will he be able to hear them, condemned to a new world of silence. The stark contrast of the vision we see before us and the voice of the 39-year-old Krapp is indeed striking. The voice appears foreign, as it emanates from the darkness, almost ghost-like in its preservation, and we find it difficult to equate the voice we hear with the man we see. The arrogance of this earlier self appears to surprise even Krapp; 'Hard to believe I was ever that young whelp' (Beckett 1990: 218), and 'The voice!' (ibid.), which no longer exists, has been relegated to box three, spool five, as the passing of time no longer permits it to emanate from the mouth of Krapp, as old age has 'kindly' replaced it with a cracked utterance. Described as 'sound as a bell' (Beckett 1990: 217), and intellectually at the 'crest of the wave' (ibid.), the younger persona appears to represent a direct contrast to the Krapp we see before us, and yet within him we recognize those early tendencies which would eventually develop, resulting in the characteristics of the latter man.

Isolation has evidently plagued Krapp for many years, as the tape confirms that he once again spent his birthday alone: 'Not a soul. Sat before the fire with closed eyes, separating the grain from the husks' (ibid.). The separation of the grain from the husks is perhaps representative of the separation of light from darkness, or mind from body. At this early age he comments on his old weakness, which presumably constitutes his need for alcohol and bananas. Therefore at the age of 39, it is evident that Krapp was physically deteriorating, despite being intellectually at his peak, or thereabouts. The routine which he now follows is indeed one to which he has adhered for at least 30 years, thereby confirming Beckett's earlier statement from his essay on Proust, as he says, 'Life is habit. Or rather life is a succession of habits, since the individual is a succession of individuals' (Beckett 1965: 19).

If the individual is continually evolving, there can be no 'I', and therefore the existence of 'not I' is very much confirmed. It is interesting that Krapp states, 'With all this darkness round me I feel less alone' (Beckett 1990: 217), thereby equating light with isolation. Knowlson states that 'Light was therefore rejected in favour of darkness. And this darkness can certainly be seen as extending to a whole zone of being that includes folly and failure, impotence and ignorance' (1997: 352). And, of course, mental anguish often manifests itself physically, thereby reiterating the point that Krapp's present state cannot be equated directly with old age. Interestingly, the 39-year-old Krapp provides an insight into the younger Krapp, aged 27/29, and appears as far removed from this earlier self, as the 69-year-old is from the 39-year-old. The tribute to Bianca's eyes confirms the belief that Krapp has not been isolated his entire existence, and yet this reality magnifies the horror of the present. The aspirations and the resolutions he once possessed serve to reinforce the futility of his current existence, as no longer does he aspire to anything, bitter perhaps in his acknowledgement that old age has robbed him of youth. Krapp does not show signs of coming to terms with old age, as he chooses to continually revert to the past, unable and unwilling to live in the present. His plans for a less engrossing sexual life appear strange at the age of 27, suggesting perhaps that he is physically past his prime. The constipation, flagging pursuit of happiness and derisive attitude towards his youth suggest that at 27, Krapp was not only physically past his prime but significantly old before his time. There is a lot of evidence in Beckett's work to suggest that he was fascinated by the idea of people being prematurely old and, evidently, even as a young man Krapp was exhibiting signs of old age.

No longer able to comprehend the word 'viduity', he searches for its meaning in the dictionary which is ironically located in the darkness. Krapp himself is suffering from the bereavement of his lost selves and perhaps lamenting his current existence, incarcerated within the realms of old age and 'burning to be gone' (Beckett 1990: 222). The vision at the end of the jetty is not elaborated upon because Krapp chooses not to hear it, thereby suggesting that it is too painful a recollection, or perhaps just no longer of any interest. As Fletcher (2000: 143) says, the revelation, whatever it was, changed Krapp's life. Krapp chose to sacrifice his life for his work, and the renunciation of love prompted a move away from the physical in order to pursue the spiritual. Ironically, despite this sacrificial decision, Krapp failed to benefit spiritually, intellectually or physically, therefore proving that it was all in vain. The isolation, which he once welcomed and yet now plagues him, was of his own making, and the belief that he could triumph over the ephemeral nature of the physical body by achieving immortality through art, has essentially condemned him to a failed existence.

The memorable equinox, which proves no longer interesting, is overshadowed by the incident on the lake. This memory, entitled, 'Farewell to love' is perhaps one of the few incidents in Beckett's work in which 'love' is not portrayed as sordid. The Beckett man probably desires to be loved but is fundamentally incapable of loving. The poignancy of this passage is indeed evident and, as Krapp continues to play it, we recognize his inability to progress beyond the past. As he records the tape for his current birthday, he recognizes that age has robbed him of life – 'Nothing to say, not a squeak' (Beckett 1990: 222) – and his happiest moment of the past half million is derived from the word 'spooool'. The physical shutdown of his body is evident as he, 'Crawled out once or twice, before the summer was cold. Sat shivering in the park, drowned in dreams and burning to be gone' (Beckett 1990: 222). Old age, isolation, lost love and artistic failure leaves Krapp with essentially nothing to live for, thereby suggesting that his present recording will constitute his last.

The sexual encounter with Fanny illustrates the awkwardness of copulation for the Beckettian protagonist, and portrays the defective nature of the body in old age, as it essentially becomes physically defunct. It appears that the elderly Krapp still needs the occasional moment of sexual gratification; however, it is sordid, unattractive and virtually unpleasing. He is declining into impotence, the sexual decay functioning as a barometer of a wider malaise. The play ends with the episode on the lake and the 39-year-old Krapp commenting, 'Perhaps my best years are gone. When there was a chance of happiness. But I wouldn't want them back. Not with the fire in me now. No, I wouldn't want them back' (Beckett 1990: 223). We surmise, that if given the opportunity, Krapp would perhaps choose to 'be again'. However, with no chance of reversal, he is unyielding in his desire for termination, as no longer can he endure the life of an aged man, subject to deterioration, and condemned to an existence of self-imposed exile.

All That Fall, written between July and September 1956, was Beckett's first radio play, offering him an alternative medium in which to evoke the power of language. Beckett used this technology to convey, once again, his perception of the human condition, illustrating the futility of existence and the degradation of old age. The radio medium affords Beckett the opportunity to allow his listeners to actually hear the sounds of old age, the moans, groans and laboured breathing. Language serves as the medium through which the suffering of being can be illustrated; Beckett's language gives voice to the pain of existence.

The cyclical quality of the drama is evident, as it begins and ends with the tune *Death and the Maiden*, an appropriate choice for a play that contains abundant references to the sick and the dying, not all of whom are advanced in years. Opening with Maddy Rooney, the drama immediately forces us to acknowledge the unreliability of the body and the inability to prevent it from deteriorating through the ageing process. The sound of her dragging feet illustrates that to be physical is to be cursed, and it conveys the immense encumbrance of the physical body. The body almost becomes objectified, appearing at odds with the mind. Perhaps best described as 'that ruinous old house' (Beckett 1990: 172), it incarcerates the consciousness, and throughout old age it is beyond repair. Therefore, even if the mind is unaffected by the ageing process, we cannot prevent the deterioration of its physical vehicle, and so we may be condemned to witness our physical decay while remaining mentally sound.

The weather appears representative of the elderly body, as Mrs Rooney questions, 'But will it hold up?' (ibid.). The unreliable Irish weather may therefore be equated with our physical self, suggesting that, although it may start out promising, we can be sure that it will not last long. Again, no one is beyond the reach of some form of impediment, and as Maddy makes her way to the station to meet Mr Rooney, it becomes evident that everyone she encounters is suffering from some kind of affliction; even Christy's horse appears reluctant to move. Maddy acknowledges the detrimental effects of living, as she says 'Oh I am just a hysterical old hag I know, destroyed with sorrow and pining and gentility and churchgoing and fat and rheumatism and childlessness' (Beckett 1990: 174). Again Beckett illustrates how many of the afflictions of the elderly cannot be equated directly with their age, but are perhaps the culmination of a futile existence and condemnation to a 'lingering dissolution' (Beckett 1990: 175). Hayman states that Maddy is, 'Tired of moving, tired of her body, tired of her life, her one wish is for dissolution' (1970: 41).

It is not surprising that Mr Tyler curses the wet Saturday afternoon of his conception. Freud reiterates this point as he states, 'There must be a primal, unconscious drive toward death, and it must be present in every individual from the beginning to the end of his life' (Woodworth 1963: 277). Therefore, if there exists an unconscious drive toward death from the moment of birth, we may assume that none of us are really fully living. 'I am not half alive nor anything approaching it' (Beckett 1990: 176), claims Maddy, and Jung, who described his patient as having never really been born,[4] is essentially describing the condition that affects us all, as we are all scarcely here, because life is so fragile. Perhaps Mrs Rooney's mourning for her lost child is unfounded, due to the fact that she should have welcomed her daughter's early departure from existence, as she essentially escaped the torment of the human condition and the degradation of the ageing process: 'In her forties now she'd be, I don't know, fifty, girding up her lovely little loins, getting ready for the change. . . .' (ibid.). Here Beckett illustrates the absurdity of bodily maturity. Young girls prepare for their bodies to change in preparation for childbirth and, after enduring years of monthly agony, their bodies endure modification in rejection of the possibility of procreation. The ageing process defies them to maintain their womanhood, as they slowly adopt the attributes of the male – 'look closely and you will finally distinguish a once female shape' (Beckett 1990: 182), claims Maddy.

Again Maddy's body is portrayed as being a burden, as we recognize the difficulty she experiences in entering Mr Slocum's car. The arduousness of carrying out simple activities is the plight of the aged, and Maddy acknowledges the desirability of becoming housebound:

Would I were lying stretched out in my comfortable bed, Mr Barrell, just wasting slowly, painlessly away, keeping up my strength with arrowroot and calves-foot jelly, till in the end you wouldn't see me under the blankets any more than a board. (Beckett 1990: 180–181)

Miss Fitt acknowledges the reduction in stature of Mrs Rooney, now appearing 'So bowed and bent' (Beckett 1990: 183). Although endowed with a youthful physique at present, Miss Fitt must 'rejoice' in the knowledge that the ageing process will render her similar to Maddy, as she will ultimately become Miss Unfitt. As she helps Maddy up the hill, her impatience towards her is perhaps representative of society's unwillingness to ameliorate the lives of the elderly, preferring rather to relegate them to establishments that alleviate our responsibility. And our inclination to treat the aged as being of less importance and almost futile in their existence is highlighted by Maddy as she states, 'Do not imagine, because I am silent, that I am not present, and alive, to all that is going on' (Beckett 1990: 185).

We may assume that Dan Rooney is greatly advanced in years, appearing older than Maddy and suffering from the affliction of blindness, and to some degree memory loss, as he fails to remember that it is his birthday. One questions his ability to work, as he appears to be many years past the retirement age, and ill equipped to face the demands of society – 'do not ask me to speak and move at the same time' (Beckett 1990: 189). The train's late arrival, appearing to be of little significance, is quickly brushed aside by Dan, as his panting and stumbling illustrates that his main priority is to make it home with Maddy and her 'Two hundred pounds of unhealthy fat!' (Beckett 1990: 191). Although there is much comedy in this episode, we also recognize the tragedy of a man who is relying on his daily routine to get him through life. His desire to 'Nip some young doom in the bud' (ibid.), does not appear that absurd, within this environment, in which there appears to exist nothing but suffering and degradation. Although Hamm declares that 'The end is in the beginning and yet you go on' (Beckett 1990: 126), Mr Rooney abhors the thought of continuance and would therefore view the death of a child as a welcome alternative to the suffering of being. Perhaps he terminated the life of his own child, unable and unwilling to witness her 'lingering dissolution'.

Dan and Maddy, one of the many couplings in Beckett's work, represent together the ravages of the advancing years and convey the reality that growing old together is perhaps less painful than ageing alone. As the play culminates with the announcement that the little child has fallen out of the carriage, we question whether Dan was responsible. Our initial shock is alleviated perhaps by the 'comforting' knowledge that this child has escaped a life of misery and the horrors of ageing.

The late prose work entitled *Ill Seen Ill Said* (written initially in French between 1980–1981) exemplifies the horror of old age, illustrating once again the isolation which many of the aged are condemned to, and the hardship of enduring a body which no longer functions effectively. Throughout the text

Beckett alludes to the irony of human existence, and the inescapability of suffering, as we witness in this work the horrific prolongation of a life. The ambiguity surrounding this text prompts one to continually speculate, and we may presume that this old woman is a widow, condemned to roam the pastures alone, frequenting the grave of her lost 'love'. She appears to be a sky gazer, committed to watching the morning and evening star, symbols perhaps of the birth and death of life. Burdened by age and longing to be gone, it is not surprising that 'she rails at the source of all life' (Beckett 1982: 7). Her advance in years and physical deterioration condemn her to sit 'erect and rigid in the deepening gloom' (ibid.), with 'Such helplessness to move she cannot help' (ibid.). The darkness perhaps reflects the old woman's inner languishing and inability to exist within an environment of sunlight and fertility; however, despite her resentment of life, she is condemned to go on, as there is no alternative but continuance. Her white hair, and faintly bluish white face, provide the only contrast to the dimness of the cabin. Her face, the typical Beckettian countenance, suggests the coldness of death, and she takes her place in the gallery of Beckettian visages.

We are told that the cabin, in which she dwells alone, is located 'At the inexistent centre of a formless place' (Beckett 1982: 8), adding to the ambiguity of this woman's life; if indeed we can ascertain that she exists and has 'the misfortune to be still of this world' (ibid.). Perhaps we should place her in the same category as May from *Footfalls*, as she is just about here, condemned to linger, and therefore always ill seen. And if she is continually 'ill seen', the writer/narrator would find it difficult to express her condition, thereby conveying a narrative which is ultimately 'ill said' and therefore difficult to comprehend. A sense of illness pervades the story and indeed the words that tell it. As the stones increasingly abound outside the cabin, the infertility of the landscape is reflected in her persona, as she too appears 'doomed to endure' (Beckett 1982: 9), reiterating Cream's declaration in *The Old Tune* that 'the young pop off and the old hang on' (Beckett 1999b: 6).

The enigmatic quality of the twelve figures serves to complement the equivocal nature of the text. Perhaps representative of the Apostles or the months of the year,[5] they provide confirmation that the old woman exists, as they continue to watch her, thereby condemning her to existence, and recalling Bishop Berkeley's theory that 'To be is to be perceived.'[6] Her memory is failing, as she cannot recall if one of the twelve has advanced towards her, her age no longer permitting the mind to function efficiently. Perhaps these figures are the harbingers of death, resolute in their desire to take her from this existence, alleviating her of the confines of the physical being. Appearing similar to the tombstone that captivates her, she endures the process of degeneration. She is perhaps mostly not of this world. Even at our most vital Beckett views us as ghosts and therefore re-conceptualizes death through his portrayal of presence and absence. The narrator tells us that 'There was a time when she did not appear in the zone of stones. A long time. Was not therefore to be seen going out or coming in. When she appeared only in the pastures' (Beckett 1982: 13). The pastures are perhaps suggestive of youth and fertility, as Beckett illustrates the inability of remaining youthful and the unavoidability of the transition to the infertility of old age and the zone of stones. The visits to the stone are habitual, but they are also little journeys towards her own finality; she longs to be among the stones, as the cabin represents her provisional home, not her ultimate one.

The shadowy album serves the same function as Krapp's tapes, in that it provides a glimpse into the past, conveying memories which highlight the horror of the present, and reminding her that she is no longer part of a couple, relegated by time to a singular existence. She is ultimately a decaying shadow of her former self. Isolation has condemned her and now 'On the snow her long shadow keeps her company' (Beckett 1982: 15). Dressed in black, she wears the clothes of mourning, providing a stark contrast to the whiteness of the snow. Again we wonder if this old woman is still of this earth? Or does she perhaps exist in some other realm? – The condition between life and death which must ultimately be labelled 'old age'. This text does not imply stagnation, but illustrates how death can take so long, and as Knowlson states, 'the 'dark lady' is endowed with a quiet dignity and a nobility that manages to survive imminent disintegration and decay' (1997: 670). Her face, which is perhaps best equated with the death mask, appears full of contradictions, due to the fact that despite her age, it is lacking in wrinkles. Described as a 'Calm slab worn and polished by agelong comings and goings. Livid pallor. Not a wrinkle. How serene it seems this ancient mask. Worthy those worn by certain newly dead' (Beckett 1982: 25). Perhaps this is not a study of old age but rather a study of lifelessness. Time's decaying influence prompts the face to become expressionless, and the expressionless face of the dead is often worn by the living in Beckett's work.

Beckett again presents us with a picture of waiting; 'Seated on the stones she is seen from behind. From the waist up. Trunk black rectangle. Nape under frill of black lace. White half halo of hair. Face to the north. The tomb' (Beckett 1982: 29). Perhaps she is awaiting death; decked out in her black lace she laments her continuance. Similarly, we too are condemned to wait, forced to view her from behind, we are denied the image of her face and the lifeless quality of her eyes. She appears to be engaging with the tomb, accepting that it does in reality represent her destiny and the place where she will again perhaps be reunited with her loved one. We question if she is becoming a part of the landscape, so deteriorated in her appearance we fail to recognize her womanly features, suggesting that her womanhood has been obliterated by her advance in years. Becoming a stone among stones, she is preparing for the ultimate physical breakdown and the 'release' of death.

Eros, the principle of life and growth, does not exist in the Beckettian world, as Thanatos, the principle of decay and death, appears prevalent. The many false endings throughout the text function effectively so that the actual reading of the work mimics the slowness of dying and the deceleration of the physical framework attributed to old age. The 'Slow systole diastole' (Beckett 1982: 31), implying the dilation of the heart, auricles and arteries, shows that she is nearing death. But life still exists within her, producing the 'Rhythm of a labouring heart' (Beckett 1982: 32). Labouring to continue functioning or perhaps labouring to cease. The mind is not willing and the body is weak. As her steps barely leave a trace and the snow fails to fall on her, we question again whether she is fully here, remaining forever ill seen. This old woman has reached the age, 'when most people cringe and cower, as if to apologize for still being present' (Beckett 1994: 200).

The narrator tell us that 'One evening she was followed by a lamb. Reared for slaughter like the others it left them to follow her' (Beckett 1982: 36). Beckett's representation of the human condition suggests that we are all essentially reared for slaughter. We are born to die and everything that comes in between, including the pain, suffering and lost love, is basically worthless. The ironic juxtaposition of extreme elderliness with extreme youth is evident here. Adorned in black she provides a striking contrast to the purity and whiteness of the lamb, and yet it too will ultimately join with her in the common destiny of death. It is Beckett's sense of the brevity of life, coupled with the paradoxical sense of how long it takes to die, that informs his presentation of the mysteries of old age.

Appearing 'Well on the way to inexistence' (Beckett 1982: 54), her old body surely cannot endure. And yet Beckett denies satisfactory termination, as 'the place of the skull' (Beckett 1982: 57), representative perhaps of Golgotha,[7] suggests death and indeed resurrection. Therefore Beckett may be implying that old age will condemn us to physical mortality but spiritual oblivion cannot be assured. And if nothingness can be achieved, Beckett would perhaps wish for 'One moment more. One last. Grace to breathe that void. Know happiness' (Beckett 1982: 59). The text ends like a prayer, yearning for a fleeting moment to appreciate that one is about to pass into oblivion. Old age is thus like a burden or millstone that we might cast off in death. Perhaps happiness exists only in that post-death state, when we have one split second to know that death has arrived and released us from the burden of elderliness.

Beckett's representation of the physical implications of old age is a reminder that life is difficult and the ageing process is often intolerable. Growing old is not a period of enjoyment or relaxation, but ultimately the culmination of life's suffering, in which isolation often takes precedence and memories serve to reinforce the horror of the present. And yet despite the physical degradation, Beckett's characters continue, having no alternative but to endure the often unbearable condition called life – 'you must go on, I can't go on, I'll go on' (Beckett 1994: 418).

Chapter 3

The Decaying Landscape

warmth of primeval mud impenetrable dark

How It Is

The Beckett protagonist perhaps finds it difficult to ever escape from the world in which he exists, as ultimately he does not find himself irreconcilable with the environment in which he dwells. If we look closely at the Beckettian world we fail to locate the beautiful summer days often located in Romanticism for example. Warmth and vitality rarely exist within these landscapes, and the sterility, which has become dominant, offers no hope of renewal. Everything appears to be in decline, as Beckett presents the natural world in a state of degradation. Inside these landscapes, which appear, at times, apocalyptic, the reality of the void becomes even more apparent. The ruination of buildings and the representation of corpses, forces one to view the Beckettian world as almost horrific, where corrosion takes precedence over vitality. Beckett uses these physical images to represent decay and essentially emphasize the erosion of human life. The environment is therefore confirmation about how these characters feel internally, and we question how life could possibly get any better for them, when the world in which they exist is itself degenerating, with the external erosion emulating their inner decay.

A Piece of Monologue, written in 1979, is chiefly concerned with the notion of death, and the images employed throughout the narrative exemplify the central theme of decline. Originally entitled 'Gone'[1], the play produces an atmosphere of dejection, in which the central protagonist appears almost ethereal, with his ghostly presence suggesting that the only solid component of the play lies within the strength of the monologue itself. The sparseness of the setting and the faint diffuse lighting emulates the 'life' that exists within it, and we recognize in the protagonist that lack of identity so often attributed to the Beckettian character. The speaker appears preoccupied with memories from the past and possesses no imminent future. He exists perhaps somewhere between the physical world and the metaphysical reality of the void, as Beckett returns to his preoccupation with the fragility of life.

The opening line of the play ('Birth was the death of him' (Beckett 1990: 425)) is suggestive of the concept that life and death are not two separate domains, but exist side-by-side, one often merging into the other to form a collateral fusion of existence. If death becomes the reality of life, then the new-born becomes the 'new dead', and as we are brought forth in the horizontal position, so too will we depart from this existence. The images employed here all point towards death, and as the speaker has journeyed, 'From funeral to funeral. To now' (ibid.), we are reminded of the struggle to survive each day, to continue onwards and to cope, as we near the grave every second, with each day ultimately signifying a mini-death. 'Born dead of night. Sun long sunk behind the larches. New needles turning green. In the room dark gaining' (ibid.). The juxtaposition of the fertility in the outside world, with the darkness invading the room (which has just witnessed the birth of new life), is a striking image, illustrating that the fertility within the room is portrayed through darkness and is suggestive of death. Born into the dark is a significant image in Beckett's work, as the characters often appear metaphorically blind, endeavouring always to find their way in a world which appears devoid of meaning.

The black void, that encases the room in which the speaker exists, is indicative of the emptiness that he feels within his own life, as memories of past 'loved ones' serve to reinforce his complete feeling of isolation. The reality of the external void, encroaching upon his very existence, thereby heightens his ghost-like persona. The black emptiness, in which nothing stirs, prevents the intervention of natural light, and darkness therefore assumes priority by eliminating the effulgence, which would undoubtedly provide some degree of relief. However, the speaker appears reluctant to fully accept his current situation, and his progression towards the window is perhaps suggestive of his desire to discover some reality within the void that incarcerates his being. He stares out, possibly searching for something to alleviate his suffering, looking for light to infiltrate his darkness, and confirmation that nature is not in a state of decay.

The 'nothingness' which surrounds him externally, appears to be taking precedence internally, as everything is gravitating towards extinction, thereby highlighting Democritus' idea that 'nothing is more real than nothing'.[2] The artificial light, which provides some relief from the darkness of reality, is also difficult to sustain and he finds it hard lighting the lamp as each, 'Match goes out' (Beckett 1990: 426). This means of obtaining artificial light cannot endure indefinitely, and as each match extinguishes, his hope of achieving some degree of relief also dwindles, with the flicker of the flame, from barely visible to non-existent, conveying the state that he himself probably aspires to. His 'Dying on' (ibid.) is a process that he must endure, and is representative of the fact that death does not come easily and, similar to the struggle of life, one must experience the struggle of death. This state of being or 'non-being', where one is existing somewhere between life and death, is illustrated well through this artificial light, as it perhaps conveys the protagonist's 'artificial life', where reality itself appears to be running out, and to be gone is to be released.

The isolation, which the speaker conveys through his narrative, is further heightened through his own solitary position on stage, and we can assume that the tale he relays is his own personal monologue. The solitude is illustrated further as he moves to the edge of the light and confronts the blank wall, which was once covered with pictures of 'loved ones'. This reminds one very forcibly of *Not I* where Mouth emphasizes the lack of parental love and the dread of familial love. The Speaker details this purging of the pictures:

> Down one after another. Gone. Torn to shreds and scattered. Strewn all over the floor. Not at one sweep. No sudden fit of . . . no word. Ripped from the wall and torn to shreds one by one. Over the years. Years of nights. (ibid.)

This eradication of 'loved ones' may have be an attempt to erase the memory of their existence, due to the fact that their constant presence further confirmed the isolation that he now endures. The wedding day picture was perhaps difficult to look at, as it may have been a reminder of the company he experienced with his parents, and also illustrated that 'happy' time before his birth – predating the moment he was 'ripped' from blissful pre-existence. This collection of memories is slowly being obliterated as they are 'Swept out of the way under the bed and left. Thousand shreds under the bed with the dust and the spiders' (ibid.). The years of nights to which the speaker refers, is suggestive of the fact that daylight no longer prevails, and an eternal blackness lingers over this semi-existence. However, despite this endless succession of eternal nights, sleep appears to be prohibited and, although the speaker is dressed in his night attire, he is denied this form of escape. Instead, he is condemned night after night to reiterate his story, as slowly everything around him disintegrates.

Along with the darkness comes the intensity of the silence, as it too takes precedence, and we are told that there is 'Nothing to be heard anywhere' (ibid.).[3] Perhaps this piece of monologue, which he recites every evening, is an attempt to deny silence the supreme status which it assumes within the emptiness of the void. His talking is therefore his contribution in confirming his own 'existence' and, as everything deteriorates around him, he struggles to maintain the narrative, as 'Words are few' (Beckett 1990: 425). He turns and faces east, perhaps waiting for the sun to rise, or possibly waiting for his life to end, but ultimately waiting for something to take its course. However, the dawn never arrives and the hope of a new beginning or 'final ending' is denied, and he is left with 'Nothing. Empty dark' (Beckett 1990: 427). Beckett's use of imagery exemplifies his interest in the theme of decline, and explores the hopeless endeavours of the self to prevent the gradual deterioration of the body and mind, as one cannot disassociate oneself from the effects of the world in which one exists. The duality of death is therefore represented through the decline of body and mind, but also through the deterioration of man and nature conjunctively.

The arrival of a discernible glimmer, offered from the hand with the lighted spill, denotes perhaps a little hope, as the darkness is momentarily parted by the lamplight. But the faint glow is difficult to sustain, as the wick is turned low and will eventually fade. 'Birth the death of him' (ibid.), is uttered once again, suggesting that death will be his birth, if he can ever reach the stage of termination and cease to exist within this void. As everything is running out ('Window gone. Hands gone. Light gone. Gone. Again and again. Again and again gone' (Beckett 1990: 428)), he and his monologue are the only components to remain constant. Although his physical presence is barely visible in the faint light, his consciousness strives to confirm his existence, perhaps refusing to acknowledge the degeneration of his physical being.

The lack of colour in this play is evident, as the grey light is the only alternative offered within the darkness. Beckett's work is rarely black and white, but often a fusion of these two opposing colours, resulting in a shade which does not possess the solidity of a primary colour, but exists somewhere in between. The colour grey is therefore a useful metaphor for the state in which many of Beckett's protagonists exist: a fusion of life and death signifying the inability to fully live, or completely die.

It is interesting that, despite the implications of death so clearly visible from the imagery in this monologue, the first word that gathers in the Speaker's mouth is 'birth'. The juxtaposition of birth and death calls into question the viability of either component and illustrates the brevity of life. 'Stare beyond through rift in dark to other dark. Further dark' (ibid.). Each dark represents the transition from womb to tomb, and death signifies the birth from life. However, perhaps this is a premature death for the Speaker, as the whiteness of his physical being ('White hair catching light. White gown. White socks' (Beckett 1990: 429)), appears in direct opposition to the environment in which he exists. His whiteness, mingling with the blackness of the void, produces a feeling of dejection and exemplifies his spirit-like persona. It is not surprising that Beckett originally entitled this play 'Gone', as the notion of 'goneness' is clearly visible throughout. However, as the light again begins to fade towards the end of the monologue and deterioration prevails, 'The word begone' (ibid.), is denied; and although degeneration continues, we may presume that the monologue will remain constant and the speaker, similar to the globe, although 'Unutterably faint' (ibid.), will continue to be alone but not gone.

The evanescent nature of the Beckettian environment is clearly visible from Beckett's play *That Time*. Written between June 1974 and August 1975, it possesses many of the characteristics of *A Piece of Monologue*. Again we are presented with the dark stage contrasted with the whiteness of the Listener's old face and long flaring white hair. And once again Beckett presents us with a narrative whose complexities are to be found in the content, as well as in the technical staging, of the drama.

That Time, like much of Beckett's work, explores the implications of memory, as the protagonist, whose head is illuminated in the darkness, listens to three accounts of episodes in his isolated life. The title therefore conveys the idea of remembering past events, but it also performs a further function. Time is paramount to physical decay, and its importance within this play and significant presence in the title, forces one to acknowledge its status, as Time metaphorically assumes its role as a non-existent character and dominating force. Beckett's early treatment of this influence for deterioration is clearly illustrated in his essay on Proust:

> There is no escape from the hours and the days. Neither from tomorrow nor from yesterday. There is no escape from yesterday because yesterday has deformed us, or been deformed by us. The mood is of no importance. Deformation has taken place. (Beckett 1965: 13)

As the protagonist listens to recollections of different periods of his life, it emerges that two factors have remained constant throughout his existence. He appears to have been always isolated, despite the presence of others and, although his location has varied, his surroundings have constantly been plagued by ruination. The three voices labelled A, B and C are his own, and although heard externally we may assume that they derive from his consciousness. The three voices suggest a trinity and the complexities of a personality that is more than a simple singular entity. Although it is difficult to suggest the exact period which each voice describes, Beckett, according to Knowlson, explained that, 'The B story has to do with the young man, the C story is the story of the old man and the A story that of the man in middle-age' (Asmus 1977: 92) quoted here from Knowlson (1997: 601). Therefore, although the voices are 'distinct', they work in unison providing the complete picture of a fragmented life.

By examining the recollection of voice B, which illustrates the life of the young man, it becomes clear that youth is not made up of eternal summers, when one believes the day will never end, and love blinds us from the prevailing degradation of the outside world. Beckett denies this idyllic setting, possibly because it never really exists, and instead forces us to acknowledge that corrosion must ultimately take precedence over vitality, as B's story of 'love' moves through images of pollution and death. The rural setting is indicative of the isolation that the protagonist endures, and despite the presence of a 'lover', his solitude is not even momentarily eclipsed, as the couple remain 'not touching or anything of that nature' Beckett (1990: 388). With the 'wheat turning yellow' (ibid.), in the sun, we presume that this encounter takes place in late summer; and yet Beckett denies the ideal, as the fertility of the environment is juxtaposed with the infertility of the relationship. Late summer is therefore emblematic of a dying relationship. And, as they sit on the stone together, the coldness of the scene takes precedence over the warmth of the season. The silence, which clearly dominates this encounter, provides a glimpse of the void, which will eventually incarcerate the protagonist, confirming the reality that had existed throughout his life.

Beckett fails to use normal parameters of time, as the protagonist remembers scenes from 'way back in childhood or the womb worst of all' (Beckett 1990: 390). The elusive nature of time and memory is clearly highlighted, and the uncomfortable nature of the protagonist's life evidently existed during the pre-birth stage. The womb ultimately becomes the tomb, and the sterility of the 'life-chamber' prepares the newborn for the infertility of existence. As the darkness encroaches upon the Listener's life, he attempts to deny silence the supreme status it assumes within the emptiness of the void by endeavouring to create tales: 'one of those things you kept making up to keep the void out just another of those old tales to keep the void from pouring in on top of you the shroud' (ibid.). The void, which will ultimately incarcerate his being, is the reality of life, and as life recedes and death takes precedence, the void within the ground represents the final 'resting' place, as emptiness follows us from life into death. This notion of inventing tales prompts one to question the viability of any past event recalled by any Beckett protagonist, and suggests that the credibility of memory is indeed questionable. Perhaps Beckett's characters feel the need to invent an ideal past in order to help them cope with the reality that living among degradation is the only alternative to not living at all. Beckett often portrays a moment of perfection, momentarily luring one into the misguided notion that life can be good, and raising hopes in expectation that the ideal does exist. However, this moment of apparent Utopia is quickly shattered, as Beckett once again illustrates the harshness of reality by employing imagery denotative of decay. Therefore the dead rat, which drifts downstream into the sinking sun, forces us to acknowledge that infertility and death are forever lurking 'in the reeds' (Beckett 1990: 391), of life, and a moment of apparent bliss is only one instant in a lifetime of impoverished existence. Beneath the ostensibly beautiful face of Nature lies a deeper reality characterized by death, ugliness and decomposition.

The fact that there was 'always space between' (ibid.) the couple highlights the solitary confinement which the protagonist grows accustomed to. The irony of the situation is indeed evident, and we realize that the one time he had someone in his life, he remained fundamentally alone. Beckett is perhaps illustrating the reality that despite company, we are ultimately solitary and the presence of others can only alleviate our isolation momentarily. Even during the flushes of youth the protagonist appears resigned to his fate. His acceptance that words cannot be sustained indefinitely, and that silence must ultimately reign supreme, perhaps forces him to give up:

> gave up there by the window in the dark or moonlight gave up for good and let it in and nothing the worse a great shroud billowing in all over you on top of you and little or nothing the worse little or nothing. (Beckett 1990: 394)

The darkness, which has begun to take hold, emulates the black void, which incarcerates him internally. The dejection, which he exudes, manifests itself through the corrosion of the external world. As the play progresses his circumstances deteriorate, as Mother Nature appears to don her clothes of subversion. Malone clearly illustrates how the first signs of darkness perhaps denote the beginning of the 'end': 'A little darkness, in itself, at the time is nothing. You think no more about it and you go on. But I know what darkness is, it accumulates, thickens, then suddenly bursts and drowns everything' (Beckett 1994: 190).

The complex structure of the play is similar to that of *Krapp's Last Tape*, as the memories are not conveyed through a chronological order but instead jump back and forth, resembling the rewind or forward function which the tape recorder provides. However, this is the tape recorder of the mind, selecting spools which denote deterioration and providing memories steeped in isolation. As we listen to Voice A, which details the story of the middle-aged man, we see the development of the theme of decline, and Beckett's notion of 'goneness' manifests itself through the narrative. Years have passed and the protagonist's situation has progressively worsened, with the environment that surrounds him evidently conveying further signs of ruination. The Voice recalls how he returned to the place where he 'hid as a child' (Beckett 1990: 388), perhaps in an attempt to lay old ghosts to rest and move on with his present existence. The image of the boy taking refuge among the ruins is a poignant one, as Beckett juxtaposes an image of decay with the vitality of youth. Again the protagonist chooses the coldness of stone on which to sit, therefore seeking comfort amid sterility. Perhaps this child feels secure in the midst of the wreckage, because within this space he is confronting the situation that he himself must ultimately become – ruined.

The sun has long since vanished, and the day, lacking in colour, has no alternative but to assume that in between state of darkness and light, resulting in a grey day. The weather that is described throughout this section, suggests the period just preceding winter, when the landscape prepares itself for the harshness of the final season. The fact that the protagonist is now middle-aged is significant, as he has moved from the youth of summer into this grey period, awaiting the coldness of the winter years, which denote the cruelty of old age. Everything is in decline, as the trams no longer exist leaving only 'the old rails all rust' (Beckett 1990: 389). The corrosion of the tracks exemplifies the erosion of his spirit, as he fails to find alleviation from the isolation which has now haunted him for many years. Foley's Folly, which provided some comfort for him as a child, perhaps represents his feelings of deterioration, as the weeds have claimed supremacy and the area now lies abandoned: 'bit of a tower still standing all the rest rubble and nettles where did you sleep no friend all the homes gone' (ibid.). The pilgrimage, which the protagonist takes to discover the memories of childhood, forces him to confront the reality of life, as the declining landscape represents an apocalyptic scene, where he appears to be among the last survivors. The world around him is essentially disintegrating and he remains powerless to prevent it: 'that way all closed down and boarded up Doric terminus of the Great Southern and Eastern all closed down and the colonnade crumbling away' (Beckett 1990: 391). We are told he then gave up, and we assume that within this abandoned structure he recognizes his own isolated self. And as his feelings of dejection are epitomized through his surroundings, human nature fails to comfort, and we realize, within this recollection, that even the lesson from the parable of the Good Samaritan has long since faded, as the people choose to 'pass by on the other side' (Beckett 1990: 392), ignoring his isolation and melancholy persona. As Knowlson says, Beckett has presented a 'concentrated image of human isolation in a world that is hurrying about its business, ignoring the signs of decay, disintegration and death with which it is surrounded' (Knowlson and Pilling 1979: 216). Therefore, the middle-aged man resembles the boy from childhood as, sitting on the doorstep, he re-enacts, 'that time on the stone the child on the stone where none ever came' (ibid.); however, his own disintegration now complements his surroundings and we no longer see the stark contrast of youth amid the ruins. 'Away to hell out of it' (Beckett 1990: 395) is his cue to leave this scene and enter an environment that further exemplifies this central theme of decline.

Winter now takes precedence and the coldness of the season metaphorically denotes the harshness of ageing, as life enters the final stage, completing the cycle in preparation for death. Voice C, details the story of the old man, who has reached this final season, and the isolation, which he has endured throughout his lifetime, follows him towards death. It is now 'always winter' (Beckett 1990: 388), and the persistent rain forces him to take refuge within the Portrait Gallery. Again he is drawn to the sterility of stone and seeks comfort on the marble slab awaiting his clothes to dry. No longer do we see the contrast between the protagonist and his surroundings, as the sterility of the stone complements the infertility of the body. Human nature cannot provide relief from the isolation, and if loved ones existed they are now 'all gone long ago all dust the lot' (Beckett 1990: 389). The protagonist now in the pre-death phase ironically adopts the pre-birth position, as he embraces himself, resigned to the fact that no one else can afford him comfort. Within this place of preservation the effects of decay cannot be denied, and one is forced to acknowledge that this deteriorating process cannot be withstood and must ultimately reign supreme. As he views 'a vast oil black with age and dirt' (ibid.), of some, 'young prince or princess of the blood black with age' (ibid.), we recognize that lack of colour so often attributed to Beckett's work. Of course, we can presume that the picture is black due to its age, but the structure of language here permits us to surmise that the blood is black with age; the redness of the blood, unable to maintain its vitality, succumbs to the darkness, which takes precedence in the veins. And as the painting shows the protagonist's reflection, he too becomes encased among the dust and dirt. His failure to recognize his own reflection perhaps illustrates the mind's reluctance to acknowledge the physical breakdown, over which it has no control. The image presented before him is no longer representative of the man he used to be, as the decaying influence of old age has resulted in deformation. The 'portraits of the dead black with dirt and antiquity' (Beckett 1990: 391), exemplify the play's theme of decline and death, illustrating the evanescent nature of the Beckettian world and the approaching fate of the protagonist. Despite efforts to alleviate his solitary position, public places, such as the Library and Post Office, reinforce his feelings of isolation and he fails to attract company. He appears almost removed from 'civilization', incarcerated within a void in which time has slowed and confronting the cold reality that life is passing him by: 'always winter then endless winter year after year as if it couldn't end the old year never end like time could go no further' (Beckett 1990: 393). The limbo in which he now dwells prevents him from fully living or completely dying, as time condemns him to existence. The Library, a place of preservation, does not provide refuge from the decay, and with 'the whole place suddenly full of dust' (Beckett 1990: 395), the protagonist is forced to confront what he himself must ultimately become, as he prepares to return to the ground. Perhaps his presence is not noticed due to the fact that his existence is not verifiable. The ghostly persona we see before us on stage perhaps suggests that the isolation, which plagued his 'existence', may be attributed to the fact that he failed to exist. The Listener's face, with the long flaring white hair, appears indicative of a death mask, and despite the occasional blinking of the eyes it fails to convey any real signs of life. This disembodied image may represent the breakdown of the physical body through time, illustrating the evolution of the protagonist's existence alongside the deterioration of the environmental landscape. However, it may be suggested that the image we see before us is denotative of what he has always been, a personification of consciousness, lacking the solidity of physical form, but nevertheless striving to survive in a world destined to decay. The final words – 'gone in no time' (ibid.) – suggest that he exists outside the influences of time, where his consciousness will remain alone, but will perhaps defy the notion of 'goneness'.

Beckett's preoccupation with imagery of physical decline is not reserved solely for his later works, but is evident also throughout his early publications. *First Love*, one of Beckett's earlier post-war novellas, was written in French during 1946. This short prose fiction provides a useful illustration of the physical deterioration surrounding us in everyday life, and explores the absurdity in believing that love could exist in a world which is itself perishing. It is not surprising that Beckett's representation of love is by no means idealized, and one feels slightly bemused at the idea of a text entitled *First Love* beginning in the confines of a cemetery. In fact Lulu, the object of the narrator's 'desire', does not make an appearance until 12 pages into the text. Beckett's decision to begin this tale of 'love' within the graveyard is a poignant one, highlighting that the only real certainty that exists in life is death, and that a true beginning is ultimately found among the ruins of the necropolis.

'Personally I have no bone to pick with graveyards' (Beckett 1999c: 8). The narrator obviously acquires some sort of contentment from the visits to his father's grave, and the black joke sets the tone of cynicism that characterizes the text. The imagery that Beckett employs right from the beginning turns the conventional perception of graveyards on its head, and instead illuminates the grotesque nature of the living:

> The smell of corpses, distinctly perceptible under those of grass and humus mingled, I do not find unpleasant, a trifle on the sweet side perhaps, a trifle heady, but how infinitely preferable to what the living emit, their feet, teeth, armpits, arses, sticky foreskins and frustrated ovules. (Beckett 1999c: 9)

As the narrator continues, it becomes evident that his preoccupation with images of physical decay highlights his relationship with life and death, and substantiates his satisfaction with his own imminent interment. He waits the day when the epitaph he has carefully constructed can be reared above his head.

Again Beckett denies the warmth of the summer months and places the protagonist within the cruel reality of winter. The extreme coldness, which exists externally, is clearly exemplified in the narrator's treatment of love, and the desire for isolation further confirms his contempt for life. As he sits among the tombstones he states, 'It was December, I have never felt so cold, the eel soup lay heavy on my stomach, I was afraid I'd die, I turned aside to vomit, I envied them.' (Beckett 1999c: 13). These lines illustrate the reality that his first love is not the woman he copulates with; his first love in life (his primary most prevalent love) is essentially death.

As the couple first meet on the banks of the canal, one is fooled into believing that this ideal romantic setting may provide a welcome alternative to the landscape of decay found within the cemetery. However, the Beckettian environment appears to deny any such beauty and therefore one's initial perception of an idealized location is quickly eradicated:

> It was a well situated bench, backed by a mound of solid earth and garbage, so that my rear was covered. My flanks too, partially, thanks to a pair of

venerable trees, more than venerable, dead, at either end of the bench. It was no doubt these trees one fine day, aripple with all their foliage, that had sown the idea of a bench, in someone's fancy. (Beckett 1999c: 20)

Love in Beckett's work is denied the privilege of being nurtured within an environment of beauty and fertility, but is instead forced to come to fruition in a world where solid earth and garbage replace the elegance of Wordsworth's yellow daffodils. However, this is not an environment that has always been subject to decay, for Beckett often displays these landscapes (similar to the people who inhabit them) as having seen better days. As the trees, once adorned with foliage, now stand barren and past their prime, thereby no longer serving the purpose for which they were planted, we recognize in them the representation of one's own life, as time passes and damns us to deterioration; and we too become like 'old leaves that have known the long joys of summer and now are good for nothing but to lie rotting in a heap' (Beckett 1994: 232). The declining quality of Beckett's landscapes clearly reflects the flawed and imperfect nature of the characters, and the relationships they have with others. The 'frosted mound, facing the icy water' (Beckett 1999c: 36), and the cold which 'embossed the path' (ibid.), illustrates the cruelty of the elements which dominate this landscape, and creates an atmosphere full of dejection in which the landscape, solidified by coldness, offers no hope of renewal; the narrator co-exists with Lulu at a point of frozen isolation, thereby highlighting the apathetic nature of their apparent 'love'. The 'waning love' portrayed throughout this text illustrates Beckett's preoccupation with 'goneness'. It is interesting how many of Beckett's protagonists appear to prefer the darkness ('I was alone at last, in the dark at last' (Beckett 1999c: 52)), taking refuge in its stillness and embracing the isolation which becomes even more prevalent within that dark void. Perhaps the blackness, contrary to conventional belief, provides some form of solace, as it prevents one from perceiving the degeneration which is occurring within one's surroundings, and therefore momentarily alleviates the melancholy effects of physical decay. Or perhaps it is the final and necessary encounter with silence and acceptance of death, darkness and the void.

The inability to sustain life and prevent deterioration has constantly bemused man, making it difficult to accept that we have no control over our own physical condition and no power to prevent the degeneration of the environment. The withering of the hyacinth[4] clearly illustrates the impossibility of preservation and creates a feeling of dejection within the reader, as we realize that this common houseplant metaphorically represents our future, as we too will eventually undergo this decomposition. As this tale of 'love' draws to its conclusion, the onset of winter prohibits any chance of imminent improvement. However, Beckett uncharacteristically offers some degree of hope, as the narrator declares that 'One should not dread the winter, it too has its bounties, the snow gives warmth and deadens the tumult and its pale days are soon over' (Beckett 1999c: 60). This degree of optimism suggests a determination to struggle on in the hope that things could possibly get better. The poignant image of human nature endeavouring to cope and continue onwards in an environment destined to decay, illustrates the paradoxical nature of Beckett's work. As Knowlson says 'it is often forgotten that Beckett's work is as much about persisting and continuing as it is about ending' (1997: 680).

One often questions what it is that makes Beckett's characters continue onwards, and persevere, despite the difficulties that are continually placed in their paths. Although this question is never fully answered, we may assume that they continue because there is no alternative but to continue ('Suicide represented for [Beckett] an unacceptable kind of surrender' (Knowlson 1997: 569)). However, this driving force, which condemns these characters to 'continual existence', appears almost absurd, due to the fact that they are surviving in a world that is disintegrating. The imagery examined throughout this chapter clearly exemplifies Beckett's interest in the theme of decline, as it explores the failure of the self to prevent the gradual deterioration of body and mind, and illustrates the reality that one cannot disassociate oneself from the effects of the world in which one exists. The characters exist in an environment devoid of meaning where everything appears to be gravitating towards extinction. However, although the images all point towards death, they ultimately fail to suggest termination, thereby incarcerating the protagonists in a state of limbo which offers no hope of renewal. 'The winter's tale', which many characters reiterate, is perhaps an attempt to confirm their own existence, and despite the decay which incarcerates them, they cling to the one thing which they believe can be sustained – words. However, as the speaker in *A Piece of Monologue* confirms, 'Words are few' (Beckett 1990: 425), and similar to everything else, they too will eventually fade, as the void becomes the reality. We are reminded of the words from Revelation: 'And in those days shall men seek death, and shall not find it; and shall desire to die, and death shall flee from them' (Rev. 9.6). Therefore, damned to existence the characters will continue, having no alternative but to keep on, and perpetually witnessing the deterioration of man and nature simultaneously, as death appears forever elusive.

Chapter 4

Moribund Man
Beckett and Death

But what matter whether I was born or not, have lived or not, am dead or merely dying, I shall go on doing as I have always done, not knowing what it is I do, nor who I am, nor where I am, nor if I am.

Malone Dies

Beckett's interpretation of death prompts one to view it, not as a sudden and terminal event, but rather as a process that must be endured if one is to reach that final stage of closure. However, to describe death in Beckett's work as providing a satisfactory conclusion is problematic, due to the fact that many of his characters exist in a limbo which appears to linger somewhere between this life and the next. This representation of death therefore suggests that, although the physical body will eventually die, we cannot be sure if the consciousness also discontinues. Christopher Ricks is right when he says that Beckett 'is the great writer of an age which has created new possibilities and impossibilities even in the matter of death' (1993: 33).

Death dominates Beckett's writing from the early years right up until the period of his own demise. Much of the work illustrates that ardent desire to comprehend the meaning of death, and we see through the writing that continuing need to probe the boundaries between this life and the next (if a subsequent life exists) in an attempt to uncover the true implications of mortality, and explore the mind's reaction to the imminence of physical degeneration. Life in Beckett's work is often viewed as a punishment; perhaps the pain of living provides sufficient atonement for the sin of having been born.

Throughout *Malone Dies* (published in French 1951) Beckett explores the mind of a dying man, allowing us access to a place that is essentially private, as we witness the degeneration of Malone's physical and mental faculties. Once again Beckett's use of language provides a new complexity to this prose piece and, despite it being entitled *Malone Dies*, it is somewhat difficult to pinpoint the exact moment of the protagonist's death. Malone, similar to the Speaker in *A Piece of Monologue*, appears to be 'Dying on' (Beckett 1990: 426), thereby illustrating that death rarely occurs instantaneously and, similar to living, it too becomes a struggle. For Beckett, to be alive is to be necessarily in the process of dying. The one entails the other.

It is difficult to determine Malone's exact location and we question whether the room in which he now 'subsists' is situated in a nursing establishment or indeed some type of sanatorium. Without clarification of his exact whereabouts, the room itself takes precedence and we realize that, within this enclosed space, Malone must ultimately face death alone. The proposal that people dwell above and below him highlights the idea that he resides in a kind of limbo, appearing suspended between two worlds, as the room resembles that in-between state of life and death. Beckett appears to represent death not as an ending, but rather as a further stage of being and, quite probably, an even more tortured one in which it resembles a 'finality without end' (Beckett 1994: 112), and a birth into a more terrifying realm. Malone declares, 'I shall soon be quite dead at last in spite of all. Perhaps next month. Then it will be the month of April or of May' (Beckett 1994: 179). Ironically, spring usually represents a period of renewal. Malone may therefore view it as being an appropriate time to die, as he imagines death to offer a welcome alternative to the pain of living. It is interesting that he says, 'I could die to-day, if I wished, merely by making a little effort. But it is just as well to let myself die, quietly, without rushing things' (ibid.). Contrary to popular opinion, Malone's statement suggests that he himself is in control of death, consequently claiming ownership over a process in which we essentially have no control. Beckett's essay on Proust highlights this idea as he says, 'Whatever opinion we may be pleased to hold on the subject of death, we may be sure that it is meaningless and valueless. Death has not required us to keep a day free' (Beckett 1965: 17). Subject to the influences of time and degeneration, Malone's quest for death takes precedence over his desire for life, and as he resolves to await death, acknowledging that he cannot determine the specific moment of his demise, he chooses to invent stories in an attempt to pass the time.

Here bodily death appears dislocated from mental decline, as the physical degeneration occurs more rapidly than mental deterioration, and the dualism of body and mind becomes highlighted. Malone is effectively paralyzed, unable and unwilling to move from the bed, which now incarcerates his physical being. The body is therefore useless and may be viewed as a hindrance, thereby appearing similar to a machine that has essentially broken down. As Malone says, 'My body is what is called, unadvisedly perhaps, impotent. There is virtually nothing it can do' (Beckett 1994: 186). The Cartesian theory of, 'I think, therefore I am', is clearly highlighted throughout this text, and only with the demise of conscious thought will Malone effectively die. Striving to cope with the situation which now confronts him, Malone adopts the device of storytelling, in an attempt to occupy his mind, until the moment of release, when the mind no longer covets mental stimulation and essentially ceases to function. It is important that Malone chooses to transcribe his stories, thereby providing further stimulus for the consciousness and allowing the microcosm of his mind to take precedence before his eyes. However, the act of writing also provides confirmation of existence, proving more durable than the spoken word, which is subject to misinterpretation and fades instantaneously. The written word will endure the passing of time and therefore, even after his death, a small part of Malone's mind will continue to exist.

One may therefore argue that Malone's preoccupation with storytelling (a characteristic of many Beckettian protagonists) is an attempt to achieve a small portion of immortality, as the legacy of his conscious thought will transcend the degenerative nature of his physical being; hence we are consequently reminded of the ambiguity of the human attitude towards mortality. However, the need to transcribe is hampered by the dwindling of the pencil lead and we are reminded that everything is subject to degeneration. To write about another's life in an attempt to comprehend the complexities of one's own, or as a means of escapism, suggests a crisis of identity and an inability to confront the difficulties of one's own existence. Malone says, 'And on the threshold of being no more I succeed in being another' (Beckett 1994: 194). To tell one's own story through an imaginative character provides distance, thereby allowing us to examine our lives, while simultaneously denying that the narrative we relate exemplifies our own existence. And as we shall see in Chapter 7, the 'I' is therefore conveniently replaced by the 'not I', and we are content to relay our life-story in the delusion that we are not in fact conveying our true self, if at all a true self exists.

Through his stories, Malone attempts to confront the nature of death, and although they temporarily provide a release from the monotony of living, they do not offer escape from the inevitability of his own demise. Malone's creative mind is abundant with references to death and, although one may see the negativity of his apparent obsession, Malone himself views his chosen theme as liberating. He may not be able to control death within the macrocosm, but within the microcosm of his mind he becomes omnipotent, enabling him to control a force, which in reality he is subject to, and ultimately condemned by. Malone's figments essentially embody the dualism of life and death, and through his narratives we witness his preoccupation with the descent into the self, which Murphy similarly aspires to. At first glance his stories appear purely fictional, but as they progress we recognize that the lives of his characters merge with his own existence and are perhaps congruous with his own situation. Therefore, as Malone writes about the lives of the Lamberts and his main protagonist Sapo, who later becomes Macmann, we identify his ardent desire to confront the nature of death, due to the fact that his narratives personify the degenerative nature of the physical being and illustrate death in its most potent form. The images of mortality which occur throughout Malone's stories are indicative of the fact that life and death are not two separate domains, but must be viewed as analogous, with each one representing an incongruous state of 'being'. Pozzo reiterates this point, as he declares 'one day we were born, one day we shall die, the same day, the same second, is that not enough for you?' (Beckett 1990: 83).

It is interesting that, on the verge of death, Malone, who describes himself as an octogenarian, chooses to characterize himself as a foetus. However, the comfort of the womb has been replaced by the harshness of the room, which now incarcerates Malone's physical form, only this time he awaits the release of death, offering an alternative freedom from the release of birth:

> Yes, an old foetus, that's what I am now, hoar and impotent, mother is done for, I've rotted her, she'll drop me with the help of gangrene, perhaps papa is at the party too, I'll land head-foremost mewling in the charnel-house, not that I'll mewl, not worth it. (Beckett 1994: 226)

This poignant image of unconventional birth is indicative of Beckett's attempt to continually equate life and death. Being described as an old foetus prompts one to view Malone as having never really been born, (a condition once proposed to Beckett by Jung),[1] and indeed it may be suggested that, although he has experienced conventional birth, he has not yet been liberated by the new birth which occurs at the instant of death. To die is essentially a rebirth into yet another phase of 'existence' or non-existence, the latter appearing preferable to most Beckettian protagonists.

As death appears unattainable, Malone again uses the device of storytelling to portray his preoccupation with mortality. Sapo (perhaps derived from *Homo sapiens*) has assumed a new identity in the form of Macmann, who finds himself gaining consciousness 'in a kind of asylum' (Beckett 1994: 257), labelled number 166. At this point of Malone's narrative we find ourselves questioning Malone's own location, due to the fact that, although Malone and Macmann's stories appear distinct, the similarities between the two soon become apparent, and we sense that Macmann's existence is indicative of Malone's. The number attributed to Macmann suggests that he is, perhaps, a prisoner. The implications of Macmann's imprisonment are reflective of Malone's current situation. Although Malone may not be incarcerated in the conventional way, he is undeniably subjected to the confines of his physical form. However, his conscious mind also serves to incarcerate him within this existence, condemning him to function mentally within a body that declines to function physically.

Macmann's 'love' interest, Moll, epitomizes the degenerative nature of the physical form, successfully illustrating the absurdity of the body, and the grotesque constitution of the individual at the point of death: 'The sight of her so diminished did not damp Macmann's desire to take her, all stinking, yellow, bald and vomiting, in his arms' (Beckett 1994: 266).

To live forever is often the aspiration of the young, oblivious of the effects of degeneration and the brutality of ageing. The severity of existence has not yet encroached upon the optimistic nature of youth, and the contemplation of one's own epitaph appears absurd. To linger indefinitely between this life and the next, as Malone is effectively condemned to do, forces one to confront death as a means of deliverance from the absurdity that we choose to call living. The desire to die, coupled with the need to go on, is the dilemma facing many Beckett characters. Malone's eagerness to complete the story of Macmann is symptomatic of his attempt to assert control over an existence in which he reigns supreme, and provide closure on a story which reflects his own. As he endeavours to consummate his narrative, it is evident that his life force is diminishing. The irony that his quest for death is nearly complete at a time when he strives for continuance is typical of the Beckettian protagonist. Beckett successfully illustrates, through the structure of the text, that Malone is slowly fading, as he implements shorter paragraphs which are indicative of Malone's struggle to transcribe his story. We may assume that Malone's energy is languishing, as the paragraphs appear laconic, suggesting an impatient desire to conclude, and an uneasiness that his life will be over before his story has been told.

With his consciousness continuing, Malone uses his few remaining breaths to provide closure for Macmann. As he details Macmann's excursion with Lemuel and the other inmates, we recognize once again Malone's ardent desire to confront the brutality of death. As Lemuel ruthlessly murders his patients, offering death to those who do not seek it, we may question Malone's desire to end his story in such a negative way. However, what we may perceive to be a cruel ending would, in Malone's eyes, be a liberating experience. Malone has confronted death within the mind and, as his characters die, Malone too embraces mortality. Although Beckett fails to stipulate the exact moment of Malone's death, we may assume that he has ceased to function, as the words are effaced. However, to assume that Malone has achieved total termination is somewhat problematic, because although his story has ended, his consciousness may continue to function, and he may subsist in an alternative state of being:

> I am being given, if I may venture the expression, birth to into death, such is my impression. The feet are clear already, of the great cunt of existence. Favourable presentation I trust. My head will be the last to die. Haul in your hands. I can't. The render rent. My story ended I'll be living yet. Promising lag. That is the end of me. I shall say I no more. (Beckett 1994: 285)

With the feet protruding forth, followed eventually by the head, it may be suggested that within this breech birth/death, Malone recognizes that he has one foot in the grave, and acknowledges the difficulty in terminating the mental faculties. In the midst of life there appears to exist only death, and only by confronting the implications of this reality may we comprehend our existence, as we continually question:

> Wherefore is light given to him that is in misery, and life unto the bitter *in* soul; Which long for death, but it *cometh* not; and dig for it more than for hid treasures; Which rejoice exceedingly, *and* are glad, when they can find the grave? (Job 3.20-22)

Reaching the grave therefore becomes man's priority, as it constitutes that final 'resting place' in which termination is perhaps assured. To return to the earth from which we came may in theory suggest a relief from the suffering of being. However, as Beckett illustrates in *Happy Days* (written in1960) Mother Earth is not always welcoming. The irony of the title is indicative of the absurdity of living, as we essentially endure each 'happy day' subject to decline in anticipation of death.

Winnie's optimism cannot be denied, and it serves to reinforce the individual's helplessness to withstand the pull of mortality in an environment where sterility takes precedence over renewability. Again we see how birth and death are not polar opposites for Beckett, but facets of the same experience. Macklin clearly illustrates this point as he says, in his essay 'The teller and the tale: Narrating the narrator in Samuel Beckett's *Cendres, Pas moi* and *Pas*', 'Frequently in Beckett's theatre the demarcation line between life and death is eclipsed and one is left uncertain as to the status of the characters and voices we encounter' (Cardy and Cannon 2000: 116). To perceive death, as the moment of physical extinction is justifiable; however, as Beckett illustrates, physical mortality does not always entail mental termination and therefore the theory that death is a protracted and complex process is confirmed.

The dismembered human image presented to us in Act One is perhaps Beckett's perception of a middle-aged woman who is undoubtedly past her prime and prone to deterioration. The blonde hair, low bodice and big bosom suggest a woman who is 'well preserved' and Winnie is undeniably maintained in her current situation, as the earth tightens its grip around her. Immobilized from the waist down, Winnie is physically restricted, as her body, subject to decline, has begun the process of degeneration, and she readily declares 'woe woe is me' (Beckett 1990: 140). As character and set merge in this drama to form an image which appears absurd, we recognize the reality it signifies, as death awaits us all and Mother Earth provides the burial ground: 'In the sweat of thy face shalt thou eat bread, till thou return unto the ground; for out of it wast thou taken: for dust thou *art*, and unto dust shalt thou return' (Gen. 3.19).

This image of life and death prompts one to view these two states of being as analogous, and therefore question the meaning of existence. If death exists in life, are any of us really living or are we all essentially dying? And the inevitability of death forces us to confront the viability of continuance. Winnie's optimism, and determination to perpetuate her life, appears pointless within this landscape destined to decay, and yet she remains committed to going on. Beckett successfully illustrates that human instinct to survive and the 'cheerful' disposition, which is often located in the dying individual, and rarely discovered in those who are left behind.

The items in her bag help occupy Winnie's time, but primarily they serve to occupy her mind, providing material for her to talk about. Words are vital in maintaining Winnie's existence, and similar to Malone's, they reinforce a certain reality and confirmation that life still prevails. Winnie's fear of solitude cannot be negated despite the fact that she appears capable of surviving alone. Indeed she is capable of passing the time unaccompanied, but the fear of having no one to confirm her existence weighs heavy upon her. We do not know the cause of Winnie's predicament, and can only speculate about her end, but what is clear is that time is passing. Without the passing of time, change cannot occur and to deny that change takes place in this drama is flawed. Winnie's situation constantly deteriorates, as gravity pulls her further into her tomb and her life expectancy dwindles. Endeavouring to comprehend the implications of time the Unnamable questions:

> why it buries you grain by grain neither dead nor alive, with no memory of anything, no hope of anything, no knowledge of anything, no history and no prospects, buried under the seconds, saying any old thing, your mouth full of sand (Beckett 1994: 393)

Evidently this environment is subject to time, and Winnie herself resembles the hourglass, and more specifically the grains of sand inside, slowly slipping away through time denoting change. Knowlson reinforces this as he says, 'For however unchanging and apparently endless Winnie's existence might appear to be, change *is* present in the shape of decline, degeneration and deceleration' (Knowlson and Pilling 1979: 95–96).

'The way man adapts himself. [*Pause*] To changing conditions' (Beckett 1990: 153), is indeed admirable, and Winnie's acceptance of further deterioration is evident by the second act. As the earth slowly deprives her of her powers, her life force is degenerating. No longer does prayer comfort her, and the optimistic clichés are used less frequently, as we essentially witness Winnie's live burial. Spiritually deadened, Winnie appears almost resigned to her fate, welcoming death as an acceptable alternative to the pain of life. Her inability to turn her head prevents her from looking at Willie, and the restriction of her arms impedes her usage of the mirror. Without confirmation of her presence, Winnie's existence is limited, and she recognizes that the end is near, as she faces death amid extreme solitude. Beckett frequently insists upon solitude as a *sine qua non* of the experience of dying, and again he successfully illustrates the duality of body and mind. Despite being physically defunct, Winnie remains mentally articulate, therefore highlighting the theory that physical death does not constitute absolute termination if the consciousness survives. However, in this drama there is no assurance of termination and therefore no confirmation that death will occur. We may speculate that by a third act Winnie may have completely disappeared, her physical body no longer visible, but clarification of complete termination would be impossible, as her consciousness may cling to existence.

Willie's presence may be viewed as almost sinister, especially within the final stages of the drama. We question why he fails to provide aid to Winnie, appearing almost resigned to her fate; and it is exactly this inability to provide help which should prompt us to feel sympathy towards Willie. Winnie has begun the death process, a journey that she must ultimately take alone, and a state from which no one can save her. Willie is therefore condemned to witness his wife's death, tormented by the knowledge that he is powerless to prevent it. He therefore fails to act, simply because there is nothing he can do. Perhaps this is why Willie's presence is not prevalent in the play, as Beckett attempts to illustrate that dying is a solitary process. Hence, Willie takes his place behind the mound, assuming the position which he will adhere to after Winnie's death, as he himself will effectively be 'left behind', the not so 'merry widower'. Perhaps this is why he reaches for the gun; unable and unwilling to go on without her, he is possibly comforted in the knowledge that death is at his fingertips. The company that they shared throughout life may therefore continue after death and, as they look at each other, the poignancy of this drama is portrayed. This is not Romeo and Juliet, and yet the reality that Beckett captures is perhaps just as moving. Dramatizing the death of a middle-aged woman with her husband as witness is undoubtedly affecting. To sum up *Happy Days* as a play about death is rather problematic, as it indubitably constitutes more than this. However, one cannot deny the existence of mortality, despite the fact that Beckett provides no assurance of total termination.

The desire to comprehend the complexities of death through writing remained with Beckett throughout his life, and we can see through the later texts that continual probing into the implications of mortality, despite the vastly different prose style. 'For to end yet again' and the other *Fizzles* portray that descent into the self, which confronts the problems of beginning and ending, and questions the theory of existence. The turbulence surrounding these voices in the dark creates an atmosphere of dejection, and a desire to provide closure in a world that appears interminable. During this latter period of writing an impression was evolving that Beckett was moving toward silence. Undoubtedly Beckett's writings were becoming condensed, ultimately exploring the void where silence must logically reign supreme. But Beckett does not often give credence to logic, and the silence that one expects to uncover at the end of these texts remains elusive, as termination is inevitably denied.

'For to end yet again', written initially in French and published in 1976, is ironically the first text in the compilation of *Fizzles* which all explore the concept that to end completely is an impossibility.[2] This initial narrative, similar to the subsequent texts, has the appearance of an unfinished work, and the voices, which appear indistinguishable from each other, add a complexity to these works which can make them appear, at times, beyond comprehension. This work appears to be analogous to a text published six years previously, entitled *Lessness*. Beckett explored in this earlier text the difficulty of dying and the struggle with continuance, in a landscape dominated by sand. However, in 'For to end yet again', Beckett's transition from sand to dust creates a greater feeling of dejection, in an atmosphere of claustrophobia, illustrating that the text *Lessness* paradoxically contains 'moreness'. If we acknowledge that 'For to end yet again' is a progression from *Lessness*, the title appears more comprehensible; due to the fact that the earlier text was endeavouring to provide a termination (an ending) and was unsuccessful, Beckett once more attempts in this text to achieve some form of closure and essentially 'to end yet again'. However, Beckett problematizes 'ending' and by extension death, suggesting therefore that final closure may be forever elusive.

The opening line, similar to the majority of the text, is full of funereal vocabulary, and Beckett appears to be exploring what (if anything) occurs after the physical body has died. The image of the skull, isolation and darkness, all suggest burial and illustrate the horrors of interment, and the juxtaposition of beginning and ending is apparent. The turbulence surrounding this narrative, and the urgency to provide clarification on the state of being is evident from the initial stages of the text. It is initially difficult to ascertain whether the 'expelled' is living or deceased and we question if in fact he 'exists' somewhere between the spheres of 'being' and 'non-being'; Beckett is perhaps suggesting that there is a third state to be added to Sartre's categories of 'being' and 'nothingness'. It is evident that this living–dying entity is perplexed by the inconceivable prospect of witnessing one's own physical degeneration, while remaining mentally articulate. Hence, Beckett's preoccupation with exploring the effects of death on both the physical and mental attributes of the human being is clearly evident: 'skull alone in the dark the void no neck no face just the box last place of all in the dark the void' (Beckett 1999d: 11). The box, which is suggestive of the casket, holds and withholds the disembodied image that Beckett presents in much of his work. However, without discernible features, the head is reduced to nothing more than the cranium and the consciousness ultimately takes precedence and cannot be localized.

Beckett focuses on the skull in an attempt, perhaps, to place emphasis on the physical, while also suggesting the metaphysical, thereby illustrating the duality of mind and body. We are therefore presented with an internal and external landscape of ruins, where degeneration takes precedence. The duality of death is represented through the decline of body and mind, but also through the deterioration of man and nature conjunctively. The representation of a dehumanized world may be indicative of the transitional period from this life to the next, where physical degeneration can be ascertained and mental continuation cannot be denied. This 'Place of remains' (Beckett 1999d: 11), as it is referred to in the text, is therefore suggestive of the decayed physical state, where one imagines the remnants of the decomposed carcass to be located. However, it may also be indicative of the impossibility to move on, as one is condemned to 'remain' and ultimately endure, continually endeavouring to 'end yet again', and quintessentially aspiring to end absolutely. The image of the still man, incarcerated within the void, in a landscape of despair, appears unsettling as no hope is offered to him. The arrival of dawn is indicative of renewal, but this 'leaden dawn' (Beckett 1999d: 11) denies the possibility of regeneration: it is a heavy, almost burdensome awakening, as it also refutes the consolidation of absolute and final death.

Change is occurring in this landscape dominated by ruination: 'First change of all in the end a fragment comes away and falls' (Beckett 1999d: 12). The expelled is therefore witnessing his own demise, conscious of the fact that he cannot prohibit the physical breakdown of his 'being'. The second change occurs when the grey is momentarily broken by the appearance of the two white dwarfs. The significance of the dwarfs is rather ambiguous, and we question whether the expelled is aware of their presence. They provide a contrast to the monochromatic appearance of the landscape, as their whiteness momentarily alleviates the monotony of the greyness within this black void: 'Long at first mere whiteness from afar they toil step by step through the grey dust linked by a litter same white seen from above in the grey air (Beckett 1999d: 12). Their Swiftian appearance further complements the absurdity of this 'other world', and we question whether they exist within the external landscape or within the internal landscape of the mind. The oddness of their physical being ('Monstrous extremities including skulls stunted legs and trunks monstrous arms stunted faces' (Beckett 1999d: 13)) prompts one to question the viability of the physical body and accept the inevitability of its demise. The dwarfs function as one unit, representative of the body/mind collaboration, as they search the landscape for 'the dung litter of laughable memory' (ibid.). The absurdity of the physical is now counteracted with the sometimes ineffectual nature of the mind, as memories are reduced to nothing more than excremental waste. However, dung is often used as a fertilizer, preventing degeneration; perhaps this is why the consciousness of the 'expelled' cannot expire and is condemned to 'remain'. The ritualistic nature of the dwarfs' exercise is evident, as the 'Bone white of the sheet' (Beckett 1999d: 12), denotative of the shroud, and the 'pillow [which] marks the place of the head' (Beckett 1999d: 13) are suggestive of the preparations for burial, primarily the interment of the mind.

To achieve the finality of absolute death, the termination of the consciousness represents perhaps that 'last desert to be crossed' (ibid.). The unreliability of the mind is again emphasized, as the voice appears to have forgotten that which it has already uttered, and proceeds once more to detail the first change. However, further decline is inevitable and the final change renders the 'expelled' parallel with the earth: 'Last change of all in the end the expelled falls headlong down and lies back to sky full little stretch amidst his ruins' (Beckett 1999d: 14). This shift from the vertical to horizontal position appears analogous with death, but clearly not an ideal death, as we are told that 'Breath has not left him' (ibid.). This representation of death, with the mind still functioning, is an unbearable concept, analogous with live burial. The end of this text fails to provide closure, and as the final sentence states 'Through it who knows yet another end beneath a cloudless sky same dark it earth and sky of a last end if ever there had to be another absolutely had to be' (Beckett 1999d: 15), we recognize that the 'expelled' will remain subject to dying, as he is condemned to an eternity of 'ending yet again' in an environment dominated by decay, forever emulating 'some dreg of life' (Beckett 1999d: 14).

The process of dying appears almost as intolerable as the process of living, and we question the desirability of birth. 'I gave up before birth' (written initially in French) dates from the end of 1973, and examines the consciousness, exploring once again the concept of death with the mind still functioning. This text appears to allude to the end of *Malone Dies*, as the mind appears reluctant to accept termination. The problem of identity is explored, as the 'I' of the consciousness struggles to dislocate itself from the 'he' of the physical. Pilling says, ' "Afar a bird" and "I gave up before birth" attempt to reduce the "he" of the "I–he" dichotomy to bones, in order that the "I" may achieve independent, authentic being' (Knowlson and Pilling 1979: 134).

The opening sentence states, 'I GAVE up before birth, it is not possible otherwise, but birth there had to be, it was he, I was inside' (Beckett 1999d: 45). To give up before birth is probably the most viable option when condemned to existence, as one will not then be disappointed when expelled from the womb. It is interesting that the 'I' attempts to focus blame for its existence on the 'he' of the physical body, and the power of the mind appears to transcend the strength of the physical, as the consciousness dominates. There seems to be a shift in attitude towards termination, as the desire for death is replaced by the acceptance of continuance. In earlier texts we have witnessed the consciousness' struggle for completion, endeavouring to embrace some form of closure. However, in this narrative, the 'I' takes satisfaction from the prospect of its survival, achieving an independence and liberation from its incarceration within the human body, appearing almost to mock the physical form in its degeneration: 'it's he who will rattle, I won't rattle, he who will die, I won't die' (ibid.). The voice seems to have contempt for the physical structure, suggesting that the body's disintegration perhaps offers freedom for the conscious mind.

The decomposition of the carcass represents termination of the physical, and yet the consciousness, free from matter, cannot be condemned to decay. The metaphysical can therefore achieve prolongation, despite the degeneration of the physical, and we question whether this constitutes a blessing or a curse: 'he'll rot, I won't rot, there will be nothing of him left but bones, I'll be inside' (ibid.). However, the duality of body and mind prompts one to question the viability of one component surviving independently from the other, and the consternation in accepting the possibility of witnessing one's own disintegration. Separation of the non-physical from the physical evidently cannot be achieved, as the 'I' is condemned to linger, incarcerated within his remains and therefore subject to decay, despite continuance. The 'I' is therefore subjected to a 'premature burial', as the mind is not yet willing to gravitate towards extinction.

The acceptance that to end is an impossibility is suggested, as 'I' speculates 'how will he go about it, go about coming to an end, it's impossible I should know' (ibid.). This statement therefore suggests that the consciousness has endeavoured to end and due to failure, acknowledges the unattainable. Perhaps this is why 'I' continually mocks 'he', unable to accept that 'he' will face death and termination, while 'I' will linger indefinitely. The consciousness cannot accept the confines of the physical and despite its declarations that 'there will be no more I' (Beckett 1999d: 46), the continuation of 'not I' will elude the implications of death. Beckett suggests throughout this text that perhaps we are never fully dead and that we essentially 'live on' or 'die on', ultimately enduring the process. The death of the body is only one hurdle to cross, as we struggle towards the death of the mind, the state to which we are condemned, if our consciousness survives, after our physical death.

In 'Closed place'[3] (written in French and translated by Beckett into English in 1975) Beckett's preoccupation with cylinders is evident. This work builds on previous texts such as *The Lost Ones*, *Ping* and *Imagination Dead Imagine*, conveying the claustrophobic nature of entrapment within the 'closed place' of the void. These confined spaces appear analogous with death; offering no hope of renewal, they provide the confined place in which the dying individual must continue the death process, as gradually his/her life force is compressed.

'There is nothing but what is said' (Beckett 1999d: 49), and the words therefore take precedence. As the narrative endeavours to describe 'how it is', or perhaps 'how it shall be', the inevitability of death is portrayed. The closed place consists of three circles of 'existence': the outer ditch, the track and the arena and 'Beyond the ditch there is nothing' (ibid.). The void takes precedence outside this closed space, suggesting perhaps that the enclosed place represents a refuge in the midst of nothing. Grey no longer predominates in this landscape, as the blackness of the arena is indicative of death.

The Dantean nature of this environment is evident, as paradoxically this closed place has 'Room for millions' (ibid.), and is suggestive of some form of mass burial: indicative of a holocaust and representative of death in its most potent form. Beckett's use of imagery illustrates that death is not selective, as it targets and eventually condemns all, and we see the shift from death as an individual experience towards a sense of collective or universal mortality. These millions appear to 'come and go', as they are described as 'Wandering and still' (ibid.), and their lack of identity is portrayed, as they remain incarcerated within this mass grave. Described as 'Never seeing never hearing one another. Never touching' (ibid.), these millions appear similar to the figures in *Quad*, where the individual lacks identity amidst the presence of others. Perhaps in death we are afforded no comfort, and we remain isolated in decay, as we are isolated in life; the presence of company only serves to augment our solitude. The lack of humanity portrayed within this image of death, prompts one to perceive the physical form as worthless, illustrating that in death, we are all as one: an assemblage of physical matter destined to perish.

The bed, where the millions are placed, is divided into lots. This horticultural image reduces the human form in status, presenting it as nothing more than a part of nature, in which its degeneration will condemn it to the earth, and its physical matter will provide the dust that will intern the next individual. These lots, similar to the coffin, have 'Just room for the average sized body' (ibid.). If the individual is larger he/she has to curl up and assume the foetal position. Beckett again presents death as a deliverance, and a birth into a new state of being as, ironically, in death the body must revert back to its pre-birth position. It is interesting that the 'Brilliance of the bright lots' (Beckett 1999d: 50) does not encroach upon the darkness of the others, and, therefore, there appears to be no grey existence within this enclosed space. We may assume that those bodies placed within the dark lots have reached a more total state of termination: a state that the individuals in the bright lots aspire to.

The significance of the black air towers is rather ambiguous, and we question whether they function as watchtowers, in which an omniscient presence oversees the arrangement of these bodies, as death is reduced to a controlled process, where exact precision is necessary. This prison imagery is suggestive of the inability to escape the confines of death and the difficulty of 'getting into death' before one's allotted time. The track, consisting of dead leaves, conveys degeneration. The leaves described as 'Dead but not rotting' (ibid.), are perhaps indicative of the fate of the millions, as they are preserved in death, thereby obtaining 'everlasting death' and not the promise of everlasting life. Perhaps for the Beckettian protagonist, everlasting life would represent a version of hell, offering a condemnation to an eternal state of being, and providing no release from the pain of existence. Unable to rot within this environment, which lacks moisture, the bodies are destined to crumble.

The image of death presented in these texts is undeniably horrific. The fate of the human body explored in 'Closed place' illustrates the worthlessness of the physical, and the inevitability of decline. Beckett forces us to view mortality as a process, which must be endured, if an end-point is to be attained and if indeed an end-point is attainable. The degeneration of the physical appears to not always constitute an absolute end and, only with the expiration of the consciousness, may 'nothingness' perhaps be achieved. By analysing the death of the physical we are confronted with an exploration of other deaths including the death of the mind, spirit and, ultimately for the writer, the death of language itself. Death within the physical realm constitutes only one of the many facets of mortality that Beckett explores, and it undoubtedly serves as an outlet into the more enigmatic regions of this much explored territory. If physical death does not constitute absolute termination within Beckett's world, we must therefore turn our attention to the representation of the mind, and explore the effects of decay within the microcosm.

Part II

Mental Decline and Spiritual Attrition

Chapter 5

The Trap of Memory

A voice comes to one in the dark. Imagine.

Company

Beckett's work refrains from idealizing memory, forcing one to re-conceptualize it as a decaying influence within the mind, as it continually revolves past experiences, prompting degeneration within present existence. However, as with all things in Beckett's work, memory is prone to erosion. It is evident that Beckett's characters often idealize memories and, in some instances, they feel compelled to invent memories in an attempt, perhaps, to eradicate the pain of past experience and therefore reduce the suffering of present existence. It is clear that memory serves as a negative influence, as the characters cannot escape the past, nor alleviate the pain attributed to it. The detrimental effect which memory produces therefore influences the characters' well-being, and forces one to acknowledge it as a representation of decay within the mind.

Written in English and finished at the beginning of 1959, *Embers* is Beckett's second radio play and undoubtedly one of the most enigmatic pieces in the Beckett canon. This newly adopted medium allowed Beckett the freedom to probe further into the implications of mental deterioration by successively employing disembodied voices, which serve to represent various aspects of the consciousness, helping the drama to become internal, and ultimately more difficult to comprehend. Beckett himself conceded the ambiguous nature of the text; after hearing the initial recording he commented, 'Good performance and production but doesn't come off. My fault, text too difficult' (Harmon 1998: 56). However, despite the complexity of the drama, one cannot resist attempting to negotiate the intricacies of Henry's mind.

There exists a thin line between normality and insanity and we often question what constitutes reality, if indeed, a reality can be ascertained. Estragon was intuitive in his declaration that 'We all are born mad. Some remain so' (Beckett 1990: 75). Henry's mental state is questionable and we wonder if he can control the voices/sounds within his mind. If we accept that Henry can control the voices in his mind then we must acknowledge that 'voluntary memory' constitutes the only form of memory explored in this drama. Beckett's essay on Proust claims that 'voluntary memory (Proust repeats it ad nauseam) is of no value as an instrument of evocation' (Beckett 1965: 14), describing it as 'the memory that is not memory' (Beckett 1965: 32). We presume that Beckett would have refrained from creating a drama that explores only one facet of the memory process, and consequently acknowledge his exploration of the effects of 'involuntary memory'. Proust himself placed more emphasis on the effective nature of involuntary memory, suggesting that it was a more accurate form of memory.[1] However, if involuntary memory is a more credible mechanism for comprehending past experience, then one must be willing to consent to a loss of control within the mind in order to permit 'involuntary memory' to be prolific. And does this loss of control within the mind facilitate the onset of some form of psychosis?

Sounds are paramount in this drama, and the sea is perhaps the only thing that exists externally. It possesses a certain reality, providing the setting for the play and constituting the one element that appears to take place outside of Henry's skull. However, although it appears to exist externally, Henry's inability to block out its sound suggests that the noise of the ocean exists also within his mind, despite his proximity to the coast. The sea is torturous, functioning as a constant reminder of his father's death and serving to reinforce the horror of the present. Its tides 'mark time' and with the passing of time the strand becomes eroded, constituting the physical alternative to the corrosion of Henry's mental faculties. We presume that the sea has drowned Henry's father, although we can only speculate whether his death was accidental or intentional. And now it seems that Henry tries to drown the sound of the ocean with the sound of his words, appearing committed to blocking out its presence and its memory from his mind. His compulsive talking, despite his motivation for it, prompts one to question the stability of his mind, and endeavour to analyse the nature and provenance of his 'destructive' memory.

The memory of his father evidently haunts Henry, and yet he appears to welcome the possibility that his father's presence may be with him: 'My father, back from the dead, to be with me' (Beckett 1990: 253). Again we see Beckett's continual probing into the implications of death; he suggests in his essay on Proust, that our memory functions as a mechanism for denying potential rest to those who are deceased, as he says that 'the dead are only dead in so far as they continue to exist in the heart of the survivor' (Beckett 1965: 44). Perhaps Henry yearns for his father's approval, being unable and unwilling to move beyond the confines of past experience, as he is haunted by the knowledge of his father's disappointment. He once used the device of storytelling as a means perhaps of exploring painful past experience, while at the same time denying that the story was a fictional representation of his life ('I usen't to need anyone, just to myself, stories' (Beckett 1990: 254)). However, the stories are now failing to act as a calmative, suggesting that his fictions can no longer suspend the feeling of solitude, as words alone are an insufficient mechanism for coping. Again we witness the Beckett protagonist adopting the art of storytelling in an attempt to comprehend past experience. Memory will not permit present existence, as it continually instigates the revisiting of lapsed experience. As previously suggested, the displacement of the self onto a fictional character prompts the denial of 'I', and one is satisfied to relay one's life story in the delusion that the tale being told does not represent one's self. Henry's story involving Bolton and Holloway is therefore not a device for passing the time, but rather his attempt to comprehend memories, which are too painful to confront as 'I'.

The implications surrounding the Bolton/Holloway story are somewhat enigmatic and it is therefore difficult to ascertain its precise meaning. However, it may be suggested that Henry's narrative does exemplify a past experience that he deems too painful to confront as himself. It may be suggested that Bolton and Holloway epitomize Henry's psyche, thereby clearly illustrating that his mind is subject to suffering. The elements contained in the narrative are in direct contrast to Henry's 'surroundings'. The Bolton story takes place indoors, suggesting that it signifies an internal suffering. Light refuses to penetrate the scene, permitting only an atmosphere of darkness and an impenetrable gloom, representative of the memory that Henry fears to confront. The fire provides a direct contrast to the sea and, as it fades, we recognize the degenerative nature of Henry's memory and his apparent wish for death. 'Standing there in his old red dressing-gown' (Beckett 1990: 254), Bolton desires the one thing that Holloway refuses to administer – a release from life perhaps? Although Bolton is possibly representative of Henry's alter ego, it may also be suggested that he epitomizes Henry's father's desires. If one accepts this interpretation, one must therefore acknowledge that Henry's father probably did commit suicide. Henry is perhaps plagued with guilt, feeling somehow responsible for the death, as he did not live up to his father's expectations and failed to accompany him on that final swim. The theme of solitude and company intersects with Henry's memories and his obsession with the past. He may in some way feel responsible for his father's death, but even more important is his sense of never having pleased his father. He appears to need someone from the past to help him cope with the present ('someone who . . . knew me, in the old days, anyone, to be with me, imagine he hears me, what I am, now (Beckett 1990: 255)) or perhaps to provide clarification on past events. This desire for recognition and acceptance possibly stems from feelings of unworthiness and rejection that he experienced as a child.

The unreliability of Henry's memory is portrayed as he questions whether his father had known Ada ('I can't remember, no matter, no one'd know her now' (Beckett 1990: 256)). We question why no one would know her now, surmising perhaps that she is no longer of this world; or is it Henry who dwells beyond the normal parameters of existence? His recollections of his wife are not endearing and yet he appears to welcome the sound of her voice. As Henry calls to her she 'responds', providing him with the comforting knowledge that someone can hear him, but also serving as a continual reminder that he has failed in his relationships. Memory therefore does not comfort Henry but instead functions as a negative influence on his present 'existence'. It serves only as a positive influence in so far as it reduces the sound of the sea in Henry's mind, as he effectively replaces the sound of the ocean with the soothing rhythm of his words. However, as time goes by, Henry will find that his memories will become increasingly faint, and his words will no longer be able to eradicate the sound of the ocean, thereby causing him further mental torture.

Henry's tormented existence has been displaced onto Addie, the child who evidently did not wish to be born, and yet they 'kept hammering away at it' (Beckett 1990: 261). Henry's declaration that 'It was not enough to drag her into the world, now she must play the piano' (Beckett 1990: 259), reminds us of the lines from *Waiting for Godot*: 'To have lived is not enough for them. They have to talk about it' (Beckett 1990: 58). This statement sums up Henry's affliction and his inability to suppress the voices within his head, remaining incarcerated in the past, instead of functioning within the present. Despite the negative influence of the ocean, it may be suggested that it constitutes the one element that can alleviate Henry's problems. Perhaps by embracing the sea completely, and allowing himself to be submerged in it, Henry could ultimately escape its sound and be reunited with his father. ('It's only on the surface, you know. Underneath all is as quiet as the grave. Not a sound. All day, all night, not a sound' (Beckett 1990: 261)). It is interesting that the darkness, silence and coldness of the ocean are elements reminiscent of Bolton's room. Undoubtedly there is a connection between Henry's story and his life, as Ada urges him to see Holloway, suggesting that Holloway is real and does not exist solely in Henry's fictions. Pountney says that

> the sea becomes the consciousness Henry seeks to avoid, as in *Not I*, where the 'buzzing' of the subconscious continually questions the story Mouth is telling, in order to try to bring it to her attention that the story is her own. (1988: 111)

Henry, similar to Mouth, is reluctant to acknowledge that the story he relates is his own; perhaps he cannot accept that Bolton's pain exemplifies his own. He cannot face the reality that 'stories' is all he has now, his life being void of companionship. He appears incapable of admitting that he is ultimately alone, incarcerated within an existence of failed relationships, and fails to recognize the fact that Holloway cannot alleviate the pain. There is no one to listen to him now; ultimately he is isolated in his suffering, and we see how memories are an inadequate substitute for the presence of another living being: 'The time will come when no one will speak to you at all, not even complete strangers. [*Pause*] You will be quite alone with your voice, there will be no other voice in the world but yours' (Beckett 1990: 262).

Memories cannot be sustained indefinitely and Beckett is perhaps suggesting that they should be viewed as complementary to living, and not conceived of as compensatory. Henry has failed in the past and continues to fail in the present. He finally admits to the 'nothingness' which exists in his life – 'Nothing, all day nothing. [*Pause*] All day all night nothing. [*Pause*] Not a sound' (Beckett 1990: 264) – suggesting that the voices we here are indeed fabrications, and that Henry is now fundamentally alone. The mind ultimately cannot cope with the reality that there is nothing left to live for, and becomes damaged by the memory of past regrets. There is nothing worse than remorse.

Beckett again tackled the implications of memory in his apparently simple but, in fact, rather profound drama *Ohio Impromptu*, written in 1981. Here we witness memory represented in a new form, as Beckett continually confronts the boundaries of the mind and questions identity and the self. Through the central protagonist, we recognize the pain of bereavement, the suffering of loneliness, and the immense desire to invoke the memory of lost love.

The Listener and Reader, described as 'alike in appearance as possible' (Beckett 1990: 445), don long black coats, contrasting effectively with their long white hair, and producing the black and white imagery which is evident throughout much of Beckett's work. In this drama we witness the contrasting nature of the static image on stage with the movement through time, evoked by the narrative. The visual representation of the Listener and Reader produces an image of 'separated togetherness', as we acknowledge that the Reader is not 'other', and that both figures are in fact one and the same: the confrontation of self and self. It could be that Beckett is dramatizing our ability to populate our own solitude here. The Reader functions as the protagonist's memory and is symbolically a manifestation of his consciousness. Memory consequently becomes externalized, functioning as a 'fictional narrative' that is ultimately based on reality and reiterated to the Listener by himself; thereby ensuring that the drama becomes interior and is ultimately the drama of the mind. Lyons says 'This separation of figure and voice, isolating the functions of speaking and listening, produces twin images in *Ohio Impromptu*: one who, apparently, initiates a retrospective act and the other who presents the words that constitute that memory' (1983: 182). Beckett therefore presents the self as creator of fictional selves, suggesting that the 'dear face' has not sent the Reader to comfort him, but rather, through the projection of the self, the protagonist has found a mechanism for coping with his loss. The reality of the external world subsequently loses its significance, as the memory of 'past togetherness' becomes paramount in sustaining present existence.

As the play begins with 'Little is left to tell' (Beckett 1990: 445), we recognize that this narrative has been recited for some time, and Beckett is successful in using this technique to give credence to the fact that this event has perhaps taken place during many previous nights, and is now slowly drawing to its conclusion. As the Reader conveys the tale of a man suffering from lost love and loneliness, we clearly recognize that the fictional tale he narrates does in fact exemplify the life of the Listener. We question the dramatic effect of the book and its function in the drama. It conveys the art of storytelling, which is paramount throughout the play, as the story the Reader tells acts as a calmative for the Listener. The book serves a similar purpose as the tape recorder in *Krapp's Last Tape*, due to the fact that it contains past memories which are easily accessed. However, we question why Beckett's protagonists rely on these external devices, concluding perhaps that their minds, due to deterioration, cannot successfully recall past events at will. Although memories are often idealized by Beckett's characters, the profundity of *Ohio Impromptu*, and the tale that is narrated, appears to contain a truthfulness and a sincerity which makes it impossible for one not be moved by the power of this drama. The genuine feeling evoked in the play may be attributed to the fact that Beckett conceived of the 'dear face' as representing Suzanne; Knowlson states that Beckett said 'I've imagined her dead so many times. I've even imagined myself trudging out to her grave' (1997: 665). The reality of his imaginings are conveyed successfully throughout the drama, as the protagonist clearly portrays the magnitude of bereavement:

> In a last attempt to obtain relief he moved from where they had been so long together to a single room on the far bank. From its single window he could see the downstream extremity of the Isle of Swans. [*Pause*] Relief he had hoped would flow from unfamiliarity. (Beckett 1990: 445)

However, the relief the protagonist so longed for was not achieved, and he recognized the futility of trying to escape from memories. It is interesting that initially he tried to rid himself of memories but now appears to cling to them. Unlike Henry, the Listener does not wish to erase these memories, as they provide a comfort to him, making his existence that little bit more bearable.

The Reader tells us that 'Day after day he could be seen slowly pacing the islet. Hour after hour. In his long black coat no matter what the weather and old world Latin Quarter hat' (Beckett 1990: 446). Again we are provided with evidence which confirms that the tale being told conveys the life of the Listener on stage, as the long black coat, perhaps the clothes of mourning, is still worn by him, and the hat is clearly evident on the table before him. Hence, details of the tale manifest themselves in front of the audience. Now alone, all he can manage is to walk the paths after her, taking solace in the silence which provides time to reflect. Perhaps he wanders looking for company and a distraction from the emptiness that must continually plague him. Contemplating the receding stream, he perhaps recognizes that it is representative of the couple, ('How in joyous eddies its two arms conflowed and flowed united on' (ibid.)), imagining that, despite her absence, she continues to be with him. As Knowlson (1997: 665) confirms, the image of the river's two arms flowing into one another, after they have been divided, is a clue to the meaning of this play, and is suggestive of the fact that the protagonist may be reconciled with his lost partner after death.

The tale implies that the 'dear face' has sent the Reader to comfort him and that she urged him, through his dreams, not to abandon the place where they had dwelled together: 'Stay where we were so long alone together, my shade will comfort you' (ibid.). If this interpretation is to be accepted, one would therefore have to acknowledge that the Reader is a projection of her, and this acknowledgement would be somewhat flawed. If the Reader constitutes her 'shade', it would be apparent that she forbids him to forget their time together, thereby denying him the possibility of moving on. We must presume, therefore, that it is not she who haunts him but, rather, it is he who creates this external agent to console himself. As McMullan says, 'The "shade" of the narrative crosses the boundaries between life and death and between identities (it is associated yet not identified with the "dear face") and becomes "as one" with the protagonist' (1993: 121). His contentment to dwell within memories illustrates his willingness to live in the past. Therefore the knock, which is used throughout the play, functions as a rewind mechanism. Retreating into lost time provides transportation into memories, and the continual repeating of sentences also prevents the tale from concluding too quickly. The protagonist's inability to rectify the mistake of leaving the dwelling where they had lived together is illustrated, as the Reader says:

> Could he not now turn back? Acknowledge his error and return to where they were once so long alone together. Alone together so much shared. No. What he had done alone could not be undone. Nothing he had ever done alone could ever be undone. By him alone. (Beckett 1990: 446)

Beckett appears to be illustrating the futility of the solitary individual incapable of altering the mistakes for which he is responsible. However, he is perhaps also suggesting that once the bereaved individual decides to move on and make changes in their lives, the reversal of this process is difficult to implement. Therefore Beckett gives credence to the fact that although mentally one may dwell in the microcosm of past togetherness, physically he/she must assume the new identity of 'I' alone.

Plagued with isolation and loneliness, night becomes the most difficult period to endure, as the hours of darkness magnify the feelings of loss and deny the possibility of sleep, forcing the mind to remain active and prompting 'I' to become a child of the night. His present existence now reflects his childhood days when the feelings of loneliness were possibly abated by the belief that he would achieve future company. Now he remains resolute in his acknowledgment that present existence is devoid of companionship, and only through death will he perhaps be reconciled with his lost love. And until that time, he uses the Reader, a projection of himself, to provide solace throughout the twilight hours, imagining that he has been sent by her, adorning the persona of his guardian angel. It is apparent how the sad tale evoked from the worn volume has become reality on stage, confirming that the fictional narrative is an intense personification of the protagonist's existence, and that the two characters are ultimately one and the same. We can see how Beckett establishes the presence of an image and, in the course of performance, diminishes that presence, revealing the fragility of its existence, and 'With never a word exchanged they grew to be as one' (Beckett 1990: 447), illustrating that this surrogate couple is ultimately 'I', confirming that the individual is never one self, but instead a continual succession of selves, enhanced by the memory of past experience. Smith illustrates this truth as he says, 'beyond difference from others that we all share, there is difference, dividedness and decenteredness within – the self never identical with itself' (1991: XV).

The impossibility of sustaining the memory indefinitely is illustrated, as it too, prone to deterioration, will eventually become defunct. As his mind weakens the protagonist finds it more difficult to perpetuate the image of the Reader and we recognize that he himself is probably nearing death:

> So the sad tale a last time told they sat on as though turned to stone. Through the single window dawn shed no light. From the street no sound of reawakening. Or was it that buried in who knows what thoughts they paid no heed? To light of day. To sound of reawakening. What thoughts who knows. Thoughts, no, not thoughts. Profounds of mind. Buried in who knows what profounds of mind. Of mindlessness. Whither no light can reach. No sound. So sat on as though turned to stone. The sad tale a last time told. (Beckett 1990: 447–448)

The arrival of a dawn, which brings forth no light, coupled with no sound of reawakening, is suggestive of the fact that the Listener now dwells between this life and the next. He no longer requires the comforting nature of memory, as he soon will cross the boundary between life and death, and either is reunited with his lost love, or perhaps oblivious to the implications of consciousness. The stage image again converges with the narrative; as the Listener and Reader raise their heads and perceive each other they are one and the same, and accepting of the fact that the termination of the story perhaps signifies the conclusion of their existence. Maybe the Reader acted as a bridge for the Listener between his bereavement and his own death. However, memories no longer serve any purpose, as ultimately there is 'Nothing left to tell' (Beckett 1990: 448).

Beckett's late prose work entitled *Company*, published 1980, is probably the most autobiographical work since his early novel *Dream of Fair to Middling Women*.[2] Throughout this text Beckett explores memory in new forms, and we witness the detrimental effects of painful past experience. The difference between memories in *Company* and memories in *Ohio Impromptu* is striking, as the recollections conveyed throughout this text, produce a negative impact upon the listener, evoking pain and suppressed feelings of inadequacy and failure. As Knowlson says, 'The incidents are selected like scenes in a novel to highlight certain themes, especially those of solitude and lovelessness' (1997: 652). Because of the pain attributed to them, it may be suggested that these memories are 'involuntary', demonstrating the listener's inability to control them, as they function as a form of regression therapy, forcing him to confront past experience in an attempt perhaps to elucidate present existence.

The opening line of the text confirms that the listener is situated in the darkness (an appropriate environment for intense recollection) and is visited by the voice, perceived to be an external agent, functioning as an orator of past experience: 'To one on his back in the dark a voice tells of a past' (Beckett 1996a: 8). We question who 'he' is and whether this voice is indeed 'other', or is in fact a projection of himself, his consciousness and his memory. If the voice is the voice of memory, we must adhere to the opinion that the voice is not external, but rather an internal projection of past experience, which functions as a mechanism for coping with present solitude. He creates this voice within his mind in order to achieve solace from a past that appears to manifest itself as a foreign experience. As the voice is presented as an external influence, rather than the voice of self, Beckett again explores the implications of identity and the faculties of the mind. The memories that are recalled do not provide total escapism, as they are intermingled with reminders of his current position and serve to reinforce the horror of the present. Brater suggests, 'There are, then, two voices here, the voice of memory and the voice of reason. Beckett gives rapid rhythm to the first and slow rhythm to the second, then lets them play against each other in vigorous counterpoint' (1989: 130).

The memories, which are explored, illustrate the solitude of his past existence, demonstrating the loneliness that afflicted him throughout childhood, and the feelings of lost innocence that plagued him. They therefore serve as a direct counterpart to his present existence, illustrating the loneliness of his entire life, despite the presence of others:

A small boy you come out of Connolly's Stores holding your mother by the hand. You turn right and advance in silence southward along the highway. After some hundred paces you head inland and broach the long steep homeward. You make ground in silence hand in hand through the warm still summer air. It is late afternoon and after some hundred paces the sun appears above the crest of the rise. Looking up at the blue sky and then at your

mother's face you break the silence asking her if it is not in reality much
more distant than it appears. The sky that is. The blue sky. Receiving no
answer you mentally reframe your question and some hundred paces later
look up at her face again and ask her if it does not appear much less distant
that in reality it is. For some reason you could never fathom this question
must have angered her exceedingly. For she shook off your little hand and
made you a cutting retort you have never forgotten. (Beckett 1996a: 12–13)

This memory is, undoubtedly, a disturbing recollection, demonstrating the
harshness of the mother towards the child and illustrating a further disintegration within their relationship. The boy is effectively punished for possessing an
enquiring mind and shunned for displaying artistic sensibility. This event conveys the seminal traumatic moment of his existence, evidently haunting him
still many years later, prompting him to question why he was rebuked in such
a way, and attempting to comprehend what it was he did wrong. Reproachful
feelings, which should have been experienced by the mother, have ultimately
been displaced onto the child, rendering the boy guilty, while unaware of his
'crime'.

The child's belief that he was in some way a disappointment, did not stem
solely from his mother's harshness, but was reinforced by his reluctance to follow his father's instructions:

You stand at the tip of the high board. High above the sea. In it your father's
upturned face. Upturned to you. You look down to the loved trusted face. He
calls to you to jump. He calls, Be a brave boy. (Beckett 1996a: 23)

Again we witness the memory of failure, as the child, paralyzed with fear,
exudes a greater terror of disappointing his father. We can equate the child's
feelings of guilt for failing to impress his father, with Henry's feelings of inadequacy. As the child stands on the board, we recognize that he is once again
subjected to a separation from the parent, unable and unwilling to take the
plunge that will guarantee togetherness. The act of achieving company therefore becomes a terrifying experience, and again the child is left feeling worthless. The depths of the ocean correspond to the depths of the darkness, which
now surrounds him, as the eradication of light serves to reinforce the feelings
of solitude. Lying on his back in the dark he contemplates the desirability of
speech, recognizing that it would break the deafening sound of the silence.

Returning again to his memory of childhood, it is apparent that the child's
need to throw himself off the tree is not prompted by the desire of achieving an adrenalin rush, but is perchance rather a cry for attention from his
mother. He perhaps wants to enjoy her company, which at this moment
appears reserved only for Mrs Coote. His mother's pronouncement that he
has been a very naughty boy, perhaps causes the child to experience feelings

of culpability, and possibly instils in him the notion of terror, as he anticipates the punishment he will receive after Mrs Coote has left. It is apparent
that these memories exacerbate the feelings of inadequacy and lovelessness
which the listener, now alone in the dark, must endeavour to comprehend, in
order to fully understand his present condition. Memories undoubtedly have
a negative influence on his current existence, illustrating the, sometimes, detrimental nature of the mind, and the inability to fully exorcise painful past
experience. Relief will only come when the mind ceases to function and the
desire for company is effectively erased: 'Till it the mind too closes as it were'
(Beckett 1996a: 30). However, the process of total mental shutdown, and the
eradication of conscious thought, inevitably takes time, if, in fact, it is achievable; and as the mind awaits degeneration, it is continually forced to function:
'Unformulable gropings of the mind. Unstillable' (ibid.). These 'gropings of
the mind', although recalling painful past experience, still provide escape
from the nothingness, which now surrounds the listener, maybe temporarily
alleviating the feeling of solitude.

We question the listener's state of existence, as the voice says to him, 'Your
father's shade is not with you any more. It fell out long ago. You do not hear
your footfalls any more' (Beckett 1996a: 50). The father's ghost can no longer
serve as his companion, and his inability to ascertain the sound of his footfalls
suggests that he himself has become almost shade-like. If he has experienced
physical mortality, he has not yet been subjected to total degeneration, as his
mind continues to function, denying peaceful rest. Memories of his father
appear more positive than those of his mother, and a sense of closeness is conveyed regarding his relationship with his father; perhaps this is why his father's
shade remained with him for some time. This sense of intimacy is perhaps
best illustrated in the recollection detailing their time together in the summerhouse: 'That you should try to imitate his chuckle pleased and tickled him
greatly and sometimes he would chuckle for no other reason than to hear you
try to chuckle too' (Beckett 1996a: 54). This memory does not cause him pain,
but it does serve to reinforce the horror of his present condition, as no longer
can he seek comfort in the presence of his father. The mature man has learnt
the lesson that solitude is our essential condition. We may be able to temper
it with family, friends, and lovers, but we cannot alter it definitively. No longer
can he achieve comfort in the presence of any other, apart from himself, as
he is condemned to loneliness. Therefore, this 'Devised deviser devising it all
for company' (Beckett 1996a: 64), is ultimately 'Devising figments to temper
his nothingness' (ibid.). Again we question the reliability of his recollections,
as the text suggests they function as 'invented memory'. These memories may
therefore be equated with the 'Simple sums you find a help in times of trouble'
(Beckett 1996a: 54).

The nothingness in which he dwells provides no stimulus, and he questions
whether sound, sight, touch and smell would alleviate his current condition.

However, we acknowledge that his lack of sensory capability does not heighten his feelings of solitude, and recognize that even if he could function fully, his physical efficiency would not eradicate his mental suffering. This 'conjuring of something out of nothing' (Beckett 1996a: 74), may temporarily provide relief, but it cannot overcome a lifetime's feeling of isolation, nor remove the desire to escape from himself:

> Till finally you hear how words are coming to an end. With every inane word a little nearer to the last. And how the fable too. The fable of one with you in the dark. The fable of one fabling of one with you in the dark. And how better in the end labour lost and silence. And you as you always were. Alone. (Beckett 1996a: 88–89)

It is ironic that a text entitled *Company* ultimately ends with the word 'alone'. Beckett successfully illustrates that despite the presence of others, we are all subjected to an existence of solitude. This solitude may be temporarily alleviated, but it can never be fully eradicated, as no one can completely comprehend, nor discover the depths of our consciousness. Within our minds and our memories we are damned to exist alone. Unable to prevent conscious thought, we are condemned to go on remembering, striving for the moment of mental obliteration in which we can embrace the silence. We are reminded of Ionesco's Berenger who proclaims, 'I feel out of place in life, among people' (Ionesco 1962: 24). This feeling of being 'other', a consciousness set apart from other 'consciousnesses', suggests that, despite company, we can never fully connect with those around us, as our individuality and our questionable identity force us to remain ultimately solitary.

Chapter 6

Tired Minds

Will you never have done . . . revolving it all?

Beckett demonstrates that old age is not only defined by the number of years one has lived, but is also determined by one's mental condition. The reluctance of the consciousness to become defunct forces one's mind to remain active, thereby denying peaceful rest and plunging one into continual disquisition, as the individual endeavours to comprehend the implications of existence and escape the weariness of rumination. The inability to stop thinking ultimately results in the mental weariness that is experienced by many of Beckett's protagonists, as uncertainty and lack of clarity fuse to form mental fatigue.

In his 1976 drama *Footfalls*, Beckett explores the implications of senescence, excavating the landscape of the mind in an attempt to illustrate the paradox that one's mental age cannot always be equated with one's physical age. In this play we witness the mental anguish of May, a woman who appears prematurely old, incarcerated within existence and condemned to continually revolving everything in her mind. The frustration of birth, language and self, and the inability to comprehend these factors in her life, condemns May to an eternal questioning which ultimately provides no viable answers. And this continual revolution of the mind leads to mental instability, which perhaps accelerates the ageing process, as mental erosion may facilitate physical diminution. Therefore, despite being in her 'forties', May's mental fatigue produces the characteristics of an elderly woman, as her appearance represents the externalization of an inner anguish. Her dishevelled grey hair and the worn grey wrap, that conceal her feet, add to her ghost-like persona, as she methodically paces the nine steps illuminated only by the dim lighting; thus appearing removed beyond the normal parameters of time. As R. Thomas Simone confirms, in his essay 'Beckett's Other Trilogy: *Not I, Footfalls* and *Rockaby*', 'The sense of youth and the feminine swallowed up by decay and decrepitude of existence is overwhelming in *Footfalls*' (Davis and Butler 1988: 59).

May exists primarily in her mind; unable to make sense of external reality she is confined essentially in conscious thought. Her mind may therefore be equated with that of Murphy, since 'Murphy's mind pictured itself as a large hollow sphere, hermetically closed to the universe without' (Beckett 1993a: 63). Her pacing, a solitary activity, which she adheres to with precision, is symptomatic of the need to assert some form of control over her existence. She uses the soothing rhythm of the pacing as confirmation that she can govern physical activity despite her mental weariness. She may not be capable of asserting control over her mental faculties, but she can regulate the sound of her footfalls. Due to the fact that 'She has not been out since girlhood' (Beckett 1990: 401), May's lack of interaction with the outside world facilitates her gradual retreat into the confines of mind, and exacerbates her mental fatigue, as she endeavours to comprehend the implications of existence 'alone'. The mind's inability to cope with continual questioning and restlessness perhaps results in the desire to eradicate conscious thought and alleviate mental tiredness; a state of peace that May cannot attain. As May calls to her mother, searching perhaps for an explanation for her state of being, we recognize that her mother cannot provide sufficient answers to prevent May's rumination. Awakened from her deep sleep, her mother bears witness to May's inexhaustible pacing, as she counts the number of steps she takes before turning to repeat the activity. The pacing constitutes the central image of the play, as the words lose their significance and are overshadowed by the hypnotic rhythm of the footfalls; and we are reminded of Macbeth's words:

Out, out, brief candle!
Life's but a walking shadow, a poor player
That struts and frets his hour upon the stage
And then is heard no more.
                    (Shakespeare 1967: 132)

May is undoubtedly a walking shadow, condemned to linger physically until mental eradication is achievable; her uncertainty about her age makes her existence questionable. Within the purgatory of her mind, she remains isolated and permanently absent from reality. However, Brater suggests in his essay on *That Time* and *Footfalls* that absence is the only presence (1977: 70–81). This assertion undercuts May's ghost-like persona and prompts one to perceive of her as constituting a reality. We therefore acknowledge that May's ghost-like persona is representative of us all, as Beckett views existence as a brief moment between two deaths. The individual's fragile life is reduced to a ghostly manifestation, burdened by mental turmoil and subjected to spiritual attrition. Beckett's words ('He is present at his own absence' (1965: 27)), describing Proust's visit to his grandmother who does not acknowledge his presence, aptly sum up May's condition; she is essentially present at her own absence.

May's mental weariness may be attributed to the difficult life she has endured. Apart from the agoraphobia, which incarcerates her, May's premature ageing is the result of having had to adopt an adult role and care for her dying mother. This role reversal has essentially forced May to become old before her time, as the mental strain of nursing a dying parent perhaps produces detrimental effects on the mind. May's inability to sleep is symptomatic of the fact that she was denied peaceful rest during her childhood. Mental oblivion was unachievable, as May was condemned to remain forever alert in her daily routine of 'preserving' the dying. The nine questions directed at her mother illustrate the responsibilities of her daily existence: 'Straighten your pillows? [*Pause*] Change your drawsheet? [*Pause*] Pass you the bedpan? [*Pause*] The warming-pan? [*Pause*] Dress your sores? [*Pause*] Sponge you down? [*Pause*] Moisten your poor lips? [*Pause*] Pray with you? [*Pause*] For you? [*Pause*] Again' (Beckett 1990: 400). These daily chores probably prevented mental and physical harmony in May's early life, and the nine tasks, listed above, are symbolically conveyed through her footfalls. The word 'Again' demonstrates the cyclical nature of her existence as, similar to her pacing, May's daily chores are never-ending, her mother appearing condemned to linger. And the nine beats therefore represent the music of the mind, as May's quasi-autistic persona manifests itself through the rhythm of her steps. The nine steps that she takes are also representative of the gestation ('anti-gestation') period, which illustrates that May is just about here, and no more. As Elin Diamond suggests 'May marks the time of fetal development but parturition remains ambiguous' (Oppenheim 2004: 57), suggesting that May has never really been born.[1]

The selfishness of the mother to create a life when her own was well advanced is conveyed, and she recognizes her thoughtlessness, as she asks for May's forgiveness. And as Bryden says, 'Nothing can change the fact that one has given birth to the other, a birth that has reactivated the cycle of pain' (1993: 180). May's troubled mind may be attributed to the need to understand her mother's motivation in conceiving her, and her inability to bestow forgiveness on her progenitor. She fails to conceive of any positive attributes in her existence, and her mental fatigue drains her physical vitality. 'When other girls of her age were out at . . . lacrosse' (Beckett 1990: 401), May was 'as one frozen by some shudder of the mind' (Beckett 1990: 402). The grey aura that she exudes is symbolic of that in between state in which she exists: a present absence. And so the light from the candelabrum penetrates her, as her mind, similar to her worn grey wrap, is a 'tangle of tatters' (ibid.). And therefore as the lights fade up at the end, revealing no trace of May, her ghost-like persona is substantiated and we recognize that, despite her absence, her revolving 'it all'[2] in her mind will undoubtedly perpetuate. Beckett conveys his belief that 'it all' is essentially futile and that, ultimately, one's existence is meaningless. Whether May has recognized the futility of existence we can only speculate; but perhaps by consenting to this fact will her mental fatigue be alleviated, and her footfalls forever silenced, as she would recognize the futility of endeavouring to provide meaning in a universe that is ultimately meaningless.

Five years after *Footfalls*, Beckett again returned to the theme of mental weariness, in an attempt to comprehend, and illustrate, the thought processes endured by a woman, who is described as prematurely old and actively seeking a departure from existence. Beckett entitled this drama *Rockaby*. The title undeniably has connotations of a lullaby, prompting one to envisage the child in the cradle receiving comfort from the soothing rhythm of the rocking. Our initial perceptions are therefore shattered, when we see before us on stage the image of an 'elderly' woman confined to a chair. Beckett has successfully juxtaposed the ideas of birth and death, illustrating the monotony of existence through the compulsive rhythmic act of rocking. As Knowlson says 'The woman in *Rockaby* is rocked from cradle to grave, as the poem moves through overlapping cycles of need and disillusionment into a final dismissal of life' (1997: 663).

Describing the drama as a poem is indeed accurate, as the rhythm of the words successfully correspond to the rhythm of the chair. The play itself is deceptively simple, as we witness a woman, with no given name, labelled W, listening to her own voice (V) emanating from the darkness. Beckett, therefore, takes us on a journey of the mind, in an attempt to convey what goes on inside the head of an isolated elderly woman, who is accepting of the fact that it is 'time she stopped' (Beckett 1990: 435), but appears unable to reach that termination. Hence, the mental fatigue results from the willingness to die, coupled with the inability to achieve closure. The rocking ultimately functions as a form of sedation, and the structured nature of the drama, with its succeeding stages, charts the decline of the woman into even greater fatigue and frailty. Therefore, in this drama, the woman's rocking replaces the rhythmic quasi-autistic act of May's walking in *Footfalls*, as the play becomes more focused on the mind and illustrates a further deterioration in physical capability, as bodily movement is replaced by the sole motion of the object (chair). Beckett creates a greater feeling of dejection here, as the woman, unlike May, is capable of realizing that life is ultimately meaningless and that there exists no 'other' who can alleviate her mental fatigue. She does not wish to comprehend her existence, as all she covets is an escape from it; and so we witness her mind assisting itself to essentially shut down.

W's solitariness and lack of social interaction, despite her endeavours to find 'another creature like herself' (ibid.), is perhaps Beckett's comment on society's treatment of the aged. Imprisoned within her world, W's lack of company has undoubtedly facilitated her mental decline and resulted in her prematurely old physical persona. The 'Unkempt grey hair' (Beckett 1990: 433), and 'Huge eyes in white expressionless face' (ibid.) are in fact the physical manifestations of a prematurely old mind, as the eyes illustrate the dejected spirit of a woman who recognizes that the 'close of a long day' (Beckett 1990: 435) is indeed a metaphor for her existence. Therefore, one may suggest that the word 'more', which she speaks softly four times, is not as many presume, a command for more, but is rather an expression of bewilderment, as she cannot fathom the reasons for her continuing survival.

W's isolation is illustrated by the fact that she can find no one to validate her existence. As she searches for someone similar to herself, she perhaps recognizes that no one is there to alleviate her condition and acknowledges that there are 'no eyes' searching for her. Mentally fatigued from her inability to discover 'one other living soul' (Beckett 1990: 437), she is forever condemned to speaking only to herself. It is apparent, therefore, that on one level, *Rockaby* is a dramatization of our ineluctable solitude: an essential part of what it is to be human. As she accepts the realization that there is no one there to comfort her, W succumbs to failure, remaining resolute in her decision to go back indoors and sit 'quiet at her window facing other windows' (ibid.) in the hope that someone will acknowledge her presence. However, with all the other blinds down, she fails to find another creature like herself to validate her existence. Her famished eyes behind the pane (pain) illustrate that she is starved of recognition, and her non-identity, perhaps, results in her belief that she is in fact a nonentity. Her existence is indeed futile, as she represents a worthless life amid a society that does not even recognize her presence. Perhaps it is this truth that plays on her mind, as she acknowledges that to live or die is inconsequential, due to the fact that no one would mourn her departure from this world. Mentally fatigued by continuance, she is therefore accepting of death.

W has sought company and failed to find it and therefore, tired of searching, she has succumbed to the pull of gravity, descended into the basement, perhaps, and positioned herself in the old rocker. No longer reaching out for another like herself, she accepts the reality that, in her world, no other exists except herself. Although physically she has journeyed into the basement, it is evident that metaphorically she has descended the steep stair down into her mind, where her 'own other' is representative of the company she now experiences. The rocking chair embraces her, cradling her in its arms, as its soothing movement endeavours to 'rock her off' (Beckett 1990: 442) and 'stop her eyes' (ibid.). Despite her lack of identity, she ultimately rejects her own self, choosing to assume the position of her mother who has successfully succumbed to death. Dressed in a 'Black lacy high-necked evening gown' (Beckett 1990: 433), she dons the clothes of her deceased progenitor, perhaps symbolically mourning the passing of mother, or perhaps as a manifestation of the fact that she laments her own current survival. By adhering to the rituals of her mother, she ultimately succeeds in finding another like herself, as she recognizes that she too is enduring the process that eventually sent the mother 'off her head' (Beckett 1990: 440). Although W may not have reached this point of insanity, her mental weariness and futile existence place her on the borderline between derangement and rationality. Her relationship with mother, mother rocker, and with Mother Earth, is essentially resolved, as no longer does she covet the comfort of another, nor does she desire to comprehend life. Her acceptance of death and rejection of life conveys her overwhelming desire to stop. No longer does she speak to herself; her words now directed at the chair illustrate her mental anguish as she pleads with it to rock her off.

Although Beckett creates a greater feeling of dejection in this play, it is also possible to feel liberated by W's closing words. Unlike May, W does not wish to discover the meaning behind life, as she accepts that life is essentially meaningless and only our 'own other' can provide comfort from the realization of this truth. To acknowledge this reality is therefore to be emancipated and ultimately accepting of death. 'Beckett's description of W as "prematurely old", suggests that her movement toward death is a willed renunciation rather than a physical failure' (Lyons 1983: 180). This statement is indeed accurate as, mentally, W accepts death, but physically she is not capable of dying. This turbulence, which exists between body and mind, consequently results in the mental weariness that W experiences, and although she acknowledges that it is time she stopped, her body will not permit cessation. Mentally frustrated, she ultimately rejects life through her cutting retort on existence. The words 'fuck life' (Beckett 1990: 442), uttered in a subdued tone, illustrate her contempt for living and her inability to inject passion or colour into her thoughts/utterances, as she remains imprisoned within a capable body, housing a mind incapable of going on.

If we return once more to *Ill Seen Ill Said*, we can see how Beckett again captures the futility of existence and displays the mental fatigue endured by the woman who appears suspended 'At the inexistent centre of a formless place' (Beckett 1982: 8). In this poetic prose piece Beckett details the solitary journey of an elderly woman, as she leaves the cabin where she dwells alone, to visit the tombstone of a lost love perhaps. Deprived of company, her lack of social interaction facilitates the mental weariness which she endures, and the presence of her shadow is illustrative of the fact that she is her own 'other'. Confined to a solitary life, we recognize her ardent desire to escape existence, and acknowledge that each journey to the stone will hopefully be her last, as there appears to be no reason for her continuing survival.

The pilgrimage to the stone appears to be the only ritual to which she adheres, as it constitutes the sole purpose in her existence. Beckett's protagonists welcome these habitual tendencies, as their rituals provide structure to their lives, providing them with the unsustainable notion that life is perhaps meaningful. As the woman in *Ill Seen Ill Said* travels towards the stone, she possibly recognizes, and welcomes, the reality that she is in fact journeying towards her own death, if indeed she has not already transcended the normal parameters of existence because, as Knowlson suggests, 'The woman herself may be a ghost, a memory or a fiction, or a mixture of all three' (1997: 669). We must therefore concede the possibility that the gravestone she visits is not that of a 'lost love', but is instead her own sepulchre. Denied peaceful rest and condemned to wander the pastures perceived only by the Twelve, her mental weariness stems from the reality that she exists somewhere between this life and the next; adhering to a consciousness that cannot conceive of itself as non-existing.

The temporal references throughout the text are usually to dawn or night, illustrating that she fails to exist within the hours of sunlight, feeling more at ease venturing out when twilight falls, when the deepening gloom is reflective of her mental condition. Rigid and upright on her old chair, subject and object merge before us to form a 'living inanimate' entity, a manifestation of her mental disposition. As she watches Venus rise, closely followed by the sun, it is not surprising that 'she rails at the source of all life' (Beckett 1982: 7). Venus, representative of the goddess of love and originally of spring, functions as a reminder of the fact that the woman exists within a loveless domain, isolated and stagnant, with no possibility of company. This goddess of spring appears out of place among the winter landscape and infertile pastures, which surround the cabin, appearing almost mocking, as it perhaps heightens the old woman's feelings of sterility. The juxtaposition of fertility and sterility serves to illustrate the realms of being and non-being, reflecting the woman's state of existence. Her position of prolonged existence is not honourable, and she does not feel elevated at the prospect of continued isolation, as 'Down on her knees especially she finds it hard not to remain so forever' (ibid.). The spiritual attrition from which she suffers, manifests itself through her inability to coerce her physical being to move, as her mental fatigue is corresponding to her physical exhaustion. And so she resembles the cabin in which she dwells; she is ultimately 'doomed to endure' (Beckett 1982: 9), possessing no further expectations of life.

Similar to W in *Rockaby*, the old woman ('Rigid with face and hands against the pane she stands and marvels long' (ibid.)), is maybe questioning what force aids her continual survival, as she resembles the landscape surrounding her. The circular environment, in which she exists, is perhaps a metaphor for her mind. Circular in appearance, it suggests continuance and a never-ending journey of conscious thought. Her inability to escape from the confines of consciousness results in the mental fatigue from which she suffers, and the pilgrimage to the gravestone is a metaphorical journey towards mental atrophy. She aspires to become part of the void and embrace the nothingness which she desires, rejoicing in the ultimate condition, to 'Neither be nor been nor by any shift to be' (Beckett 1982: 20). And we are reminded of the words in Job, which state as follows:

> Wherefore then hast thou brought me forth out of the womb? Oh that I had given up the ghost, and no eye had seen me! I should have been as though I had not been; I should have been carried from the womb to the grave. (Job 10.18–19)

The 'millions of little sepulchres' (Beckett 1982: 26) reinforce her feeling of isolation as she has become 'other', appearing distanced from the decay which surrounds her, as she continues to exude signs of life or perhaps 'life-lessness'. And therefore, even though at times she appears as if turned to stone, her body is in fact 'ashiver from head to foot' (Beckett 1982: 30), illustrating the contrasting nature of opposites, and ultimately the fusion of life and death. As body and mind constitute the human being, we recognize that the rhythm of her labouring heart parallels the rhythm of her labouring mind, as her footfalls on the evening snow correspond to the difficult journey her mind endures, as it is incapable of cessation. Her mental fatigue may be alleviated, as death appears to be drawing close. 'Ceaseless celestial winds in unison' (Beckett 1982: 42) may be the soundtrack to her death, as she appears 'Well on the way to inexistence' (Beckett 1982: 54). However, 'the place of the skull' (Beckett 1982: 57), suggestive of Golgotha, denotes crucifixion, but also denies the possibility of peaceful rest, as resurrection follows death. Beckett may be suggesting that although the old woman may achieve physical mortality, mental cessation may not be accomplished, and so her weariness of mind will perpetuate. She will remain forever ill seen, on the line between existence and non-existence, and incarcerated within the void, where mental fatigue will offer 'no happiness' and her journey to the gravestone will probably continue. This text exudes a tremendous restlessness, as not only does it detail the poverty of this old woman's existence but it also demonstrates the poverty of words. We witness Beckett groping for the right words; hence the old woman's struggle mirrors his. Trying to contemplate the idea of 'nothingness' must surely procure mental exhaustion, and in this text we witness how Beckett's writing reflects the unwritable nature of human experience; life cannot be told in words except 'ill said'.

If we return again briefly to Beckett's earlier prose text *Malone Dies*, which is examined in Chapter 4, we can investigate the effects of mental fatigue endured by the main protagonist. As Malone is effectively paralyzed, unable and unwilling to move from the bed, which now imprisons him, we recognize the necessity of exploring his mind, as physically he is of no importance. Therefore, the desire to die coupled with the need to go on, results in the turbulent state of mind which afflicts Malone, and determines the mental weariness that arises from his disquieting existence.

Beckett does not stipulate Malone's exact whereabouts. However, the possibility that people could dwell above and below him highlights the idea that Malone resides in a limbo state, appearing suspended between the confines of body and mind. The room itself therefore takes precedence, as we are unable to establish its precise location, and this enclosed space subsequently becomes the metaphor for Malone's mind, closed to the outside world but not inaccessible. Malone recognizes the reality that his room is analogous with his mind; he states, 'these six planes that enclose me are of solid bone' (Beckett 1994: 222). His quest for death ultimately takes precedence over his desire for life. However, his need to comprehend self and understand his existence, which includes his death, forces Malone to transcribe his narratives in an attempt to uncover his true self: 'Then it will be all over with the Murphys, Merciers, Molloys, Morans and Malones' (Beckett 1994: 237). This text is a deathbed confession, which constitutes an examination of a life, and explains why 'I' dominates the narrative. Through his narratives the microcosm of Malone's mind takes precedence before his eyes, as fiction ultimately becomes his reality. Mental fatigue consequently plagues Malone, due to the fact that his conscious mind also serves to imprison him within this existence, condemning him to function mentally within a body that declines to function physically.

Malone's desire to articulate the moment of his death cannot be achieved because, as Levy states, 'death is simply not an act that can be narrated' (1980: 57). Therefore, Malone's writing exercise is ultimately futile, as he will fail to narrate the appropriate words that will constitute his final condition, and his failure in death will parallel his failure in life. Malone is perchance mentally weary because he recognizes this truth and maybe this is why he claims that he will die 'tepid, without enthusiasm' (Beckett 1994: 180). Malone's stories ultimately fail to help him, due to the fact that displacement of the self onto a fictional character essentially denies one's identity; perhaps mental exhaustion derives from this unending search for the self. However, Malone is content to fictionalize his own reality, and his narratives are therefore a waste of time, as they fail to reveal his inner depths, and consequently defeat the purpose of his original aim, thereby heightening the tiredness of mind, which he endures, and adding to the suffering which he expects. Once again, with Malone, we have a sense of loneliness, suggesting that the lack of company may well have induced the mental fatigue.

Malone illustrates the inability of one to fully come to terms with one's position in life, and the impossibility of being able to comprehend one's existence. Hence, he appears similar to May in *Footfalls*:

All I want now is to make a last effort to understand, to begin to understand, how such creatures are possible. No, it is not a question of understanding. Of what then? I don't know. Here I go none the less, mistakenly. Night, storm and sorrow, and the catalepsies of the soul, this time I shall see that they are good. The last word is not yet said between me and – yes, the last word is said. Perhaps I simply want to hear it said again. Just once again. No, I want nothing. (Beckett 1994: 199)

A comprehension of individuals and of existence is unattainable, as an understanding of life remains forever elusive. And it is this desire to understand one's role within the universe which plagues Beckett's characters, dominating their thoughts from birth to death, and resulting doubtless in their mental fatigue. Malone's desire to write himself out of existence is futile because, with the continuance of words, conscious thought endures, and so he is imprisoned within the paradox that to end, he must ultimately continue. As death remains elusive and mental fatigue endures, Malone is left with the terrifying prospect that 'he who has waited long enough will wait for ever' (Beckett 1994: 242).

Beckett successfully illustrates the paradox that one's mental age cannot always be equated with one's physical age. He conveys the effects of time on the microcosm, illustrating the implications of senescence and demonstrating the mind's inability to cope with existence. Mental fatigue plagues Beckett's characters because their desire to end is complicated by their need to go on. Their desire to comprehend the implications of existence prompts them to continually 'revolve it all' in their minds, as they fail to acknowledge the reality that life is ultimately meaningless, and continuance is therefore futile.

Beckett illustrates that mental weariness essentially produces mental instability, as the mind, unable to become defunct, functions on the border-line between sanity and insanity. And as the mind grows increasingly fatigued, it fails to exist within the realms of reality, prompting mental degeneration and propelling the protagonist further into the realms of derangement. Throughout Chapter 7 it will be illustrated how Beckett portrays the decayed mental faculty, as he challenges the conventional representations of mental disorders, providing a further insight into the workings of the psyche.

Chapter 7

Perceptions of Insanity

We all are born mad. Some remain so.

Waiting for Godot

Insanity has often been regarded by society as an inferior mental state. Michel Foucault suggests that 'We have now got in the habit of perceiving in madness a fall into a determinism where all forms of liberty are gradually suppressed' (1989: 83). However, Beckett offers an inversion of the general perception of madness, as he pushes the boundaries of the mind and illustrates that sanity and insanity are not polar opposites, but rather different aspects of the consciousness. In Beckett's work the line between the rational and the unsound state of mind becomes effaced; he suggests that freedom is only to be located in the insane mind, where the consciousness is not restricted by conforming to society, and the mind becomes freed from the 'confines' of sanity. Much of Beckett's work details the convoluted workings of his characters' mental faculties and his writing undoubtedly prompts us to re-conceptualize the definition of the sane and insane.

Written in 1965, *Eh Joe* successfully dramatizes the process of listening, conveying the complex interweaving of the conscious and unconscious mind and illustrating the 'diseased' psyche of the main protagonist. The drama ultimately becomes internal, as Beckett excavates the landscape of the mind in an attempt to portray the confrontation of self, as through his mental processes Joe undergoes an uncompromising self-examination. Normality and abnormality (terms which have little value in Beckett's work) ultimately merge, as Joe exists somewhere between the boundaries of the sane and the insane. And so we witness a character that tries to control his mind in order to render reality more manageable.

Jack MacGowran's description of the play, as photographing the mind,[1] is indeed insightful, as the camera accentuates a sense of dramatic engagement with private thoughts. Beckett breaks all conventions of privacy, as the camera allows us access, first, to the bedroom of a character that believes he is alone, and then goes one stage further by allowing us access to the inner workings of his psyche. By forcing us to witness the mental anguish of another, Beckett is ultimately prompting us to examine our own thought processes and, perhaps, acknowledge that, if we are truthful, we ourselves are not that far removed from Joe, as we all have recourse to administer 'Mental thuggee' (Beckett 1990: 363), in an attempt to deal with unwanted memories and thoughts, and suppress personal failings. Joe's facial expression throughout the play is therefore practically motionless, due to the fact that the drama takes place behind the impassive exterior, within the tormented interior.

Despite being physically alone, Joe fails to inhabit the world of silence, as the accusatory voice inside his head forces him into an unrelenting self-analysis, prompting him to confront the unpleasantness of his personality. As the voice recalls the stories of past 'loves', Beckett successfully presents images of the past in the immediate present, similar to *Krapp's Last Tape*. Although voices in the head may be attributed to the onset of schizophrenia, it is important to question whether Joe controls this voice or does it in fact control him? [2] It may be believed that Joe experiences this voice involuntarily, thereby suggesting that he is mentally unstable, as his mind is essentially degenerating, and he is afflicted by disturbing thought processes over which he fails to assert control. Although this reading of the play is indeed justifiable, it is interesting, and necessary for a full comprehension of the work, to suggest that it is Joe who creates these voices in his head for his own erotic pleasure. And if Joe does in fact control his mind and thought processes, it becomes evident that he is more mentally disturbed, perhaps, than someone who is labelled clinically insane.

As Beckett presents the man in the room scenario we recognize the reality that this middle-aged protagonist is essentially isolated, a condition that afflicts nearly all of Beckett's characters. Therefore, if Joe does manufacture this voice inside his mind, he may be essentially 'devising it all for company' (Beckett 1996a: 64), in an attempt to block out the reality that he is in fact alone and that his body is beginning to degenerate. It may be suggested that although the voice causes him discomfort, without it he would have nothing, and the prospect of the silence may be more unbearable than the pain of self-confrontation.

Joe's preparation of the room is congruent with his preparation of mind, as he ensures that he is safe from outside intrusion ('No one can see you now. . . . No one can get at you now' (Beckett 1990: 362)), in order to procure maximum mental climax, by succumbing to the voice in his mind. As the voice mocks him ('You know that penny farthing hell you call your mind' (ibid.)), we recognize that for Joe, his mind represents a state of purgatory in which he must confront ghosts from the past, including his mother and father. And, paradoxically, his mind affords him pleasure, as his 'masochistic' thought processes appear to produce a cathartic response from him. Of course we cannot be assured that the story the voice tells does in fact constitute the truth, and we recognize that these past 'loves' may in reality be a complete fabrication of Joe's 'diseased' mind; it is difficult to comprehend why Joe would manufacture a tale about a girl committing suicide,[3] and yet perhaps this is confirmation about the state of Joe's mental faculty. Beckett's men fail to understand the concept of love.[4] Joe may not actually derive pleasure from the tragic story, but perhaps he finds 'pleasurable' the idea that someone may have loved him so intensely, as to not be able to live without him. We get the impression that he treated these girls, and indeed everyone around him, badly; therefore it is also possible that his mistreatment of her left her with such low self-esteem that she was incapable of going on. Does he regret his past actions? Joe's concept of external reality is indeed questionable, and as he confronts himself within the mind he risks mental breakdown. By continually consenting to voices within his mind, Joe permits the intrusion of 'not I', and although they may represent authentic versions of the self (different aspects of the psyche), they prohibit 'I' from dominating the mind, thereby ensuring continued confusion of identity and mental trauma. 'Mental thuggee', as a process of the mind, is indeed effective, as it permits manipulation of thought processes and allows one to assert some form of control over consciousness, as we can choose to erase episodes in our mind which we deem painful. However, similar to our bodies, our minds are prone to degeneration and we cannot prevent the break down of our mental faculties. By permitting this voice to take precedence within his mind, Joe is relinquishing control over his psyche, and although mental thuggee is at present effective, eventually it will become futile in the struggle to murder the voices in his head.

The ending of the drama is significant; Jack Macgowran, in *Theatre Quarterly*, says 'It's a little victory he has at the end in dismissing the voice; he finally crushes it' (1973: 20), quoted here from (Pountney 1988: 171). However, as Pountney rightly points out, 'the fading image and sibilant voice disappear together' (ibid.), thereby suggesting that Joe has not achieved a minor victory. In fact, it may be suggested, that the disappearing image of Joe essentially represents the dissolution of self. The voice, which has produced mental erosion, has perhaps succeeded in eliminating Joe. We acknowledge his physical body, but mentally he is perhaps anaesthetized, as the voice of 'other' has conceivably claimed ownership over Joe's mind. 'Not I' consequently dominates, as Joe's 'identity' perhaps becomes lost in the convoluted workings of his psyche.

Seven years after *Eh Joe*, Beckett once again returned to the theme of mental disorders in his 'disturbing' drama *Not I*. This play undoubtedly pushes back the boundaries of theatre, as Beckett presents, on stage, a mouth, which pours out words that are barely intelligible. This drama prompts one to re-examine the issue of personal identity and question whether someone who fails to acknowledge 'I', may be classified as insane. Here Beckett presents us with a consciousness that is aware of its existence but dare not admit it. To tell one's own life story through an imaginary character provides distance, thereby allowing Mouth to examine her life, (similar to Malone and Henry) while simultaneously denying that the narrative she relates does in fact recount her own

existence. As stated previously, 'I' is therefore conveniently replaced by 'not
I', as identity becomes displaced and mental stability becomes questionable.
As Knowlson says, Mouth 'takes her place in a long line of split personalities,
psychotics or obsessional neurotics, who assume, nonetheless, more universal
significance' (1997: 590). It is interesting that Knowlson credits Beckett's mentally disturbed characters as having universal significance because, if we look
closely at Beckett's representation of insanity, we recognize that he challenges
conventional perceptions and presents the mentally deranged as perhaps constituting a more common reality. If we are a succession of selves, as Beckett
suggests in his essay on Proust (1965: 19), then the concept of adhering to a
fixed identity is undermined, as 'not I' is the only identity that we can assume.
Therefore the ability to know ourselves or our 'selves' fully is lost.[5]

Mouth believes she is alone and does not recognize the presence of the
Auditor. The fact that Mouth fails to acknowledge his presence confirms the
reality that she is in fact talking only to herself, and Beckett might be trying to
dramatize how we are ultimately alone in our plight. It is often assumed that
talking to oneself is the first sign of madness, and yet it may be suggested that
we all suffer from this affliction. The inability to prevent thought produces a
continual voice within our minds, and although we may not give voice to our
thought processes, they nevertheless dominate our minds, and therefore we
appear not that far removed from Mouth herself. We question whether the
human experience renders us insane.

Beckett presents language as an affliction in this drama, and the opening
word 'out' is indicative of the reality that Mouth wishes to eradicate words,
striving to evict them via this orifice, and return to the silence whence she
came. The excretion of words and the fluids (which Mouth also secretes in the
form of spittle) reduces this body part to nothing more than a waste disposal
unit. Language is therefore reduced to meaningless outpourings, as Beckett
successfully conveys his belief that words too, must ultimately fail. Mouth herself possesses no identity, as she is not attached to the recognizable features of
a face, thereby appearing almost alien, as she is separated from the confines of
body, but not yet liberated from the limitations of mind.

Beckett does not stipulate what exactly happened to Mouth in the field to
produce such an outpouring of words, and this is due to the fact that it is of
little importance. The buzzing in the ears ('in the skull . . . dull roar in the
skull' (Beckett 1990: 378)), may indeed be confirmation of mental disturbance, or it may perhaps represent the consciousness which cannot be silenced.
Unable to keep words confined to her mind, Mouth has no alternative but to
open up and release them. The theme of denial, ('what? . . . who? . . . no! . . .
she!' (Beckett 1990: 377)), which is prevalent throughout the drama, and the
inability to acknowledge 'I', may be attributed to feelings of guilt. As Murray
(2006: 7) confirms, guilt, in Beckett's work, is a persistent condition. Mouth
questions if she is being punished for her sins, and fails to realize that the

only sin she has committed is the sin of having been born, a transgression she ultimately could not control. This continual feeling of culpability has perhaps caused her mind to deteriorate; Lillian Feder's words substantiate this idea: 'Inappropriate, pathological guilt, for example, was among the most common symptoms of mental disturbance prevalent in Western civilization' (1980: 5). As Mouth's concept of external reality became confused, due perhaps to 'some flaw in her make-up' (Beckett 1990: 378), the dissolution of self was inevitable (presupposing we have a stable self to begin with) and therefore 'I' was inevitably replaced by 'not I'.

Mouth cannot progress beyond the stage at which we witness her until she acknowledges 'I' and takes responsibility for the existence she has endured. And until that moment, she will remain similar to John the Baptist,[6] as she will continue to be 'The voice of one crying in the wilderness' (Mt. 3.3), enduring a mental crucifixion and a non-identity. The agitated outpourings of Mouth seem to act as a primal scream about the horror of being alive and the madness it induces. Is Beckett suggesting here that life incites psychosis? By adhering to 'not I', Mouth metaphorically fails to exist and the mind subsequently becomes unhinged, as the consciousness cannot conceive of itself as non-existing. Perhaps Mouth exerts no control over the words and is, therefore, unable to prohibit the stream of language that flows from her:

> imagine! . . . can't stop the stream . . . and the whole brain begging . . .
> something begging in the brain . . . begging the mouth to stop . . . pause
> a moment . . . if only for a moment . . . and no response . . . as if it hadn't
> heard . . . or couldn't . . . couldn't pause a second . . . like maddened . . .
> (Beckett 1990: 380)

If the brain is begging the words to stop, then surely the mind is functioning, as it recognizes the abnormality of Mouth. However, the inability of the brain to control Mouth, suggests that it is a defective and unreliable mechanism; it appears as a disconnected force. Mouth understands that there is something she must say, ('perhaps something she had to . . . had to . . . tell . . . could that be it?' (Beckett 1990: 381)), in order to stop this flow of language. However, she fails to realize that, perhaps, it is the acknowledgement of 'I' that will end her mental anguish.

With her troubled mind, and the denial of self, Mouth will continue to endure mental decline and be afflicted with the burden of language. Perhaps Beckett is suggesting throughout this drama that language is fundamentally redundant in affirming identity. The story can never be properly told because the words are essentially ineffective. And as 'Words fail, there are times when even they fail' (Beckett 1990: 147), we will all endure the impossible task of articulating 'I', as the mind, unable to find the right word, will eventually disintegrate, condemning us all to assume the posture of 'not I'.

Written in late 1962–1963 *Play* illustrates Beckett's early attempt at conveying the disturbed workings of the mind on stage. The triangular relationship between the three characters, and the hellish setting in which they exist,
prompts one to conceive of this drama as analogous to Sartre's *In Camera*.
However, although similarities may exist between the two plays, it is evident
that Beckett offers a bleaker representation of existence, which negates any
possibility of improvement. By representing the mental torture of three individuals who believe they are alone, unaware that they reside in close unison,
and by forcing them into an unrelenting inquisition, Beckett successfully conveys how the mind reacts to mental turmoil, and illustrates that total insanity may be preferable to clarity of mind. However, although the narrative the
three characters relate may not, in itself, suggest insanity, it is the situation in
which they exist that will eventually cause them to experience mental breakdown. Beckett's Hell is clearly a psychological one that could exist, and does
exist, like Sartre's, in the pre-death state.

Bodily death appears dislocated from mental mortality, as their bodies, subject to the confines of the urns, are essentially defunct. Their bodies being,
therefore, inconsequential, forces us to focus primarily on their heads, as
Beckett successfully draws our attention to the workings of their tortured
minds. With their 'Faces so lost to age and aspect as to seem almost part of
urns' (Beckett 1990: 307), we recognize that their physical aspect represents
their mental state as, due to the continual repetition of their narrative, they
are becoming deadened and similar to the inanimate objects in which they reside. They appear similar to their predecessor Mahood who, in *The Unnamable*,
finds himself existing within a jar, with no recollection or understanding of
how he came to be there. They are similar to Mouth, uttering words in the
hope that they may perchance hit on the right ones, and so end the torturous
outpouring of language. And we can see how in the 10 years between *Play* and
Not I Beckett's work was becoming ever more reduced, as the heads in *Play* are
condensed to a Mouth in *Not I*.

The spiritual dejection that exudes from the characters in *Play*, suggests
that their position is in fact hopeless, and they know that an escape from
consciousness is unattainable. The structure of this drama is interesting, as
it appears to pivot about its middle point, gravitating from a story of adultery
to a more philosophical/metaphysical tone. The impassive faces and toneless
voices reflect the weariness of the characters, and illustrate that they have
become mentally conditioned to relate their stories without thought or reason. They are programmed to speak when the spotlight indicates, thereby
appearing similar to machines, as they continually repeat the story they
believe they must tell. This mindless, repetitive narrative, over which they
have little control, must eventually lead to mental instability, as the human
mind cannot endure the monotony of repetition, coupled with the monotony
of 'existence'.

Despite being described as a play in one act, the drama appears split into two halves. The first section, which details the events of the adulterous affair, appears similar to other dramas that have explored this much discussed topic. Beckett has used the many clichés in order to undermine the significance of their past lives, thereby prompting us to conceive of their current situation as the dominant factor in this drama. It is the situation in which they now exist that makes Beckett's play stand apart from other dramas which explore the relationship between husband, wife and mistress. Consequently, the second half of the drama, which details the characters' reactions to their current predicament is undoubtedly the more interesting for the purposes of this chapter.

In the second half of the play, the spotlight continues to provoke anxiety in each of the characters, reducing them to nothing more than helpless victims, unable to gain control over their minds. This inability to control speech or attain silence would undoubtedly have been Beckett's conception of hell, where the endless repetition of meaningless words would represent an unequalled kind of torture. However, with the pauses between the light, there exist periods of respite for the characters and temporary moments of silence, during which they can reflect on their horrendous situation. And although W2 asserts that 'There are endurable moments' (Beckett 1990: 312), these periods of silence would be as excruciating as the incessant talking, because each character realizes that the silence cannot last, as eventually the light will require them to speak again. This light, which effectively switches on and off speech, illustrates the fallibility of the brain, as no longer can their minds control their mouths, and so they are subject to the disposition of an external agent that essentially plays with their heads. And as M states 'All this, when will all this have been . . . just play?' (Beckett 1990: 313), he fails to recognize the reality that 'all this' is just play, and although he is a part of the game, he does not control the moves. He participates in the game by producing words, which are inconsequential and cannot alleviate nor change his present situation, and yet he is compelled to speak. As Paul Lawley says, in his essay 'Stages of identity: from *Krapp's Last Tape* to *Play*', 'The heads speak not just in response to the light but in an attempt to get it off themselves, hence words for them are a defence-mechanism, a set of blocks necessary less for meaning than for their abstract function' (Pilling 1994: 99–100). They are prisoners of language similar to Mouth in *Not I* and Lucky in *Waiting for Godot*, and it is this inability to control one's current existence that facilitates mental erosion, as spiritual dejection gives way to depression of mind. W2 recognizes that her mind is becoming disordered, as she says 'Yes, perhaps, a shade gone, I suppose, some might say, poor thing, a shade gone, just a shade, in the head' (Beckett 1990: 307). And as Knowlson affirms, 'W2 hopes that madness might provide her own form of release from torment' (Knowlson and Pilling 1979: 117). It is not insanity that Beckett illustrates as horrific but rather the refusal of the mind to go

blank, ('How the mind works still!' (Beckett 1990: 313)), that is the most har-
rowing aspect of this drama.

The need for recognition facilitates the mental weariness they endure, and
as W2 asks 'Are you listening to me? Is anyone listening to me? Is anyone looking at me? Is anyone bothering about me at all?' (Beckett 1990: 314), we recognize the panic in her voice. This need for recognition, which many characters
possess, causes feelings of insecurity, as the mind is incapable of conceiving
that it is essentially talking to itself and mental instability therefore appears
inevitable. With their questions unanswered and their torture unrelenting,
these characters appear condemned to an eternal outpouring of meaningless
language. If they are perhaps a little 'unhinged' already, they may decide to
relinquish any stability of mind and embrace insanity, in the hope that, mentally deranged, they would be better equipped to deal with the realities of
this existence. By relinquishing control over their minds and by ending their
continual questioning, they would essentially be freed from the confines of
sanity. As Beckett pushes the boundaries between the sane and the insane, he
forces us to conceive of insanity as perhaps a more bearable state, and so we
turn to his early work *Murphy* in which he illustrates that the 'insane', possibly,
possess a more cultivated mind than the mentally sound, and are therefore to
be envied.

Murphy, published in 1938, was Beckett's first published novel and possibly
one of the most accessible fictions that he has written. As Beckett presents an
inversion of the general perception of madness, we recognize that he pushes
the boundaries of the mind and forces one to confront the reality that perhaps
'sanity' is an inferior state of mind, where we conform to the regulations of
society, dwelling primarily in our bodies and avoiding transcendence of the
physical. By embracing 'insanity', the confines of the physical body disintegrate and we are free to wander through the landscape of our minds, where
contemplation procures happiness and being oblivious to the outside world
secures peace (Although many of Beckett's later works illustrate the suffering
caused by continual introspection). It is in this state of being that one perhaps
discovers 'self', and where the conscious and unconscious minds merge to
produce the feeling of catharsis. And we therefore question whether Beckett's
representation of the insane in *Murphy* can be classified as a representation of
decay due to the fact that, despite conventional perceptions of insanity, Beckett
illustrates it as a supreme cultivation of mind.

The novel evidently revolves around the central protagonist Murphy, an
individual who has a deep sense of alienation from the outside world. It is
interesting that Bion[7] (Beckett's analyst for two years) wrote some papers in
which he argued, as Cronin states

> that there were cases in which psychological birth occurred before bio-
> logical birth, while the people concerned were still in the womb. The

result was that actual biological birth did not necessarily bring mental separation from the mother. There were people who suffered trauma due to 'mismanaged birth' and who remained throughout their life with a sensation of still being in the womb because no proper caesura had taken place during biological birth. (Cronin 1997: 222)[8]

These people were perhaps unable to fit into society, believing themselves to be removed beyond the normal boundaries of conventional existence. Their minds are not equipped to deal with day-to-day living; therefore withdrawing into themselves procures the reality that they find lacking in the outside world. Although Beckett fails to detail Murphy's birth, it may be suggested that his state of mind could perhaps be the result of the trauma experienced during the birthing procedure.

Although Murphy is unable to live fully in the world and interact successfully with others, he is also unable to live outside of it, and so he achieves the balance of necessary social interaction coupled with withdrawal into the confines of his mind. For Murphy 'The mental experience was cut off from the physical experience' (Beckett 1993a: 64); subject to the confines of his physical body, Murphy endures the 'separated togetherness' of mind and body, where the body represents incarceration and the mind offers liberation. Murphy, therefore, embodies the Cartesian dualism as 'he felt himself split in two, a body and a mind' (ibid.). R. D. Laing suggests that when an individual is insecure, in his/her own being, such people 'experience themselves as primarily split into a mind and a body. Usually they feel most closely identified with the "mind"' (1990: 65). Therefore, we question whether living this dual existence, in which identity essentially becomes divided, can be labelled insane. Even though the novel details Wylie and Neary's search for Murphy, we acknowledge that this external search is secondary to the internal search within Murphy, who is essentially in pursuit of himself. As Pilling says 'everything in Beckett's first published novel depends – as the very title of the book implies – on one figure, and on one figure only. Without Murphy, there could be no *Murphy*' (1997: 125).

We are told that 'Murphy's mind pictured itself as a large hollow sphere, hermetically closed to the universe without' (Beckett 1993a: 63). It is therefore evident that Murphy's mind is similar to that of Belacqua who, in *Dream of Fair to Middling Women*, conceived of his mind as a 'wombtomb' (Beckett 1993b: 121), and the only place in which he could withdraw into himself. To describe Murphy as a solipsist is indeed justified, as essentially he does not believe in anything outside of himself. But surely a withdrawal into one's mind, where one can escape the pain of living, is a preferable state of existence and a quietism that is indeed enviable. In fact, this type of existence appears more rational than one in which we try to condition our minds in the hope that we can conform to society's expectations by living a 'normal' life. This novel demonstrates a supreme cultivation of mind, as Murphy is able to discipline his mind to function as a place as well as an instrument. His strain towards mental sublimation allows escapism, and he is justified in declaring, 'I am not of the big world, I am of the little world' (Beckett 1993a: 101).

The three zones – light, half light and dark – that constitute Murphy's mind correspond, as Cronin points out, to Jung's assertion that 'the mind is made up of concentric circles becoming ever darker till we reach the final darkness of the unconscious' (Cronin 1997: 221). It is in this dark zone that Murphy conceives of himself as a 'mote in the dark of absolute freedom' (Beckett 1993a: 66). To reach this level of unconsciousness, where one attains freedom, demonstrates a supreme cultivation of mind, not a disordered mental faculty. Geulincx states, '*Ubi nihil vales, ibi nihil velis*', meaning 'where you are worth nothing, you will wish for nothing';[9] and we recognize his acknowledgement that in the mind alone, man can perhaps be free.

The Magdalen Mental Mercyseat represents sanctuary for Murphy, as it constitutes the visual representation of his psyche. Although the patients all suffer with some form of mental condition, we are told that 'They caused Murphy no horror. The most easily identifiable of his immediate feelings were respect and unworthiness' (Beckett 1993a: 96), for the simple fact that they had achieved what Murphy longed for: total emancipation of mind. Beckett is unconventional in his representation of this sanatorium, as he prompts us 'to think of the patients not as banished from a system of benefits but as escaped from a colossal fiasco' (Beckett 1993a: 101).

Mr Endon, 'whose name is the Greek word for "within"' (Kenner 1973: 68), constitutes the deluxe version of Murphy.[10] Described as a 'schizophrenic of the most amiable variety' (Beckett 1993a: 105), he is representative of everything Murphy aspires to. We are told that Endon's inner voice 'did not harangue him, it was unobtrusive and melodious' (Beckett 1993a: 105). However, it is evident that after this novel, Beckett's protagonists who experience inner voices mostly endure a troubled existence. Murphy's inability to achieve Endon's state of 'sub-consciousness' essentially leads to his demise. As the narrator says, 'The last Mr Murphy saw of Mr Endon was Mr Murphy unseen by Mr Endon. This was also the last Murphy saw of Murphy' (Beckett 1993a: 140). A supreme cultivation of mind therefore becomes destructive, as the Cartesian dualism of mind and body cannot be sustained. Therefore, to endure this existence, one element of self must become secondary, as body and mind cannot co-exist on an elevated plane. And so we question whether it is rational to adhere to the conventions of society and refrain from withdrawal into the mind, where freedom is perhaps guaranteed.

Watt, may possibly be described as an illustration of the human mind in ruins. Or perhaps it is better to view it as an extreme representation of how it is to be alive when our minds function at such an elevated level in the pursuit of comprehending the complexities of existence. Is Watt insane? Or is he perhaps an extreme representation of us all? Alvarez suggests that Watt is more mentally affected than Murphy; he says:

> Watt, in his turn, is a stage beyond Murphy. Where Murphy idealized the schizophrenics from the outside, Watt is one. He tells his story to a man called Sam, like Beckett himself, who is a fellow-inmate of a lunatic asylum much like the Magdalen Mental Mercyseat. What he tells and how he tells it are, in their different ways, symptoms of his condition. (1992: 41)

Like many of Beckett's protagonists Watt appears to be a wanderer. He exists on the fringes of society, beyond the confines of 'normal' existence, appearing strange to anyone who perceives him ('Perhaps he is off his head' (Beckett 1976: 17), comments Mr Hackett). It is not surprising, therefore, that Watt ends up in an asylum because, similar to Murphy, he probably wants to escape from the outside world, as the impossibility of comprehending existence has perhaps had a detrimental effect on his mind. Watt represents what May shall become, as his continual 'revolving it all' has possibly produced mental breakdown. We wonder if, in fact, Watt was on his way to the asylum when he came across Knott's house, perhaps mistaking it for the refuge that he was seeking; because, as we are told 'Watt never knew how he got into Mr. Knott's house' (Beckett 1976: 35). It is Watt's need to know which has essentially affected his mind. He appears to suffer from obsessive-compulsive disorder, continually questioning the significance of objects and events. As Pattie affirms, this is a 'narrative voice that is pedantically and comically caught up in the precise nuances of the everyday' (2000: 60). Hence, we recognize that life and the inability to understand it, ultimately causes mental affliction. The complexity of Watt's mind is illustrated in the sequence detailing Watt's reaction to the pot:

> Looking at a pot, for example, or thinking of a pot, at one of Mr. Knott's pots, of one of Mr. Knott's pots, it was in vain that Watt said, Pot, pot. Well, perhaps not quite in vain, but very nearly. For it was not a pot, the more he looked, the more he reflected, the more he felt sure of that, that it was not a pot at all. It resembled a pot, it was almost a pot, but it was not a pot of which one could say, Pot, pot, and be comforted. (Beckett 1976: 78)

It may be concluded from this that Watt is insane, but it is also possible to suggest that he possesses a mind which is more acute than the average mind; hence his desire to comprehend existence is so elevated that his mind breaks down when it realizes that life is beyond understanding. 'For to explain had always been to exorcise, for Watt' (Beckett 1976: 74–75); consequently when an explanation is not found, 'unknowability' procures mental deterioration. As Davies suggests, 'perhaps Mr Knott is a tranquil man because he is content with being rather than hankering after knowledge' (1994: 40) – unlike Watt.

This need to explicate is seen throughout the novel especially in the Lynch family and Louit interpolations. These episodes are used as an illustration of a point, and yet they are so lengthy that one tends to forget the original point that they are used to illustrate. The description of the Lynch family,[11] which continues for 11 pages, is used to illustrate how Knott's food is disposed of. And the Louit episode,[12] which lasts approximately 28 pages, is used to explain why Bando (a remedy for impotence) can no longer be obtained. These episodes are fascinating and extremely comical, as Beckett pushes language to its limits, prompting it to appear absurd, as the countless permutations included in these sections serve to make the words appear almost meaningless, as they become essentially hypnotic. However, as Beckett says, 'art has nothing to do with clarity, does not dabble in the clear and does not make clear' (Beckett 1983: 94). The rhythmic quality of the words is illustrated in this small excerpt from the 'looking' episode:

> Mr. Fitzwein looks at Mr. Magershon, on his right. But Mr. Magershon is not looking at Mr. Fitzwein, on his left, but at Mr. O'Meldon, on his right. But Mr. O'Meldon is not looking at Mr. Magershon, on his left, but, craning forward, at Mr. MacStern, on his left but three at the far end of the table. But Mr. MacStern is not craning forward looking at Mr. O'Meldon, on his right but three at the far end of the table, but is sitting bolt upright looking at Mr. de Baker, on his right. (Beckett (1976: 173)

Episodes such as these appear to come from a mind which is in turmoil, but the interesting thing is that they do not all come from Watt. Arthur, for example, relates the Louit episode to Mr Graves. It may be suggested, therefore, that everyone in Knott's house is either mentally deranged or mentally gifted, as they are able to reason out such complex situations; it is of course suggested that genius is akin to madness. Consequently, it is perhaps not surprising that Watt entered Knott's house believing it to be the lunatic asylum. If the people in Knott's house are in fact mentally exceptional, the fact that 'nothing changed, in Mr. Knott's establishment' (Beckett 1976: 130), could have had a detrimental effect on Watt and the other servants, as their enquiring minds would not have been sufficiently challenged. Therefore, once they had understood the workings of Knott's home their minds may have become lethargic.

However, we can only speculate about Watt's state of mind because Beckett further complicates things by stating, in the third chapter, that the story is, in fact, narrated by Sam, a lunatic whom Watt meets in the asylum. Hence, we recognize that the narrative is not chronological, as one would expect chapter three to be located at the end. However, this technique serves to heighten the confusion of the narrative, as it becomes 'clear' that Watt's story is told by a man (Sam) in a lunatic asylum, who himself was told the story by Watt (a possible lunatic) but may not have actually heard the story correctly because his hearing was failing. Hence, Beckett is again illustrating the unreliability of narrative and the difficulty of expression.

As Sam details his meetings with Watt, he comments on how Watt's speech began to deteriorate, thus resulting in the fact that he missed some key facts: 'Thus I missed I suppose much I suspect of great interest touching I presume the first or initial stage of the second or closing period of Watt's stay in Mr. Knott's house' (Beckett 1976: 163). He goes on to tell us how he also missed the second, third, fourth, fifth, sixth, seventh and eighth stage of the second or closing period of Watt's time in Knott's house.[13] Hence, Beckett successfully illustrates that language is prone to failure and is perhaps ultimately futile, as the difficulty/impossibility of expression is conveyed through Watt, as he begins to invert letters in words and words in sentences. Even though, ironically, he is described as a 'very fair linguist' (Beckett 1976: 208), Watt's words (as recalled by Sam) illustrate a linguistic decay and perhaps a mental breakdown. As Sam says 'The following is an example of this manner: Lit yad mac, ot og. Ton taw, ton tonk. Ton dob, ton trips. Ton vila, ton deda. Ton kawa, ton pelsa. Ton das, don yag. Os devil, rof mit' (Beckett 1976: 165). We cannot be sure whether these episodes are confirmation of Watt's insanity or Sam's. Perhaps neither is insane. The difficulty in reading *Watt* stems from the fact that it is not just Watt's story re-told by Sam; there is evidently another omniscient narrator who relates the conversation between Mr Hackett and Tetty, and who comments on the goat that watches Watt making his way to the station. It is not surprising that Pilling says, '*Watt* is definitely fragmentary' (1976: 40). However, despite the complexities of the novel we continue to read it, endeavouring to comprehend its meaning, hence, we assume the position of Watt in our quest for understanding. Perhaps, therefore, it is not the characters that are disturbed, but the reader who tries to make sense of it all.

Beckett illustrates that the actual experience of living gradually impairs our mental faculties, resulting in mental decay, which, combined with physical degeneration, must ultimately lead to spiritual attrition. Chapter 8 examines how Beckett's protagonists function when the will to live has left them.

Chapter 8

'I Can't Go On, I'll Go On'
The Ebbing Spirit

I listen and the voice is of a world collapsing endlessly.

Molloy

To define spirit is a difficult task; perhaps Beckett would describe it as 'whatever it is, that gives us the strength to live on and on with our wounds' (Harmon 1998: 142).[1] However, the futility of existence and a lack of hope forces the spirit to gradually decline, until the weariness of living eventually erodes it, and one collapses under the monotony of life, unable and unwilling to continue. Beckett successfully illustrates this attrition of spirit and demonstrates that without strength of spirit, one is metaphorically dead. To reach an 'absolute end', physical death and mental death must be joined by spiritual death, as only by giving up the will to live, can one perhaps successfully discontinue.

Nacht und Träume, a television play, written in 1982, captures the acuteness of spiritual attrition, as the central protagonist, Dreamer (A), finds solace from his dreamt self (B). The title, meaning 'Night and Dreams', epitomizes the darkness which envelops the dreamer's spirit, as no longer can he find comfort during waking hours and, thus dejected, he turns only to himself for company. The drama, which includes no dialogue, conveys the feeling of isolation which the dreamer endures, and illustrates the compassion he craves. Unable to find partnership, he embraces himself through his dreams, as he essentially becomes his 'own other'.

The dark empty room, in which the Dreamer sits, conveys the feeling of isolation which evidently plagues him, as there exists nothing or no one to alleviate his feeling of despair. His grey hair suggests that he is an aged character, who perhaps recognizes that life is drawing to a close, having offered him little worthwhile. Without the possibility of improvement, his spirit appears to succumb to erosion, as his feeling of dejection ensures spiritual decline and facilitates the process that he must endure before the life force expires. With essentially nothing to live for, his dreams provide escape from the harshness of existence and alleviate the weariness that plagues him during waking hours.

It is only his dreams that prevent his spirit from giving up completely, and while he can dream, he perhaps retains some of his will to live. The dream affords him consolation, as the play implies that such solace is not available in conscious daily existence.

Seated at a table, he is perhaps too weary to confront the bed, unable to move from the position at which we now witness him. The table, where perhaps he once indulged in artistic creation, now serves as a platform on which to rest his fatigued head. Only in dreams can his imagination now serve him, as the hours of darkness become temporarily alleviated and he is free to embrace the compassion which exists only in his mind. As the voice softly hums the 'Last 7 bars of Schubert's *Lied, Nacht und Träume*' (Beckett 1990: 465), we recognize that he finds consolation in music; and so the tune functions almost like a lullaby, as it ensures the arrival of sleep and the possibility of dreams. As Knowlson says, this play 'evokes more clearly perhaps than any other of Beckett's plays that "purity of spirit" that had long been important in his life as well as in his work' (1997: 683). Beckett indeed captures the purity of the spirit, as the protagonist appears almost child-like in his desire for compassion. This play is therefore similar to *Ohio Impromptu*, which also illustrates the desire for consolation and the methods used for getting one through the night.

As (A) falls asleep and his dreamt self becomes apparent, he continues to remain 'just visible throughout dream as first viewed' (Beckett 1990: 465). His dreamt self (B) is situated 'on an invisible podium about 4 feet above floor level' (ibid.). As Beckett states 'He is seated at a table in the same posture as A dreaming, bowed head resting on hands, but left profile, faintly lit by kinder light than A's' (ibid.) Beckett is successful in creating A's doppelgänger and confirming the ghostly aura which surrounds this drama. B is illuminated by a kinder light than A, due to the fact that he receives the compassion which A desires, despite the fact that he assumes the initial position of dejection. However, B's spiritual decline is momentarily alleviated by the arrival of the hands, which provide the image of consolation, and administer the compassion which the dreamer fails to receive. Spiritual attrition is most acute when one is isolated and therefore the arrival of the hands temporarily suspends spiritual decline. Of course Beckett was well acquainted with Dürer's famous *Praying Hands* painting which evokes an image of solace, perhaps providing the writer with the inspiration to capture, in drama, the poignant image of consoling hands.[2]

The hands, which are disembodied, become paramount to the drama and confirm Beckett's life-long interest in the compassion that hands can administer. Hands are mentioned throughout much of his work, prominently featuring as an image of comfort. The narrator in *Company* states, 'What a help that would be in the dark! To close the eyes and see that hand' (Beckett 1996a: 26); and in *Nacht und Träume*, these hands provide help, as they comfort the dreamer physically and spiritually. The gender of the hands is not stated in the drama and we question whether the gender is in fact important. If these hands provide consolation, then surely it does not matter whether they are male or female. Although the gender of the hands is not defined in the directions, Beckett himself said, 'I think no choice but female for the helping hands. Large but female. As more conceivably male than male conceivably female' (Knowlson 1997: 683). Perhaps Beckett believed that compassion is more effectively administered by the female touch than by that of the male.

From out of the dark the left hand appears and rests on B's head, appearing similar to a blessing; its comforting touch momentarily renews the spirit, as B raises his head in contemplation of the source of this healing hand. The drama appears more profound if we accept that the hands are disembodied, thereby suggesting no fixed identity, and hence, the hands are conceived of as having universal significance and consolation. The play undoubtedly conveys a religious element, as one is reminded of the laying on of hands, which suggests healing and provides comfort in times of physical pain and spiritual weakness. The right hand, which appears with the cup, from which B subsequently drinks, has implications of Christ on the cross before his death: 'When Jesus therefore had received the vinegar, he said, It is finished: and he bowed his head, and gave up the ghost' (Jn 19.30). Again we are reminded that the erosion of spirit is a process which must be endured, until we reach that end point, where we give up the will to live and subsequently welcome death.

The cloth, which gently wipes B's brow, suggests that the protagonist is weary of existence and is perhaps ready to give up his ghost. It also reminds us, as Knowlson (1997: 682) points out, of the story of Veronica who allegedly wiped Jesus' face on His way to Calvary, offering Him compassion amidst suffering.[3] As B 'raises his head further to gaze up at invisible face' (Beckett 1990: 466), he perhaps desires to see the image that will welcome him into death. As he holds his palm upwards, it appears that he longs to be led into the unknown, where waking hours will cease to be, and the semi-conscious dream-like state will remain. As the hands join with his, the image of a 'separated togetherness' suggests comfort and provides the touch for which the protagonist longs. In Beckett's work the process of spiritual decline cannot be reversed, and despite receiving comfort, the protagonist's spirit is weak. There is no sense here that the protagonist will (re)gain a zest for life; rather, he is being comforted in his despair. Unable to go on, the hands consequently sink to the table, and B's head, in an image of dejection, is bowed to rest upon them. The comfort that he receives in dreams is not enough to renew his will to live, as he recognizes that night and dreams cannot be sustained. The dream represents a 'reality' that fails to exist. The dreamer recognizes that there are no hands to comfort him during waking hours and no touch to alleviate his spiritual decline.

The repetition of the dream in slower motion which concentrates solely on B, illustrates that A (Dreamer) is gradually fading, unable and unwilling to exist anywhere, other than in his dreams. He appears to be 'without the courage to end or the strength to go on' (Beckett 1999e: 67). As the dream again draws to a close, recovering the image of A, we recognize that the dream will probably not come again. As the dream fades out, so too does the dreamer, suggesting that he and his dreams have perhaps expired. The fading image is representative of his fading spirit, and as his dream ends, he no longer has the strength to continue without it. Night and dreams will not come again as, spiritually deadened, he almost certainly no longer has the strength to welcome them.

Beckett's 1982 drama for television, *Quad*, conveys Beckett's developing mistrust of language, as he abandons words in an attempt to create a visual image that denotes spiritual weariness and dejection. Beckett again illustrates the monotony of ritual, as the four players adorned in long gowns with cowls hiding their faces, pace the designated area, each following his particular course. Each player is methodical in his steps, ensuring the avoidance of E (a danger zone) and the other players. Hence these individuals endure a 'separated togetherness', as they are not alone throughout their journey, and, yet paradoxically, they remain isolated. We are told that the players must be of similar build, illustrating the uniformity of appearance, analogous with the uniformity of the pacing. Despite the fact that the players wear different coloured gowns, have their own coloured light and their own percussion, their methodical approach to their designated course renders them different from each other while simultaneously the same. One must approach this drama, not just as a work of art, but also as a representation of life. It is important to remember that Beckett always endeavours to illustrate 'how it is' to be alive, and throughout this drama he represents the monotony of the life journey coupled with the attrition of spirit, which results from the weariness of living.

As the players approach the square to begin their course, they essentially come out of the dark into the light, representing an image analogous with birth. Similarly, as they leave the square to return to the dark, they illustrate the visual representation of death. Therefore, between the birth and death episodes, they are condemned to walk a particular course representative of life. As Beckett has illustrated many times, the journey from birth to death is a difficult one, where we share the company of others, but ultimately remain alone. It is for this reason that the players are prohibited from contact with each other, due to the fact that the life journey is one that must be undertaken unaided. Perhaps it is this realization, the fact that the players are isolated in companionship, destined to walk alone, with no end in sight, which fuels the feeling of dejection and the spiritual decline that exudes from them. With their backs bowed and their heads facing the ground, the players convey that visual image of dejection representative of their spirit. They walk quickly in an attempt perhaps to complete the journey, and yet the avoidance of E (which may represent death) illustrates their fear of completion. This desire to end, coupled with the necessity to go on, produces the feeling of weariness, as the spirit dwindles while the life force continues. The sound of their footfalls is

vital, in order that we can hear their journey as well as witness it, as they continually come and go. The players follow the same repeated patterns because
they have no alternative but to adhere to the ritual that has been imposed
upon them. Beckett successfully illustrates that, despite spiritual attrition,
humans will find ways of coping with the trials and tribulations of life, as we
appear almost programmed to continue despite the ardent desire to end. He
illustrates how for most of our lives we are driven forward by some indefinable
quality that helps us to come to terms with our condition and our suffering.
In his essay on Proust, he speaks of 'An automatic adjustment of the human
organism to the conditions of its existence' (1965: 20).

Describing the four individuals as players implies that they are involved in
a game, as their precision of movement is analogous with the game of chess
which fascinated Beckett. They are involved in the game of life, where each
move is perhaps predestined, affording them little control over their existence
and providing an explanation for their spiritual decline. The hellish nature of
the ritual to which they must adhere is not alleviated by the colourfulness of
their gowns, or the sound of their percussion; in this drama, neither colour nor
music can alleviate the attrition of spirit. It is interesting also that the players
always go to the left to avoid collision. Knowlson says that 'Beckett explained
to his Polish translator, about *Company*, that "Dante and Virgil in Hell always
go to the left (the damned direction), and in Purgatory always to the right"'
(1997: 673). If the players are therefore damned it is not surprising that they
reflect their erosion of spirit, as perhaps they no longer possess the will to continue. With their backs bent and their heads bowed they go on because they
must go on, not because they wish to, and so they appear spiritually deadened
while physically alive. The fact that they rush about in the first half is comic
and yet it also appears absurd and almost unsettling. They seem somehow
manic; perhaps their frenzied movements convey the possibility that that they
are hurrying through life in an attempt to get it over with more quickly.

The second part of the drama illustrates a further progression in decline in
which Beckett returns to his normal palette and uses only black and white. With
the coloured gowns and percussion removed, we witness a more hellish state.
The 'colour' white, which has always been associated with strength and purity,
takes on a new significance, as here it represents a sense of nothingness. Their
gowns, now uniformly white, suggest a loss of hope and appear like shrouds.
And with slower steps they exude a greater sense of apathy. Condemned to go
on with no end in sight, the players appear like the living-dead, existing without the will to live.

The *Texts for Nothing*, which Beckett wrote during one of his most product-
ive periods, (1947–1952) illustrate the redundancy of language coupled with
spiritual decline. However, unlike *Nacht und Träume* and *Quad*, the attrition of
spirit, which is evident in these texts, results primarily from the impossibility
of successful artistic expression combined with the difficulty of articulating

'I'. These texts undoubtedly suggest a need to assert a cohesive self, and once again we witness Beckett grappling with the intricacies of identity or lack thereof. Similar to the Unnamable, the narrator (narrators) of the 13 texts endeavours to tell a story which perhaps does not exist, and so he is trapped in the relentless task of giving silence a voice and expressing that which is, perhaps, beyond expression. One is therefore left with 'The expression that there is nothing to express, nothing with which to express, nothing from which to express, no power to express, no desire to express, together with the obligation to express' (Beckett 1965: 103). It is this failure to adequately express, coupled with the necessity of continuance, while simultaneously desiring end, which produces the attrition of spirit that is evident throughout. These texts appear to have no beginning, middle or end; they are essentially voices emanating from the darkness.

The title *Texts for Nothing* perhaps suggests that these writings have little worth. However, it could also imply that these texts are about 'nothingness', and illustrate the difficulty in endeavouring to express the void/silence. As Pilling affirms, 'The unique form of the *Texts* is a reflection of their uniqueness of subject matter' (Knowlson and Pilling 1979: 44).[4] They are not works of failure but instead texts about failure. Beckett expresses many things throughout these texts which make them a significant work in his canon, as to talk about 'nothing' paradoxically requires that you talk about 'something'. Therefore, if Beckett is expressing nothing, he is expressing the one true reality that exists: the sense of nothingness which surrounds us all from the moment of birth to the moment of death. Perhaps it is this sense of nothingness and lack of hope, which causes the spirit to fade. As Estragon says, there is 'Nothing to be done' (Beckett 1990: 10), and so we witness the suspension of 'doing', which is subsequently replaced by the commencement of 'waiting', and it is during this waiting period (life) that the protagonists endure a continuing feeling of dejection. It is not quite clear whether each text is narrated by the same voice; however, what is apparent is that spiritual decline runs throughout all of them, with each text appearing faintly more disconsolate than its predecessor. As Levy states, each narrator 'is not trying to do anything but merely go on giving up' (1980: 72). The paradox is evident here, as to go on giving up implies a continuance in ending. Consequently, 'Through the Text narrator, Beckett fulfils his aesthetic of failure' (Levy 1980: 75), and the failure corresponds to the inability to end.

Lying in a quag at the top of a hill, the voice of text one questions his existence and the imperative force, which condemns him to continue, despite his desire to end. ('How can I go on, I shouldn't have begun, no, I had to begin' (Beckett 1999f: 7)). He recognizes the necessity of continuance despite the spiritual attrition that plagues him, and so his mind becomes the battleground between the spirit that drives him onwards, and the spirit, which accepts the worthlessness of life. We recognize his inability to move forward, as he appears stuck in a mental quagmire. He states, 'I should turn away from it all, away from the body, away from the head' (ibid.). It is interesting that he refers to the body and head as being separate almost, as if they are not an essential part of him, suggesting perhaps that he conceives of 'himself' as being disconnected from body and mind. Is this where 'I' is located, existing somewhere independent of mind and body? He goes on to say that it would not matter if body and head ceased, he would still be there; suggesting that it is he ('I') who would have to end. Can 'I' perhaps be equated with spirit? Hence, until he rejects the spirit, or 'I', he must continue to embrace the body and mind, as only by rejecting body, mind and spirit, will he perhaps be able to discontinue. Exhaustion of spirit is possibly the necessary prelude to physical and mental extinction. His acceptance that life is incurable and that existence is incomprehensible erodes his will to live, and as he states, 'I'll never try to understand any more' (Beckett 1999f: 10), we recognize that hope appears to have been abandoned. The narrator seems to be acquainted with the reality that life is incurable, and the memory of his father, reading to him the story of Joe Breem, perhaps reinforces the veracity of this fact as, now alone, this memory can only temporarily procure happiness. He affirms that memories of his father have helped him survive until now; however, there is a suggestion that this can/will no longer sustain him. This represents the first stage in the process of spiritual decline and, as the texts progress, we witness a further abandonment of will. Although Beckett does demonstrate, as H. Porter Abbott suggests, 'an aesthetic of recommencement' (Pilling 1994: 109) throughout the texts, celebrating the strength of the human spirit, it is evident that he also illustrates the impossibility of going on when one continually experiences feelings of dejection. Human nature can only be resilient for so long until hope deferred results in lassitude, as one accepts that there is no possibility of improvement. The narrator of text one illustrates how each of us are in the same hopeless position, and how none of us can alleviate the suffering of our fellow man; he says 'we're of one mind, all of one mind, always were, deep down, we're fond of one another, we're sorry for one another, but there it is, there's nothing we can do for one another' (Beckett 1999f: 9).

Change is apparent by text two, as the narrator suggests that something is altering, perhaps in the head. However, he also draws our attention to words themselves, affirming that they are failing and will perhaps inevitably cease.[5] This reference to language is interesting, as it suggests that words too are no longer spirited. And it is evident that as the texts progress they become more and more self-referential concentrating on the futility of language itself. By the end of the second text the narrator confirms, with some regret perhaps, that hope is dead. Does he wish that he still had hope even though the negative response suggests that he does not pity the fact that hope is gone? One wonders if he does lament the fact that all hope has vanished. The suggestion that he does appear somewhat disappointed that hope is dead implies perhaps that some form of desire is still present within him at this point. It would be best if he resigned himself to the fact that hope is a worthless feeling, as improvement is not viable in life; the sooner one recognizes this reality the more tolerable perhaps life becomes.

We witness a resigned tone in the third text, as it appears that the narrator cannot really be bothered any more. He appears child-like, as he creates his story about Bibby, the tale perhaps functioning as a calmative. The need to have done with it all is apparent, and he does not want anyone preventing him from giving up, and so rejects the idea of a fellow companion, believing that solitude will be more conducive to ending. Returning again to the idea of story, the narrator of text four believes that a story will somehow compensate for the lack of meaning which has enshrouded his existence, affording him a definite voice and 'purpose' in life. However, the reality that words alone are insufficient in alleviating misery prompts him to declare that 'a story is not compulsory, just a life, that's the mistake I made, one of the mistakes, to have wanted a story for myself, whereas life alone is enough' (Beckett 1999f: 24). The spirit has eroded further, prompting the voice to no longer desire a story to tell, forcing it to make do with language, which is itself failing. The narrator has abandoned the one goal, which kept him continuing, and now, with nothing to aim for, he appears resigned to await death in the acknowledgment that to be is to be miserable. He seems to question the thought processes and we witness how the consciousness, or the 'I', becomes fluid, as there appears to be no sense of a coherent self. Is this text suggesting that even consciousness is not self, that it too, similar to the body and mind, is other? Is it suggesting that self is something else, something that is struggling to take hold and control the body/mind? Therefore the mind continually questions identity because it can never attain 'I'; 'I' cannot be localized. 'I' perhaps doesn't exist. Hence, spiritually deadened, we recognize that the 'voices, wherever they come from, have no life in them' (Beckett 1999f: 21); these narratives are essentially diaries of despair.

Again we see how guilt appears to plague all of Beckett's protagonists and undoubtedly aids their spiritual erosion, as they acknowledge the reality, confirmed by the narrator of text five, that 'to be is to be guilty' (Beckett 1999f: 26). Suffering for a crime that was beyond their control (the act of being born) they endure the sentence of life. ('I'm the clerk, I'm the scribe, at the hearings of what cause I know not' (ibid.)). This trial takes place within his mind and he longs for birth so as to begin the death process. Is this taking place before birth or indeed before conception? Again the dissolution of language is highlighted, as we are told that he grows tired of the quill. His flagging spirit causes confusion in identity, as the mind, without the desire to live, begins to shut down. And so the narrator denies that the words he speaks are his own, as identity again becomes displaced. As the spirit declines, a sense of lethargy plagues the narrator and he attempts to deal with the monotony of existence by denying that this futile life belongs to him:

> It's tiring, very tiring, in the same breath to win and lose, with concomitant emotions, one's heart is not of stone, to record the doom, don the black cap and collapse in the dock, very tiring, in the long run, I'm tired of it, I'd be tired of it, if I were me. (Beckett 1999f: 29)

It is interesting that the 13 voices are male, and that the texts examined throughout this chapter primarily involve men. Carl Jung states that 'inwardly it is the man who feels, and the woman who reflects. Hence a man's greater liability to total despair, while a woman can always find comfort and hope' (1998: 102). Perhaps this is why the spiritual dejection, which is evident in Beckett's work, is generally conveyed through the male voice. And we therefore question whether the male spirit is generally weaker than the female. If so, perhaps this explains Winnie's forced optimism in *Happy Days*.

The motif of the search, coupled with the journey of life, is clearly illustrated throughout the 13 texts. Maybe the search is for an ending, as the voices wish to have done with it all, desiring the 'release' that they believe death will bring. For them, words have no real significance and so they become equated with pain and sorrow. 'I confuse them, words and tears, my words are my tears, my eyes my mouth' (Beckett 1999f: 40), claims the narrator of text eight, and ironically words ensure attrition of spirit. It is interesting that words are equated with tears illustrating the sorrow that language can produce. Perhaps it is the inability of finding the right words that cause him misery, or maybe the sorrow stems from the fact that he is still able to speak, confirming the reality that he still exists. He says, 'It's an unbroken flow of words and tears. With no pause for reflection. But I speak softer, every year a little softer. Perhaps. Slower too, every year a little slower' (ibid.). This slowing down renders the voice of text eight unable to move from the place in which he now exists. The impossibility of knowing, or providing definite answers to the questions he poses himself, ensures the arrival of negativity, as he recognizes the pointlessness of it all: 'all dies so fast, no sooner born.' (Beckett 1999f: 45). He exists in a world dominated by silence: 'Only the words break the silence, all other sounds have ceased' (Beckett 1999f: 40). One senses the pointlessness of his existence, when all he requires is to be allowed to end. He appears similar, perhaps, to those who are so advanced in years that they just want a release, and cannot comprehend the reasons for their continuing survival. As the voice in text eight conveys, the arrival of a new day does not inspire hope but instead fuels dispiritedness – 'But at least get out of here, at least that, no? I don't know. And time begin again, the steps on the earth, the night the fool implores at morning and the morning he begs at evening not to dawn' (Beckett 1999f: 41).

Beckett, undoubtedly, conveys the pointlessness of existence throughout this text, when the desire to live has been eradicated but the possibility of ending is denied.

Urging himself to give up, the voice of text ten recognizes that 'the heart's not in it any more' (Beckett 1999f: 50). Is this a reference to earlier days when there was some optimism? The two-phase structure of *Waiting for Godot, Happy Days* and *Quad* would seem designed to reflect this loss of hope, vitality and spirit. By giving up the will and desire for continuance, spiritual decline progresses more rapidly, as the redundancy of living and the pointlessness of existence confirm the futility of remaining optimistic. The isolation and loneliness, which plague the narrator, force him to wish for death. He acknowledges the futility of language and accepts the impossibility of uttering anything of value. He complains about words, ironically choosing to express himself through the medium that he despises and thinks worthless. His self-disgust and world-weariness fuel his desire to be gone and he says, 'he'll have done nothing, nothing but go on, doing what, doing what he does, that is to say, I don't know, giving up, that's it, I'll have gone on giving up, having had nothing, not being there' (Beckett 1999f: 52). Hence, the 'optimism' of earlier texts has long since faded and we are moving towards an inevitable end. The voice of the final text, despite growing weaker, desires to leave a trace and so we are left with a voice barely murmuring: 'For the narrator, now almost absent, this is the end of the farce of making, of the silencing of silence, of the wish to know, an acceptance of death and of the inevitable failure of his attempt to create himself' (Ackerley and Gontarski 2006: 567).

The *Texts for Nothing* paradoxically culminates in the desire for nothing, as these multiple selves endeavour to discontinue. The supposed 'lifeless words' (Beckett 1999f: 60), which constitute this personal essay are strategically used in the defence of 'nothing'. They serve the purpose for which they are used, primarily, to illustrate the journey of life, the attrition of spirit, which results from that journey, and the futility of language itself. The texts are endless, as no conclusion is ever reached; similar to 'nothing' they possess no end-point but do illustrate a 'progression in decline'. They are perhaps 'texts for silence', a series of dead voices speaking lifeless words that dramatically affect the reader, prompting us to question the point of existence. And so we are left with no questions and no answers, only the deafening silence that lingers after the final voice has stopped. Ironically, we are left with 'nothing', as the voice of text thirteen says 'what has become of the wish to know, it is gone, the heart is gone, the head is gone, no one feels anything, asks anything, seeks anything, says anything, hears anything, there is only silence' (Beckett 1999f: 63).

The reality that 'there is only silence' prompts Beckett to continually explore new ways to illustrate this truth. His desire to give 'silence a voice' and illustrate 'nothingness' culminates in an artistic contraction, where minimalism allows Beckett to strip language of non-essentials, further depicting the void, and illustrating that less is, often, paradoxically more. This linguistic/artistic contraction is fully explored in Part III, where it is illustrated that form is as fundamental as content.

Part III

Death of the Word

Chapter 9

Minimalism and Reductionism
Advancing Towards Lessness

I realised that my own way was in impoverishment, in lack of knowledge and in taking away, in subtracting rather than in adding.

Beckett[1]

Beckett views language as an inadequate mode of expression and yet it is the medium through which he chooses to express. The love/hate relationship with language, which Beckett has always evinced, illustrates both his respect for language and his mistrust of the word. The accepted conventions of narrative and drama ultimately limited Beckett, as he endeavoured to give 'silence a voice'. By adopting a minimalist approach and by stripping language of non-essentials, Beckett is able to implement the use of the 'non-word', illustrating that what is not said becomes as effective as that which is clearly defined, and *how* you express becomes as fundamental as *what* you express. Beckett's minimalist work demonstrates that form is as important as content, and the innovations in style in his shorter works, and powerful use of language, prompt one to acknowledge these pieces as fundamentally important in the Beckett canon.

In this chapter it will be illustrated that, in Beckett's use of minimalism and reductionism, he effectively demonstrates that less is paradoxically more. This chapter serves as an introduction to this final part, as it is used to establish theories and pose questions on the topic of linguistic/artistic contraction, and identify the concept of the 'decay of language', which is explored further in the following chapters. It appears that Beckett set out to destroy language in the hope that a new language could be discovered in the process: a language that would illustrate the reality, or Nothingness, of existence, and encapsulate the failure of both life and words simultaneously. Beckett details his approach to language in a letter (dated 1937) to Axel Kaun:

And more and more my own language appears to me like a veil that must be torn apart in order to get at the things (or the Nothingness) behind it. Grammar and Style. To me they seem to have become as irrelevant as a

Victorian bathing suit or the imperturbability of a true gentleman. A mask. Let us hope the time will come, thank God that in certain circles it has already come, when language is most efficiently used where it is being most efficiently misused. As we cannot eliminate language all at once, we should at least leave nothing undone that might contribute to its falling into disrepute. To bore one hole after another in it, until what lurks behind it – be it something or nothing – begins to seep through; I cannot imagine a higher goal for a writer today. (Beckett 1983: 171–172)

We recognize from Beckett's letter that his writing would, undoubtedly, gravitate towards 'lessness'; it would be pre-disposed to reductionism. The 'reductionist' process in Beckett's work forces one to acknowledge the 'tragedy', (failure, inadequacy) of language, as words become subdued in an attempt to capture the formlessness of both life and art.

The play *Come and Go*, which Beckett describes as a 'dramaticule', meaning a playlet or miniature, was written during early 1965 and consists of a mere 121 words. However, although the play is brief, it still manages to convey many things due to its artistic precision. Beckett illustrates throughout this drama that language is not essential in defining meaning, as non-linguistic techniques become powerfully suggestive, and Beckett conveys meaning through his use of language coupled with the 'non-word'. Hence, Beckett's dramatic 'language' is both verbal and visual; and although one may argue that this is true of all drama, one cannot deny the fact that Beckett's use of silences and implied discourse are as fundamentally important as the spoken word; a *modus operandi* which sets him apart from other dramatists.

Everything in this play is pared down, from the stage setting to the characters' names, which are abbreviated to Vi, Flo and Ru in accordance with the minimalist nature of the drama. Form complements meaning and, as the characters literally come and go on stage, their actions metaphorically represent birth and death. Consequently this play has a universal significance, as the stage is representative of life and the characters represent ourselves, illustrating that we are born and that we die, and in between there exists nothing of any real value. Again we recognize the biblical element which is often found in Beckett's work, as Psalm 121 states, 'The Lord shall preserve thy going out and thy coming in from this time forth, and even for evermore' (Ps. 121.8). If Beckett is illustrating the brevity of life, then the form of the drama, with its minimalist structure, clearly complements its thematic implications. Beckett can therefore convey meaning simply through the actions of his characters, thereby using language to complement his use of non-linguistic techniques and not as his primary mode of expression. By combining language with aesthetically strong non-linguistic techniques, Beckett is successful in creating a dramatic experience, which may on the surface appear minimalist, but which is fundamentally innovative, transcending accepted theatrical conventions. Of course all drama may be described as being a blend of language and image; however, Beckett simply redefines the equation/relationship between them. The title of the play illustrates the temporary nature of life and conveys the cyclical quality of human existence; and we are reminded of the words from *Watt* – 'for the coming is in the shadow of the going and the going is in the shadow of the coming' (Beckett 1976: 56). Hence, with three simple words (come and go) Beckett essentially captures the fundamental aspect of human existence and conveys the brevity of life.

The stage, stripped of non-essentials, is reduced to a softly lit playing area which accommodates the narrow bench-like seat without back, which is perhaps evocative of schooldays, and, therefore, useful in providing a striking reminder of how time has passed. Beyond the bench, darkness envelops the stage, prompting the audience to focus solely on the three characters, as the non-elaborate stage setting ensures that the eye will not wander. An image of three women, advanced in years, but age undeterminable, portrays the theme of friendship, as their minds, in retrospect, transport them back to girlhood. As they come and go their 'separated togetherness' confirms their unity, while simultaneously conveying their loneliness, as youth has passed them by and death steadily approaches. The darkness, surrounding the softly lit playing area, perhaps equals the state of non-being, the state that encapsulates their future, or perhaps, present condition. As Oppenheim (1994: 170) suggests, darkness in the late short works is an intrinsic part of the work, representing more than the normal theatrical blackout. *Come and Go* represents the well-advertised Beckettian theme of solitude and company but, technically, it comes close to a tableau, thereby illustrating Beckett's increasing interest in non-linguistic art forms. With their hands combined, the women represent a trinity, independent and yet joined. They are individually themselves and yet an image of each other. Perhaps this is why Beckett chose to use a bench-like seat, which is undoubtedly uncomfortable, in order to convey the temporary nature of this meeting, as the three characters appear to be in transit.

The full-length coats, which the characters wear, are dull in colour and, coupled with the 'Drab nondescript hats with enough brim to shade faces' (Beckett 1990: 356), Beckett ensures that the three women retain a sense of anonymity, as they appear as 'alike as possible' (ibid.), reminding one of the players in *Quad*. Costume is therefore used to conceal, negating any possibility of the women revealing personal identity or facial characteristics; a 'mask of sorts', as Levy (1990: 44) points out. This minimalist drama therefore goes so far as to strip the women of any sense of character, prompting them to appear devoid of expression. And yet what they express through their minimalist gestures, and speech, ensures a drama that is not lacking in profundity.

Everything on stage including their costumes, their speech, even their movement is lacking in expression and yet we sense their emotion behind the physical anonymity. The characters communicate with each other through whispers. Beckett states that the voices should be 'As low as compatible with audibility. Colourless except for three "ohs" and two lines following' (1990: 357). Language itself becomes pared down, as Beckett uses only the words that are necessary in conveying meaning, choosing to discard longer speeches that he employed in his earlier plays. Language is reduced here to a point where one can easily imagine its disappearance. However, this stifling of language only seems to amplify the tragedy of the threesome, the tragedy being their imminent deaths and their individual obliviousness to this reality. Language is the defective vehicle by which to express, it is not used by Beckett as a celebration of the word. In Beckett's view language is to be mistrusted because it is pre-disposed to failure, therefore to use it sparingly becomes, perhaps, the safest way to use it and, possibly, the most effective.

It is interesting that at the beginning of *Come and Go,* Ru states, 'Let us not speak' (Beckett 1990: 354), suggesting almost that to say nothing would be for the best. Ironically it is the very thing that is not stated in the play that functions as the primary theme behind it. *Come and Go* is a play about death, and yet death is never mentioned, as Beckett conveys its presence through various methods; therefore what is not said becomes more powerful than that which is clearly defined. As Knowlson says, 'The theme is suggested rather than stated, sensed behind the words rather than contained within them' (Knowlson and Pilling 1979: 125). A dramatist who can convey a theme without actually stating it has undoubtedly grasped the power of the 'non-word', as he sets up the implied meaning and permits the audience to draw its own conclusions. By using this technique the drama becomes open for various interpretations. By implying meaning rather than stating it, Beckett ensures that his work remains ambiguous while simultaneously engaging; and as everything becomes reduced, we recognize that in his work 'linguistic decay' perhaps facilitates artistic progression, and it is here that the paradox lies. As Brater says, 'Minimalism, an abstract and by some measure even a geometric art form, at best aims to do more and more with less and less' (1987: ix).

Through his use of language, Beckett is able to suggest that each of the three characters is suffering from a terminal illness. The irony in the drama stems from the fact that each character is conscious of her friends' illnesses but unaware of her own condition. Beckett is able to suggest that each character is terminally ill by using phrases such as, 'Does she not realize?' (1990: 354), followed by, 'God grant not' (ibid.). Consequently, 'Death reveals itself through omission, as "non-matter"' (Pilling 1994: 149). Beckett chooses not to mention death throughout this play and yet he manages to present us with three women on death row, ignorant of the fact that death is coming for each of them, but ironically aware that death is coming to the other two. As Vi, Flo and Ru sit and await death, Beckett is able, visually, to illustrate the human condition, as the three characters take on universal significance and are therefore representative of us all. Of course, as with all of Beckett's work, it is possible that the three women are in fact already dead and are unaware of this reality. As they hold hands Flo states, 'I can feel the rings' (Beckett 1990: 355); however, the stage directions state 'No rings apparent' (1990: 356). With his use of words coupled with non-existent props, Beckett is able to imply the character's ghost-like personas. The rings, to which they refer, may be the circles of Dante's hell, which would confirm that they are in fact already dead. Of course the rings may have a romantic connotation (wedding rings?), suggesting perhaps a past happiness, and illustrating the degeneration effected by passing time, as we surmise that their husbands are already deceased, or that they, themselves now ghosts, continue to feel the imprint made by the wedding bands. The rings may also suggest 'age', relating to the theory of dendrochronology and again therefore highlighting the women's advance in years.

Beckett's innovations in minimalism, and his reduction in language, permit a drama of 121 words, with approximately 4 minutes playing time, to convey multiple thematic implications. What at first appears to be a simple dramatic experience turns out to be a dramatically engaging, profoundly moving one. *Come and Go* portends the development of Beckett's drama in the 1970s and 1980s. It is another new form for timeless ideas. As Malone says, 'The forms are many in which the unchanging seeks relief from its formlessness' (Beckett 1994: 198). As everything becomes reduced on Beckett's stage, including language itself, we question whether language is in fact necessary in defining meaning, and whether characters are in fact essential in the creation of drama. As Beckett's plays progress, he appears committed to taking drama as far as it can possibly go, experimenting with various body parts, for example Mouth in *Not I*, in an attempt to create the ultimate dramatic experience, which would, in theory, illustrate 'nothing' and paradoxically convey everything. Beckett therefore faced the complex task of creating a drama that would have no characters or any dialogue – a wordless communication. With *Breath* Beckett achieved the very thing which many people deemed impossible, defying previously accepted theatrical conventions, and demonstrating his theory which he states in his early essay on Proust that 'The artistic tendency is not expansive, but a contraction' (1965: 64). If language is not essential in conveying meaning, what implication does this hold for modern drama and ultimately for language? If progression is only to be achieved by contraction, as Beckett believed, then surely the fundamental goal is to attribute a voice to silence and essentially embrace the void.

In *Breath* (original text first published in *Gambit*, vol. 4, no.16, 1970), form complements meaning, as Beckett achieves the ultimate in minimalism, creating a 35-second play without language. Lighting, shape, rhythm and timing are essential in creating this type of expressive drama, which offers a scathing comment on the brevity of existence and on the chaos of the world into which we are born. Lasting 35 seconds, the play has stage directions which take longer to read than to execute. It is possible to draw a parallel between

Breath and a painting, or a form of modern art perhaps, as Beckett, through this drama, conveys an image – a wordless art form, a still life.

Beckett's style was continually evolving as he searched for the best medium through which to convey his theories on life. Although he was using fewer words, he was still managing to convey exactly 'how it is', illustrating the brevity and difficult nature of existence, while demonstrating man's ability to cope with hardship and ultimately to go on. By manipulating language and syntax and by experimenting with minimal forms, Beckett was able to convey exactly the same message in 100 words, a message that in his early work would have perhaps taken 1,000 words to illustrate effectively. It is therefore evident that, as Beckett's language becomes reduced, his meaning very often becomes more concise, illustrating the paradox that in Beckett's work, reduction facilitates artistic progression. Beckett's later minimal style is perhaps more of a natural progression than a conscious objective. His theory that everything in life is essentially running out, as illustrated by Hamm in *Endgame*, is indeed reflected in his writing style, as his form complements what he is expressing thematically. However, it is difficult to ascertain whether this was a natural progression or a desired objective, as Fletcher (2003: 13) suggests.

Without the use of language, *Breath* is able to convey the same message as Pozzo's, 'They give birth astride of a grave' (Beckett 1990: 83), speech. It appears that *Breath* is reducing the genre to near non-existence in favour of a tableau. It impacts upon modern drama in the way that it illustrates that neither characters nor dialogue are essential in the creation of a dramatic experience. But it is important also in that it provides an insight into Beckett's later drama, in the context of form and structure. Light, which plays a primary role in *Breath*, becomes paramount in Beckett's later work. As he experiments with the increase and decrease of light in this short drama, we witness that the futility of existence can be conveyed through sound (instant of recorded vagitus) coupled with effective lighting and miscellaneous rubbish without a word being spoken. Hence, in 35 seconds Beckett successfully illustrates the futility of our existence.

Of course, Beckett's reductionism is not confined solely to his drama but is clearly evident in his prose work, where the manipulation of language and form serve to produce some of his best and most complex work. Moving towards a wordless drama was perhaps more straightforward since Beckett still had characters, lighting and objects to work with. However, the prose shorts represent a different form of minimalism because they depend exclusively on words. Many would ask why Beckett did not move into drama exclusively, as it allowed him to be artistically creative without depending totally on words. But one must remember that Beckett was never fully satisfied with anything he created; thus he had to continue experimenting with both drama and prose in an attempt to find a form for formlessness, continuing to push each mode of expression to its limits. As the work evolves, language becomes contestable, and we question whether it is an adequate mode of expression and whether it truly conveys what the author is endeavouring to communicate. To this question Beckett would probably offer a definitive 'no'. As Brian Finney asks, in his essay 'Samuel Beckett's Postmodern Fictions', 'In a world deprived of meaning how can the linguistic artist express this meaninglessness with words that necessarily convey meaning?' (Richetti 1994: 842). In his discussions with Georges Duthuit, Beckett (1965: 103) clearly states that he feels he has 'nothing' to say, that he must express 'nothingness', but that there exists no suitable medium through which to say it; and yet he experiences that imperative to create. Conventional narrative was inadequate; therefore, for Beckett to satisfy himself artistically he would have to create a new style of writing which would accommodate a new kind of language, culminating possibly in what he called the 'literature of the unword' (1983: 173). His later texts are perhaps best described as 'word-less poetry', as this term encapsulates the silence which Beckett was writing towards and encompasses the rhythmic quality of his language. Of course, the term 'word-less' also encapsulates the notion of 'less words'. Beckett's later prose works illustrate his 'Assault against words in the name of beauty' (ibid.). To express the beauty of silence was the challenge that faced Beckett, and it is the area that will be examined in the final chapter. By manipulating language and discarding conventional style and syntax, Beckett moves closer to minimalism, silence and ghosts, into the world of memory and imagination, where the thought processes of his characters are portrayed through new techniques and the discarding of conventional narrative.

To state that Beckett experiments with form and minimalism solely in his later texts would, of course, be flawed. From the beginning, Beckett has been subverting traditional prose narrative. Though the majority of his shorter texts appear in the latter part of his career, it is evident that some of his early writing experiments with the style and form that Beckett later adopts. For example, 'The Expelled', written in French in October 1946, is approximately 15 pages long and provides an insight into the works to come, as it conveys the difficulty of existence and questions the viability of narrative. We recognize in this text the protagonist's lack of identity, as the 'I' becomes dominant. Beckett, of course, destabilizes the 'I' throughout his work, divesting it of fixity and certainty. Thought processes are explored, as the protagonist's retrospective narrative conveys one episode from his existence, and we recognize how life consists of many little stories. Again the conventions of the ordinary novel are discarded, as Beckett illustrates a story that fundamentally has no beginning, middle or end; it is a fragment from an undoubtedly fragmented life. This is an experimental fiction designed to capture the formlessness of experience and so conventional structures are jettisoned. The protagonist's story is a simple one in which he describes his expulsion from the house where, we presume, he lived as a child, his wanderings and meetings with various insignificant people, one of whom, a cabman, takes pity on him and allows him to stay in his stable overnight; and in the morning he leaves. These are the main facts of the 'story'. The whole idea of 'story' is, of course, central to the Beckettian enterprise but he revolutionizes 'how' the story is told. Telling stories is a coping mechanism used in the quest to discover self, an endeavour to comprehend 'I'. Beckett's use of language demonstrates the futility of existence, as 'The Expelled' has universal significance, describing each individual at the moment when he/she is evicted from the womb, in preparation for his/her journey to the tomb. Therefore 'the atrocious life that was his' (Beckett 1999e: 16), is a representation of human existence, and the 'I' narrative functions as the reader's personal story.

The protagonist appears set apart from his contemporaries. Even as a child he viewed himself as being other, almost superior to those around him in his intellectual pursuit of self. His desire to discover self, ('I whose soul writhed from morning to night, in the mere quest of itself' (Beckett 1999e: 7)), even at a young age, is evident. Perhaps soul can be equated with 'I' here, and this search for self is a search for meaning in his life, a sense of identity perchance. However, he ultimately lacks identity, as, nameless and now homeless, he assumes the role of wanderer, destined for a journey of uncertainty. Solitary, and in search of meaning, he encapsulates the Beckettian man.

Memories function largely in this text, transporting the protagonist back to the past and forcing him to recall events which were not particularly happy. It is not surprising that he thinks 'Memories are killing' (Beckett 1999e: 5). The difficulty of expression is highlighted, as the protagonist, while recollecting the day his father took him to buy a hat, asks, 'How describe this hat? And why?' (Beckett 1999e: 7). Here he captures the difficulty of expression, combined with the futility of expression. 'The Expelled' is ultimately an account of a life and, despite its relative shortness, Beckett has implemented everything that is essential in creating this moving piece of narrative. The difficulty of being able to express oneself is, again, captured at the end, as the protagonist admits to the ineffectual nature of his story – 'I don't know why I told this story. I could just as well have told another. Perhaps some other time I'll be able to tell another' (Beckett 1999e: 20). This is perhaps Beckett's harsh statement on his own writing, conveying his feelings of failure as a writer and illustrating his obligation to continue his struggle with words. The end of the text succeeds in devaluing the artistic effort.

The difficulty of achieving successful artistic expression is again illustrated in 'As the Story Was Told'. Written during 1973, it consists of five pages and appears, at first glance, similar to a child's book with its large print. The text is ambiguous, appearing almost beyond comprehension, as Beckett discards accepted conventions of narrative. This obscurity appears to be an inevitable consequence of an increasingly dense and compressed style. Although punctuation is used, the text consists of no paragraphs, leading the narrative to appear almost like a monologue, thereby adding to its complexity and heightening its density. In this work the story is not easily told and the reader is left feeling rather dismayed and confused. Although appearing deceptively simple, 'As the Story Was Told' is linguistically complex, as its thematic implications are located among the 'non-words', and the narrative appears cryptic. Familiarizing oneself with Beckett's work, as a whole, enables one to a certain extent to comprehend this evasive text, as in it we recognize the recurring theme of the failure of language.[2]

The text conveys the difficulty of narrative. The theme of the text is therefore reflected in its form, as we find it difficult to comprehend the story that is being told. Beckett, therefore, successfully reflects the thematic implications of the narrative in the actual form of the writing. Hence his theory that artistic expression is arduous is portrayed on two levels. However, one questions Beckett's methods of illustrating the difficulty of artistic creation, due to the fact that his language and form often become so reduced that its complexity very often conceals its meaning, to the point where Beckett's 'message' is perhaps lost. Illustrating the difficulty of expression through a work that is itself written in a difficult style, perhaps defeats the primary objective. However, Beckett would perhaps argue that creating a work that appears elusive and beyond comprehension is, in itself, an illustration of the futility of language and the difficulty of artistic expression. The paradox is evident – Beckett uses language in his illustration of the ineffectiveness of that medium, and yet he does so successfully.

The opening sentence of 'As the Story Was Told' ('As the story was told me I never went near the place during sessions' (Beckett 1999g: 5)) immediately captures the elusive nature of the text. The 'I' is not identified and we witness no character development throughout the narrative. The lack of detail enhances the text's obscurity, as the protagonist fails to state what place he is referring to or the exact nature of the 'sessions'. Details such as these, which other writers rely on to develop narrative, are simply discarded by Beckett because they are deemed to be inconsequential. It is evident how Beckett's reductionism rejects everything that is in fact superfluous to his own style, despite the breakdown in conventional form. Perhaps Beckett is trying to suggest that the human experience is a formless and confusing 'narrative' that is ultimately prone to decay. It is a story which is never properly told; 'It is a tale/ Told by an idiot, full of sound and fury,/ Signifying nothing' (Shakespeare 1967: 132).

The sessions, which take place in the tent, are obviously designed to extract some form of information from a man, who, similar to the narrator is nameless. We are reminded of *Rough for Radio II* where Fox undergoes a type of torture, albeit self-imposed, in an attempt to find the words that will appease the Animator. Here again we see the fallibility of words, as the narrator deems that the sheet of writing, extracted from the man in the tent is ultimately worthless: 'for as I watched a hand appeared in the doorway and held out to me a sheet of writing. I took and read it, then tore it in four and put the pieces in the waiting hand to take away' (Beckett 1999g: 8). However, the failure of words has dire consequences for the man, as it ultimately results in his death. We wonder if the narrator is suffering from a sense of guilt, as his destruction of the sheet of writing inevitably leads to the man's death. However, language ultimately fails, as writing cannot alleviate the pain of living, nor can it convey the true harshness of existence. As Pilling says, 'The written word is not, for Beckett, a medium that can absolve the crime of being, and nor is the spoken word' (Knowlson and Pilling 1979: 184). For many writers, the act of writing is never a source of relief or satisfaction. The inability to capture in words the very thing that one wishes to express is clearly illustrated by Beckett in the closing lines of this complex little text – 'I did not know what the poor man was required to say, in order to be pardoned, but would have recognized it at once, yes, at a glance, if I had seen it' (1999g: 9).

Beckett's minimalism illustrates his search for the words that he will recognize, for the language that will successfully express that which he is trying to say. But perhaps the reality of the human experience is fundamentally beyond expression. Hence, the superlative text does not exist and could not possibly be produced. Experimentation with form and minimalism results in some of Beckett's most beautiful and complex work, which will be examined in the following chapters. Beckett's frustration with language pushes him further into minimalism where the silence of the Real is perhaps best located and the objective of implementing the non-word is perhaps achieved. In these shorter texts Beckett endeavours to write himself out of language, into the void and the silence of Nothingness.

Chapter 10

Dramaticules

It seemed to me that all language was an excess of language

Molloy

In her essay, ' "Make Sense Who May": A Study of *Catastrophe* and *What Where*', Annamaria Sportelli says that 'Language is the discontinuous *par excellence*, language is the vehicle of catastrophe' (Davis and Butler 1988: 123). Beckett would, undoubtedly, acknowledge that language is the vehicle of catastrophe because, like everything else in the world, it is subject to decay, and hence pre-disposed to failure. As discussed in the previous chapter, Beckett's minimalist work demonstrates that form is as fundamental as content and the implementation of non-linguistic techniques serves to challenge language to the point where it often acknowledges its own futility. This chapter focuses on the shorter drama and illustrates how Beckett's linguistic/artistic contraction is used effectively to demonstrate the 'impossibility' of successful artistic expression. Here we witness the fundamental tragedy of language itself.

Words and Music, a radio play completed towards the end of 1961, illustrates Beckett's interest in non-linguistic art forms and demonstrates his inherent mistrust of the word. The drama is relatively difficult to comprehend and, although it may not be regarded as minimalist, in comparison with a play such as *Breath*, it does demonstrate a linguistic crisis, as words are challenged by the non-linguistic medium and the inadequacy of language is conveyed. The play dramatizes the difficulty of reconciling words and music; hence we witness the confrontation of the verbal and the non-verbal, suggesting that the drama could have been called 'Words or Music'.

'Radio-dramatic writing requires an economy of effects not essential in the novel or stage play' (Oppenheim 1999: 273). With no visual aspect, radio drama must be succinct in order to be effective. Therefore superfluous language must be rejected if one is to achieve maximum dramatic impact. And in *Words and Music* words themselves become challenged to the point where they acknowledge their own sterility and recognize the pointlessness of verbal expression. This play, like several others, takes as its theme the anguish of artistic creation.

It contains very little plot development; however, as Levy states, 'Its structure is a clear and sophisticated case of serving as a metaphor to the self-referential meaning' (1990: 72–73), as Beckett uses his words to convey the impossibility of successful artistic expression and the inability to capture in words, and perhaps any art form, the very thing you wish to articulate. Therefore, here we witness the tragedy of language, as Beckett uses language, a medium which he deems ineffectual, in order to illustrate the ineffectiveness of that medium.

Three 'personalities' exist in this drama as Words and Music are given the status of characters under the command of Croak, who forces them to formulate expressions on topics such as love, age and 'the face'. Croak functions as a type of conductor who manipulates both mediums in an effort to make them express his emotional state. Croak's name suggests that he is little more than a 'sound effect', and his monosyllabic speech confirms that he needs both Words and Music to fulfil his obligation to express, as the failure to create beauty/harmony is reflected in his name. Words and Music must convey what Croak feels, and a tension emerges between the two mediums, as each struggles to be the primary mode of expression and each subsequently fails. One senses tension, frustration and suffering here, emotions which are undoubtedly experienced by the creative artist. Words and Music question each other's ability to express adequately, to the point where the desire to communicate, coupled with the necessity to express, take precedence over what is actually being articulated. Therefore what is said becomes secondary and words function as mere sound effects that ultimately signify very little. Language is used for the sake of speaking and not for the celebration of the word, hence it turns on itself, advertising its own inadequacies and acknowledging its failings. Both mediums struggle to work together endeavouring to find some way to unite and ultimately create song. Beckett illustrates that trying to combine two modes of expression, in an endeavour to communicate, may ultimately lead to artistic failure, as the work slowly falls apart. Hence the artist (Croak) must recognize that to express oneself successfully, one must acknowledge the impossibility of successful expression and 'admit that to be an artist is to fail, as no other dare fail, that failure is his world and the shrink from it desertion' (Beckett 1965: 125).

'In the beginning was the Word' (Jn 1.1), and yet Beckett chooses to begin his drama with the sound of music, thereby giving precedence to the non-linguistic medium and perhaps acknowledging Words' inability to successfully open this piece for radio. Music, for Beckett, is an elevated art form and he describes it in his essay on Proust: 'music is the Idea itself, unaware of the world of phenomena, existing ideally outside the universe, apprehended not in Space but in Time only, and consequently untouched by the teleogical hypothesis' (1965: 92). However, Beckett as an artist is essentially confined to words, even though his works often take on a musical character. Nevertheless, Beckett probably hoped that in the end there would be no words, as the non-word would take precedence and the silence of the Real (the silence that underlies everything) would be achieved.[1]

Despite Music opening the drama, Words quickly intervenes endeavouring to express himself. As radio plays have no visual aspect, dramatists often use descriptive language in order to establish a mental setting for the listener. However, Beckett discards normal practice and fails to offer the listener any descriptive details about where this 'battle' between Words and Music is taking place. Perhaps this struggle to express takes place, essentially, within Croak's mind. This in itself is a metaphor for the inner workings of Beckett's mind, as he endeavours to progress artistically despite the decaying nature of his language. Words pleads with Music to stop, as his initial interruption illustrates, 'Please! [*Tuning. Louder.*] Please!' (Beckett 1990: 287), he cries, before questioning, with loathing, 'How much longer cooped up here in the dark? [*With loathing*] With you!' (ibid.). The darkness is representative of the artist's inability to clearly express, as both Words and Music are ineffectual in his struggle to define himself. It is evident that Music disturbs Words, illustrating the fact that Words recognizes his weaknesses and ultimately fears becoming a defunct mode of expression. Through this drama Beckett is perhaps illustrating his own uncertainties about language, believing that eventually it will no longer serve him, as it too becomes subject to the influences of degeneration. Language will expire, it is finite, and it will end. Hence, we recognize the dramatization of failure, as the play seems to suggest some ideal form of expression that will never be attained.

As Words endeavours to discuss the theme of sloth, we recognize the sterility of his language. Words lacks expression and style, forcing his speech to sound clinical and monotonous. 'He' says, 'Sloth is of all the passions the most powerful passion and indeed no passion is more powerful than the passion of sloth' (ibid.). Words is unconvincing in his explanation of sloth and we witness his failure in attempting to convey the true definition of his chosen theme. There is a lazy, apathetic aspect to his language, as it lacks dynamism, flair and inspiration. Words has failed to explicate his theme effectively through his choice of words, and yet it appears as if he has the potential for successful expression, which paradoxically illustrates that he has, to a certain degree, captured the essence of his theme, albeit unwittingly. It is interesting that he refers to Croak as 'My Lord' (ibid.), illustrating that Words acknowledges his need for proper manipulation by the artist if he is to be an effective mode of expression. But there is a great deal of irony in all of this since Words does not do his master's bidding. He needs, and wishes, to be moulded by his master, while simultaneously rejecting the efforts of the artist to help him perform effectively.

There is a suggestion of incompatibility between Words and Music and Croak endeavours to coerce them into working together saying 'My comforts! Be friends!' (ibid.). It is ironic that he refers to them as his comforts, as they appear to be anything but comforting; their unwillingness to co-operate with

each other, or to follow his instruction, results in Croak feeling incredibly dis-
couraged. It is apparent that this play captures the frustration of the artist
who puts in so much effort and yet derives so little consolation from language
and artistic creation. Music appears more willing to co-operate, probably
due to the fact that he does not feel just as threatened as Words, and is confi-
dent that he will be able to convey what Croak is wanting to communicate. As
Croak declares that 'love' is tonight's theme, we recognize that this struggle to
express is a nightly occurrence. Croak finds it impossible to express (through
either Music or Words), his inner feelings and therefore he must continue to
strive for the best way to illustrate his message. He is perhaps representative of
Beckett, as he conveys the artist's disapproval of his own artistic creation and
illustrates the continual struggle to discover the language that will accommodate the message.

    As Words attempts to define love, he rhymes off the same speech as before
but substitutes the word sloth for the word love. We question whether Words
is just lazy or is this really the very best that he can do? Croak's frustration is
evident, as he thumps his club on the ground forcing Words to work harder;
however, Words appears to become confused, using language which is not
appropriate for the chosen theme, and ultimately highlighting his inability to
express successfully. Music too tries to convey love but is forced to play louder
in order to drown Words' protestations and consequently loses all expression.
Although Croak refers to Words and Music as his balms, it is evident that both
ultimately torture him, as he recognizes their inadequacies but still continues
to work with them, as they are the only tools he has.

    The effect of the rotation of themes (sloth, age, love, the face) is to show
that Words will always fail to measure up whatever the subject, reminding us
of Winnie's declaration that 'Words fail, there are times when even they fail'
(Beckett 1990: 147). When Words tries to define age he falters, saying 'Age
is . . . age is when . . . old age I mean . . . if that is what my Lord means . . .
is when . . . if you're a man . . . were a man . . . huddled . . . nodding . . . the
ingle . . . waiting –' (Beckett 1990: 289). The pauses and hesitations register
the impossibility of finding the right verbal formula to capture what Age
actually is. However, although he fails to provide a proper definition of old
age, Words stylistically captures the essence of his given theme. As he stut-
ters and falters he manages to portray how it is to be old. Again Beckett uses
words to highlight the reality that often it is not what is said that is important
but rather how it is said. The sound and rhythm of language is perhaps more
useful than semantics.

    It is ironic that, as the drama progresses, Words' use of repetition is
replaced by his attempt to sing, and it appears that Music endeavours to
'speak', thereby implying that a role reversal is perhaps taking place, as each
mode of expression is dissatisfied with itself. Perhaps they are each trying
to find elements of the other within themselves. Music tries to help Words,

as he continually invites Words to sing and 'finally accompanies very softly' (Beckett 1990: 291), resulting in the sonnet about age. As Croak coerces them to talk about 'the face', we are given no information about the owner of the face and therefore presume that it perhaps represents a lost love. We recognize that Croak has been building towards this moment, leaving the most important theme until the end in anticipation of a climactic finish. It is apparent that *Words and Music* anticipates some of the later plays (*Ghost Trio, Ohio Impromptu . . . but the clouds . . .*), as it touches on the theme of lost love. Croak needs Music and Words to capture the 'passion/love' he feels for the face, and it is at this point that both mediums ultimately fail. The sterility of Words is overwhelming and we witness the futility of verbal expression, as Words states in a cold, disregarding voice, 'Seen from above at such close quarters in that radiance so cold and faint with eyes so dimmed by . . . what had passed, its quite . . . piercing beauty is a little. . . .' (ibid.). Words clearly has no interest in the chosen theme, and perhaps Beckett is suggesting here that language will never do justice to the human experience. Music endeavours to be sentimental but the rambling of Words overshadows his efforts and, despite his warm suggestions, Words disregards any sense of structure or meaning. When they finally collaborate, Music accompanies Words as he endeavours to sing, resulting in a 'song' that fails to convey anything about 'the face'.[2] Words' inability to convey the theme that Croak has requested suggests that he has obstinately refused to co-operate with his 'master'. Croak's impatience with both Words and Music is highlighted, as he walks away dejected, in spite of Words' calls for him to stay. Words admits defeat in the end and losing his power to express himself through language he sighs, perhaps 'content' in the knowledge that language is an inadequate mode of expression and always will be.

After completing *Words and Music*, Beckett quickly moved on to another radio play which was written in French in 1962 and entitled *Cascando*. Although structurally similar to *Words and Music*, *Cascando* illustrates an artistic contraction, as we witness in this drama a further stripping away of non-essentials. These radio plays are significantly different from Beckett's earlier pieces such as *All that Fall*, as he appears to have gone beyond 'conventional' radio drama, employing words and music as personified modes of expression, and forcing the work to become metalinguistic, as words no longer function as a storytelling device but instead serve to comment on themselves. Therefore in *Cascando* the listener is not offered conventional character development and there is very little plot of which to speak.

The title alludes to the musical term, meaning to decrease in volume and deceleration of tempo; therefore, it implies that everything in this play, as in Beckett's work in general, is slowly running out. There is a sense of diminuendo, fading away, a movement towards nothingness; and this is of course consistent with Beckett's sense of what life itself is ultimately like.

In *Cascando*, Music remains Music, illustrating that Beckett was perhaps satisfied with Music's 'performance' in the previous drama. However, Words is replaced by Voice, suggesting that Beckett has essentially rejected Words in favour of a new character. Hence, we recognize how Beckett is continually endeavouring to escape the burden of words. Of course, Voice encompasses words but it also includes timbre, which illustrates that Beckett was endeavouring to convey the possible musicality of words.[3]

Cascando deals primarily with the recurring theme of storytelling and the inability to complete the narrative successfully. The irony with Beckett's work is that, as it progresses, there appears to be less of a story and, therefore, experimentation in form compensates for the lack of plot development, as style is the embodiment of theme. The desire to end coupled with the need to go on plagues the Opener in this drama, forcing him to tell a story that can never be completed. As long as he lives he shall continue talking, and so we witness creation for the sake of creation, a story that is about the inability to complete the story, and language which comments on its own shortfalls and does so beautifully.

The radio piece begins with Opener stating coldly, 'It is the month of May . . . for me' (Beckett 1990: 297), thereby implying that for him this is a period of renewal and the moment when, once again, he will endeavour to complete a story. Katharine Worth, in her essay 'Words for Music Perhaps', says that Croak and Opener 'have apparently no creative ability as musicians yet are compelled to create through music as well as words' (Bryden 1998a: 10). This is undoubtedly true, and it may be suggested that they have no creative ability as writers either and yet are compelled to create through words. As Hesla confirms, 'Before he sets out on his venture, man as artist and man as man knows that he is doomed to fail' (1971: 226). It appears that Opener does not assert as much control over Voice or Music in the same way as Croak does, thereby suggesting that they are independent of him. However, it is probable that Voice and Music are in fact part of Opener's consciousness, and the story Voice relates about Woburn's difficult journey is therefore a metaphor for Opener's artistic impediments.

The panting rhythm of Voice suggests that the narrative moves swiftly, however, it also suggests difficulty, struggle and exhaustion, and the pauses between words, coupled with the periods of silence, and the intrusion of Music result in a narrative that appears stylistically flawed, and yet is dramatically effective, as the drama's theme is illustrated through its form. To capture in words the thing you desire to express would undoubtedly bring peace as Voice indicates:

> story . . . if you could finish it . . . you could rest . . . sleep . . . not before . . .
> oh I know . . . the ones I've finished . . . thousands and one . . . all I ever did . . .
> in my life . . . with my life . . . saying to myself . . . finish this one . . . it's the

right one . . . then rest . . . sleep . . . no more stories . . . no more words . . .
and finished it . . . and not the right one . . . couldn't rest . . . straight away
another . . . to begin . . . to finish . . . saying to myself . . . finish this one . . .
then rest . . . this time . . . it's the right one . . . this time . . . you have it . . .
and finished it . . . and not the right one . . . couldn't rest . . . straight away
another . . . (Beckett 1990: 297)

The style of this speech conveys a sense of weariness, as the pauses between the words illustrate a need for silence and a desire to end. These pauses, which are everywhere in Beckett's work, are significant, as they illustrate the disintegration of conventional narrative and function as a prelude to the silence which Beckett endeavours to express both artistically and philosophically. This is perhaps Beckett's 'voice' speaking, clearly conveying his uncertainties about his own work and questioning whether he will ever be satisfied with anything he writes. Words ironically function to undermine language and Beckett's style serves to illustrate the arduousness of the creative process, as the stop/start rhythm of *Cascando* reflects.

As Voice progresses with his Woburn story the words eventually grow repetitive and we witness an almost incoherent sequence of incomplete phrases which stylistically reflect Woburn's incomplete journey. With his 'face in the mud . . . arms spread' (Beckett 1990: 298), Woburn is symbolic of crucified humanity, and the torment of the creative process; and when he collapses in the stones he reflects the tragedy of language itself, the infertility of the stone echoing the sterility of words. The drama is poignant, as it is perhaps an illustration of the failed artist, who is oblivious and unwilling to accept failure. However, as Opener says, 'It's my life, I live on that' (Beckett 1990: 299), he implies that despite the arduousness of the creative process, and its inevitable failure, it is a task, which must be adhered to, as life is a succession of incomplete stories.

As Music begins to weaken and Voice grows static, we recognize that this story will remain incomplete. Woburn, confined to a boat with his face in the bilge and his arms spread, 'clings on . . . out to sea . . . heading nowhere . . .' (Beckett 1990: 302). He is an image of dejection and a metaphor for this never-ending story. 'As though they had linked their arms' (Beckett 1990: 303), Voice and Music endeavour to complete the creative process so that there will be 'no more stories' (ibid.); but the futility of both mediums and their inability to sustain succinct expression forces this radio piece to end even though the story will continue. The story will continue because it can never be properly told. There can be no perfection, no satisfaction, and no closure. Even though Beckett inserts '[*Silence*]' (1990: 304), at the end of the play, we know that it shall not be permanent, as despite their degeneration, the words have not yet expired. And Beckett is condemned to continue with a medium (language) he deems inadequate, forced to use a mode of expression that is essentially disintegrating before him.

In their essay, 'Working Wireless: Beckett's Radio Writing', Stanley Richardson and Jane Alison Hale suggest that, 'Nowhere has Beckett demonstrated more eloquently the failure of words, more musically the limits of music, or more successfully the art of failure than in his works for radio' (Oppenheim 1999: 291). It is interesting that three out of the four shorter dramas explored in this chapter are in fact radio plays. Of course, one may argue that the later prose fiction demonstrates the failure of words more eloquently than the radio drama, because of the poetic beauty found in the shorter prose texts. However, Richardson and Hale are right to make the point that radio drama allowed Beckett to successfully incorporate both words and music, promoting them to the roles of characters, challenging each medium to perform to the best of its ability, and illustrating that perhaps every mode of artistic expression is ultimately pre-disposed to failure.

Rough for Radio II, written in French in the early 1960s, does not have a musical element and so it differs from *Cascando* and *Words and Music*, as Beckett relies completely on language. The Animator, with the aid of the Stenographer and Dick, habitually coerce Fox to speak in the hope that he will utter the 'correct' words.[4] Ironically, the Animator does not know which words constitute the right words, suggesting, therefore, that the whole procedure is in fact ineffectual. The premise of this radio drama is quite similar to *Catastrophe* in that both plays demonstrate the manipulation of the subject by those who desire him to provide successful artistic expression. The Animator demands that Fox speaks about various episodes from his life, and hence we hear Fox telling stories about 'soaping the mole' (Beckett 1990: 277), his twin brother and Maud, recognizing that each story is ultimately brief and incomplete. The meaning behind these stories is vague and they do not satisfy the Animator's desire for the right words. As Levy suggests 'Radio II is concerned with the discrepancy between life as it is lived and the word or notion which may sum it up or explain it' (1990: 84). Hence, we recognize that *Rough for Radio II* encapsulates Beckett's belief that his words continually failed in providing an accurate illustration of how it is to be alive; the words remained insufficient. Do we conclude therefore that Fox represents Beckett in his inability to say the right thing? This interpretation could be accepted, but it is also possible that the Animator is a representation of Beckett in his failure to successfully manipulate his subject and thereby failing to create. Perhaps the four characters combined encapsulate Beckett's view of his own creative process – the Animator, who endeavours to give life to his subject, may represent the imagination; the Stenographer who writes everything down represents the pen; Fox represents the mind endeavouring to express; and Dick, who is mute, represents silence, the superlative condition. Together they embody the artist.

Initially we view Fox as a victim because he is subjected to physical violence, which is administered by Dick, with the use of a bullwhip if he (Fox) fails to speak. He appears to be imprisoned, brought out each day to undergo the same routine in the hope that he will utter something of interest. 'Fox, I hope you have had a refreshing night and will be better inspired today than heretofore' (Beckett 1990: 275), states the Animator, acknowledging the reality that inspiration is needed for artistic creation. They appear to keep Fox desensitized when he is not in use, treating him like an animal that is being hunted down, thus highlighting the irony of his name, as Fox appears de-humanized. The restrictions placed on Fox, for example the hood, gag, blind and plugs, suggest that he is a captive, held against his will. However, as the play progresses we recognize that Fox is perhaps not a victim, as he himself requests the constrictions that are placed upon him. The third of his exhortations, which the Stenographer reads, states:

'3. Kindly to ensure full neutralization of the subject when not in session, especially with regard to the gag, its permanence and good repair. Thus rigid enforcement of the tubefeed, be it per buccam or be it on the other hand per rectum, is *absolutely*' – one word underlined – 'essential. The least word let fall in solitude and thereby in danger, as Mauthner has shown, of being no longer needed, *may be it*' – three words underlined. (Beckett 1990: 276)[5]

It, therefore, appears that Fox is in fact a willing participant in this search to find the correct words, ensuring that he takes every precaution to guarantee that conditions will be perfect for each time he is in session. The gag is of extreme importance to him, as it ensures that no word shall be spoken while he is alone in case it happens to be the word they are searching for. This fear of wasting words, and the dread of not finding the right words, evidently dominates the drama. Fox acknowledges his failings and gives voice to Beckett's attitude towards his own work, as he writes: ' ". . . with pain that these dicta, like all those communicated to date and by reason of the same deficiencies, are totally inacceptable" ' (ibid.). The words are unacceptable because language is fundamentally deficient. Hence, it is not the failure of the artist (Animator) but the failure of the words (Fox). An artist cannot succeed if his tools are inadequate. This drama illustrates that language is ultimately unreliable, as the Animator, dissatisfied with Fox's story, implements his own words to the dismay of the Stenographer, who says 'But, sir, he never said anything of the kind' (Beckett 1990: 284). The words are therefore, no longer, an accurate description of Fox's experiences, and the Animator has succeeded in fictionalizing Fox's life.

Rough for Radio II ends on a note of failure as, despite the implementation of his own words, the Animator acknowledges that he has not, yet, found the words he has been searching for. We recognize the fact that he will, with the aid of the Stenographer, Fox and Dick, continue his futile search. The Animator is himself imprisoned, caught up in the quest for words that will always elude him, because the perfect phrase, essentially, does not exist. Therefore, in the final words, 'Don't cry, miss, dry your pretty eyes and smile at me. Tomorrow, who knows, we may be free' (ibid.), we recognize that his freedom will never come, and so he will remain, similar to the artist, in the continual search for perfection.

Beckett's later drama is significantly minimalist and the plays written during the 1970s and 1980s illustrate Beckett's desire to attain silence. The drama becomes extremely pared and the stage, lacking in props and colour, conveys the darker nature of these later works. Humour has long since been removed from Beckett's writing and silence appears to play a greater role. Plays such as *Quad* and *Nacht und Träume*, reject the use of language completely, and these mimes illustrate Beckett's interest in the dramatic power of the visual image. The setting of the late plays becomes internalized, and landscape is rejected in favour of darkness, as Beckett uses a small stage space representative of the mind. On Beckett's stage the macrocosm is ultimately replaced by the microcosm and we recognize the significant difference between the early drama such as *Waiting for Godot* and the dimly lit setting of *What Where*. As Beckett's drama progresses, the verbal subtext of the work becomes ever more important, and Beckett's manipulation of language ensures multiple thematic implications.

Catastrophe, written in French during 1982 for Václav Havel[6], reflects Beckett's continuing anxiety concerning the creative process. It presents the audience with a 'real' identifiable place, as it illustrates the rehearsal of a play. Consequently, *Catastrophe* is fundamentally a play within a play, an image of an actor during rehearsals for the final scene. The play illustrates the manipulation of the protagonist by the director and his female assistant and reflects the suppression of human rights, which constitutes the catastrophe. Having one's voice suppressed is of course a traumatic experience for the artist. The political overtones of the play are extremely apparent. However, it is perhaps more pertinent for the purposes of this chapter to view the play as Beckett's illustration of artistic failure. As Knowlson states, *Catastrophe* has been seen as 'demonstrating the impossibility for an artist to shape his work in such a way that it reveals what he intends it to reveal; art in the end escapes him' (1997: 679). The play is short, consisting of succinct lines spoken between the director and his assistant. Unconventionally, the protagonist is given no words to speak. Although the protagonist is often viewed as a victim, and as an icon of suffering, it is possible to view the play as a representation of the suffering endured by the artist who is subject to failure. Beckett's directions state that the director is dressed in fur coat and fur toque to match, but says that his age and physique are unimportant. Similarly, for the assistant Beckett sees age and physique as insignificant, as for the protagonist. Beckett has discarded what he deems to be non-essential details. The protagonist, dressed in black with a black hat, which serves to hide the face, is stripped of any sense of character, thereby ensuring that he appears similar to an inanimate object, devoid of any human characteristics; essentially an 'art form' to be manipulated and moulded. He appears similar to a sculpture, Beckett perhaps taking his inspiration from Alberto Giacometti's work, as he sets up the visual to upstage the verbal.[7] The protagonist is an image of human failure and despair.

As the director contemplates his work (protagonist), he is not satisfied with its initial appearance and so he begins the manipulation of his art form, endeavouring to shape it so that it will express what he wants to convey. The director appears tetchy, unpleasant, pompous and self-serving, characteristics that many would associate with the temperamental artist at work. The female assistant does not assume the role of the submissive woman, even though she delivers some of her lines in a timid voice. She appears to be very much in collaboration with the director, offering up ideas about how the protagonist can be manoeuvred in order to obtain maximum dramatic impact. The assistant appears to have her own ideas on how the protagonist should look, illustrating her own 'creative' flair perhaps. The director, however, fails to encourage this creativity and seems determined to follow his own objectives in his search for the 'perfect' image, or what he perceives the perfect image to be. He has failed to recognize that perfection does not exist in artistic expression.

As the protagonist's gown and hat are removed, we witness the metaphorical paring of the work, as everything that is deemed superfluous, is discarded. The protagonist who suffers from 'Fibrous degeneration' (Beckett 1990: 458), is in reality degenerating before our eyes, as he is stripped of clothing and sculpted into the image the director wishes to convey. His skull, which is moulting, and his hands, which are described as clawlike, serve to illustrate the deterioration of the image before us. He appears de-humanized, as his body is essentially breaking down, and the director treats him as if he is fundamentally worthless. His night attire and his few tufts of hair are described as being ash in colour, which is interesting, because the colour ash, due to its dullness, undoubtedly denotes bleakness. Moulded with intrinsic precision he embodies the meticulousness of Beckett's artistic process. Beckett uses this drama perhaps to make a scathing comment on the critics who desire his work to be less elusive, and so the director states, 'For God's sake! This craze for explicitation! Every i dotted to death!' (Beckett 1990: 459). His experimentation with lighting further reduces the stage to a dimly lit playing area where only the protagonist remains visible. The light on his body, fading slowly to illuminate only his head, serves to convey a striking visual image of dejection; an image which needs no words to highlight its intensity, and so the director states, 'There's our catastrophe' (Beckett 1990: 460). However, as the protagonist slowly raises his head we witness his defiance. His refusal to be shaped and manipulated reflects how language often fails to convey the thing you want it to express. Artistic failure is ultimately the true catastrophe represented in this drama, bringing to mind the words from *Worstward Ho*: 'Ever tried. Ever failed. No matter. Try again. Fail again. Fail better' (Beckett 1999a: 7).

Through his drama Beckett deals thematically with the difficulty of expression and the degenerating nature of language. In Chapter 11 we witness Beckett's attempt to deal with the death throes of language stylistically, through prose works that endeavour to write themselves out of words and achieve an aesthetic beauty, resulting from their obscurity and poetic quality, as the silence and the void are expressed through a language of 'nothingness'.

Chapter 11

The Miniaturist of the Word
The Shorter Prose

The artistic tendency is not expansive, but a contraction
Proust and Three Dialogues with Georges Duthuit

Beckett's later prose works demonstrate a linguistic contraction, discarding conventional narrative in favour of a new style of writing which would accommodate a new kind of language, culminating in the 'literature of the unword' (Beckett 1983: 173). These are experimental fictions designed to capture the formlessness of experience, and so conventional structures are jettisoned, as we witness an increasing poeticization resulting from this reductionism: a reductionism that was desired, but also the result of a natural, unavoidable progression. Beckett compares his language to 'a veil that must be torn apart in order to get at the things (or the Nothingness) behind it' (1983: 171). Surely Nothingness encapsulates silence, and Beckett's 'literature of the unword' was the process by which he advanced towards 'nothingness', endeavouring, perhaps, to write words out of existence. Therefore the 'literature of the unword' is dominated by silence, as silence represents the condition to which it aspires.[1]

Manipulation of language, form and syntax produces a style of writing that can often appear elusive and therefore difficult to comprehend. Although these fictions may appear enigmatic, obscurity appears to be an inevitable consequence of an increasingly dense and compressed style; a style which accommodates a language that endeavours to express 'nothing' while simultaneously conveying 'everything', and words which acknowledge their own futility and the impossibility of successful artistic expression. Throughout these later fictions we witness the tragedy of language and the aesthetic beauty located among the decaying words.

Imagination Dead Imagine, written in French in the 1960s, and consisting of approximately 1,000 words, conveys the process of the imagination and the artistic challenge of endeavouring to depict the void. This text thematically resembles *All Strange Away*, as we again witness the recurring theme of the rotunda and Beckett's interest in closed spaces. *All Strange Away*, of course, begins with the sentence 'Imagination dead imagine' (Beckett 1999h: 7), illustrating how Beckett has taken an idea from the initial text and developed it into a self-contained work.

Stylistically, *Imagination Dead Imagine* appears more succinct, as the discarding of superfluous words results in a text that is more coherent than its predecessor and stylistically more creative. The concentration of language helps illustrate the vision of an arrested decay contained within the rotunda. Beckett endeavours to convey the artistic tragedy by implementing a linguistic contraction, thereby illustrating the difficulty of successful artistic expression due to the degenerating nature of the word. Hence, the failure of human existence is illustrated through the use of language that is itself failing. Without the use of language through which to express, the imperative to create dwindles, resulting in the death of the imagination and culminating in the death of the artist. *Imagination Dead Imagine* is not just an illustration of two bodies suspended in a rotunda; it also conveys the process of the imagination and the determination to provide an illustration of 'nothing' because nothingness dominates our existence, as we cannot comprehend the reason for our being here; nor can we know what lies beyond our present condition.

The title of this text can be interpreted in various ways. Perhaps it means that the imagination is endeavouring to envisage what death is like. Maybe it suggests the death of the imagination coupled with the determination of the imagination to go on, illustrating the reality that death in Beckett's work does not necessarily represent an ending. Hence we witness the stoicism of Beckett's language despite inevitable failure, a stoicism which is evidently prevalent in his characters. Rabinovitz too acknowledges this point saying 'Ostensibly, "imagination dead imagine" is an admission of defeat, the confession of a loss of artistic power. But at the same time it can be taken as a behest to go on creating even in the face of overwhelming difficulties' (Acheson and Arthur 1987: 54). The voice in *All Strange Away* speaks of 'dead imagining' (Beckett 1999h: 23), suggesting that the imagination is unproductive, again bringing us back to the arduousness of the creative procedure. Probably the most accurate reading of the title is to accept that Beckett is endeavouring to imagine the death of the imagination and the implications of this for the artistic process. The title therefore encapsulates the primary theme of the text, as Beckett sums up in three words, that appear syntactically incorrect, the motif which dominates much of his work. As Levy says, 'the role of the imagination was to reduce the narrative world to the Nothing it tries to express' (1980: 110). And in *Imagination Dead Imagine* we are presented with a narrative world which is so concentrated, that it reflects the language that is used to describe it.

The journey from *All Strange Away* to *Imagination Dead Imagine* illustrates a 'progression in decline', as the paring of language results in a potent style that triggers the poetry of Beckett's prose and clearly illustrates the minimalism of the later prose fictions. The precision of description here produces a text that can almost be described as a type of instruction manual, as the narrator plots the points of the rotunda in which the two bodies are suspended, encouraging us to venture in and out, observing this picture of an arrested decay. As Brienza says 'the narrator requires us to visualize an image and then to dissect it' (1982: 59). The rotunda may be compared with Murphy's mind: 'a large hollow sphere, hermetically closed to the universe without' (Beckett 1993a: 63). The narrator appears almost scientific in his approach, using a tone that seems unfeeling, removed from the vision before him and hence creating a feeling of uneasiness in the reader. And this scientific approach corresponds to the predilection for mathematics, geometry, algebra, statistics, measurement and dimension that is well advertised everywhere in Beckett's work. Without the incorporation of paragraphs this text appears extremely dense, thereby heightening the feeling of claustrophobia and intensifying the impact of the language. The tonal and syntactical fluctuations, which are prevalent throughout the text, are very much evident in the opening lines, and it is this style of writing that dominates Beckett's later prose fictions. The heavily punctuated sentences produce an oscillating rhythm, preventing the text from becoming monotone, despite the apparent clinical tone of the narrator's words. Conventional narrative is inadequate for capturing the formlessness of experience and therefore it is apparent why Beckett employs a concentration of language to capture both the human and artistic tragedy. These later fictions appear to document the inability of words to capture the tragedy of the human descent into nothingness. Everything which is recognizable in conventional narrative is discarded by Beckett, and so here islands and waters are omitted only to be replaced by the whiteness of 'nothing'. Hence, features of the macrocosm are eliminated, as Beckett's work becomes increasingly explorations of the mind and the creative process. Not only are islands and waters deleted; the words 'endlessly, omit' (Beckett 1999i: 35), in the opening lines, encapsulate Beckett's approach to his own writing.

It is here amidst the void that Beckett locates the rotunda, a white hollow sphere surrounded by whiteness, invisible to the eye but undeniably present. And so we witness Beckett's creation of 'something' out of an apparent 'nothing'. If imagination is supposed dead in this text, the ability to be creative is denied, as one is condemned to imagine 'nothing'; and through the use of reductionism Beckett has successfully conveyed this 'nothingness', a task that is stylistically arduous. The paradox is therefore evident, because as Beckett's work diminishes in length it perhaps transcends earlier writings, as we witness an increasing poeticization of his fiction through this reductionism.

The contradictions and paradoxes contained in *Imagination Dead Imagine*, for example, 'No way in, go in' (ibid.), serve to make the text somewhat difficult to comprehend, while simultaneously producing a work that is stylistically innovative, creating a narrative world that can only be described as horrific. The description of the couple's position in the rotunda illustrates the precision of detail that Beckett employs throughout this text.[2] The concentration of language, and the discarding of everything which is not relevant to the creation of this visual image, serves to produce a mental picture for the reader which is profoundly intense, as we recognize the representation of a live burial or, perhaps, a vision of the foetus in the womb. It is apparent that the narrator does not appear to feel contempt or, conversely, pity for the paltry nature of the human body here.

The woman, similar to the man who lies beside her, is a visual representation of the contraction that is evident in Beckett's work. Although the couple do not appear to be subject to degeneration, enduring perhaps an arrested decay, we do imagine their stature to be smaller than the average human, as they are contained within a rotunda that appears to constrict any form of movement or growth. Despite being male and female their position within the rotunda means that there is no chance of procreation, and so they are condemned to inhabit a world of sterility, where the imagination and language itself appear to be sterilized.

Beckett's interest in breath/breathing is evident in this text, as the line 'Hold a mirror to their lips, it mists' (Beckett 1999i: 37), conveys the horrific reality that the couple are in fact living.[3] The narrator says, 'It is clear however, from a thousand little signs too long to imagine, that they are not sleeping' (Beckett 1999i: 38). Hence, they are probably conscious of the situation they are in, which makes their condition seem all the more dreadful. Perhaps their imaginations are dead, as they cannot picture anything other than the whiteness that surrounds them; they are subject to 'dead imaginings'.

These later fictions illustrate that, although Beckett's style has evolved and the medium through which he expresses himself has changed, it is evident that the themes incorporated in his later writings are the same as those explored in his earlier works. And therefore, in *Imagination Dead Imagine*, we witness the recurring themes of degeneration, isolation, death that does not constitute an end, and the recurring motif of the eyes, ('Piercing pale blue the effect is striking' (Beckett 1999i: 37)). As with all of Beckett's writings, we also recognize the 'underlying' theme of the complexity of the creative process. In fact, it is possible to suggest that language itself is the dominant theme in a text such as *Imagination Dead Imagine*. However, this text differs from others due to the negativity of the final lines, as Beckett's words provide no possibility of hope. Rarely does Beckett state so emphatically that nothing exists beyond the nothingness that now surrounds us. The sombre tone of the final lines captures the futility of existence and, perhaps, conveys the artist's acceptance that there is nothing worthwhile to express.

It is interesting that, after completing such an innovative text as *Imagination Dead Imagine*, Beckett turns his attention to a new fiction that he entitles *Enough*. With the first English publication in 1967, *Enough* 'gives the impression of having been conceived as a miniature rather than refined into a precipitate, as the other "residua" were' (Knowlson and Pilling 1979: 149). And although this text is longer than its predecessor, it is more accessible, due to the fact that it adopts a more 'conventional' style. The title encompasses the notion that there is no more to be said, suggesting perhaps that this text will represent an ending, thereby encapsulating the final lines of *Imagination Dead Imagine*, and conveying the reality that 'there is nothing elsewhere' (Beckett 1999i: 38). However, it also implies a realization by Beckett, a suggestion perchance that he recognizes that his style of writing must change if he is to advance as an artist. Perhaps Beckett realized that he had written 'enough' in the style which he had previously adopted, and accepted the need to turn towards something new. As Pilling states:

> it is only in *Enough* that Beckett discovers the prose style that breaks decisively with what has gone before, the blend of passion and blandness, straightforwardness and obscurity, that is the hallmark of the comma-less writings of the late 'sixties and early 'seventies. (Knowlson and Pilling 1979: 150)

And, although stylistically different, *Enough* incorporates the recurring motif of the couple, the journey, and the theme of abandonment. Although innovative in style, this text may also be viewed as being slightly regressive due to its use of paragraphs. However, it differs from previous works because of the absence of commas. There exist no pauses throughout the text, thereby forcing the words to become paramount. Without commas the text consists of terse simple sentences and, hence, we witness a new form of writing. As Mary F. Cantanzaro says 'Although the language appears orderly and conventionally constructed, it is marked by turns of phrase that indicate revolt, rebellion, frustration, resignation' (Smith 1991: 20).

Beckett told John Gruen in 1970 that his reaction to dead languages has been to turn 'toward an abstract language' (Worth 1975: 79), which is evident in *Worstward Ho*. Dead languages to Beckett were perhaps not just languages such as Latin, as it is possible that he considered his early writings to be illustrations of a 'dead language', due to the fact they incorporated a style which had evidently become redundant for him. *Enough* is also significant in the Beckett canon because it provides the last glimpse of the 'real world', as after this text Beckett's narrative worlds become ever more interior.

The opening paragraph of the text is, perhaps, the most interesting and indeed the most enlightening for the purpose of this chapter, as it documents the struggle of the writing process. This is, undoubtedly, Beckett speaking and he appears to be suggesting that he/we renounce all previous work and prepare for what is to come. The statement, 'Too much at a time is too much' (Beckett 1999i: 25) is perhaps a direct comment on the transition from longer works to the minimalist fictions and the shorter plays which follow this text. The inability to prevent conscious thought and curtail the imagination is suggested – 'When the pen stops I go on. Sometimes it refuses' (ibid.) – coupled with the difficulty of capturing on paper the workings of the mind. Therefore every text is ultimately a failure perhaps in the eyes of the artist. The imagination is not dead but there exists, as always, the difficulty of how to express, when the mind holds the information but the pen refuses to acknowledge it. 'Such is the silence' (ibid.) and 'So much for the art and craft' (ibid.) when the artist fails to find the medium through which expression becomes possible. Hence, the issue arises as to whether language is actually ever capable of providing the medium required. There appears to be a tragic dichotomy between experience and expression. However, the pen is all that he has and so he presses on despite the frustration and disappointment.

As *Enough* progresses we witness the 'I–he' dichotomy, as the narrator describes the man 'she' once knew, the journey they took, and the eventual abandonment she suffered. The dark tones incorporated in this fiction produce a feeling of uneasiness in the reader, as the suggestion of an 'inappropriate' sexual relationship perhaps illustrates that *Enough* is not as straightforward as it first appears, nor is it an image of conventional paradise. Similar to *Imagination Dead Imagine*, the narrator appears somewhat removed from the story she relates, as the clinical tone suggests she is slightly anaesthetized in relation to the details she conveys, appearing disconnected from the situation as it took place. She appears to have had no identity, living only in the shadow of the man who accompanied her; 'I only had the desires he manifested' (ibid.), she claims. The image of the couple may be equated with the representation of the man and woman in *Imagination Dead Imagine*, as similarly their stature is reduced. Described as 'bent double' (Beckett 1999i: 27), they journey forward in an almost crippled state, until 'In the end his trunk ran parallel with the ground' (Beckett 1999i: 26). This image of the couple journeying, with backs bowed, resurfaces again in *Worstward Ho*, representing Beckett's continuing interest in presenting the body as physically flawed; and illustrating the point that although many of his later works concentrate on the mind, Beckett continues to include details which illustrate the physical discomforts of existence and the unavoidability of atrophy.

Beckett's preoccupation with permutations in language, which he took to extremes in *Watt*, is again evident in this text, illustrating how Beckett forces words to work hard so that every possible meaning, and variations of meaning, can be extracted from the minimum of words. This is illustrated as the narrator comments on the possible forms of communication between herself and her companion,[4] illustrating Beckett's ability to convey multiple meanings with the minimum of words, and highlighting the artistic inventiveness of the shorter prose fictions.

The narrator, who is evidently now old, oscillates in tone as she looks back over her life with apparent regret, attempting to express 'how it is' and in fact 'how it was'. An acceptance of failure is apparent – 'Given three or four lives I might have accomplished something' (Beckett 1999i: 26) – as she endeavours to relate the tale of her existence. This text, undoubtedly, troubles the reader, as it raises many questions that remain unanswered. And so, one is left feeling that this writing is not 'enough', and yet, perhaps, Beckett felt that it was all he could manage. Hence, this raises the issue as to whether these texts were actually written for the reader, or do they, perhaps, just fulfil the artist's obligation to express?

Bryden acknowledges the complexity of Beckett's later prose, suggesting that some readers view it as 'perversely uncommunicative, teasingly mysterious' (1993: 137). Written originally in French, *Lessness*, published in 1970, is so enigmatic in its structure and thematics that it could easily be labelled 'perversely uncommunicative', appearing almost unreadable and beyond comprehension. The blurb from the Calder and Boyars (Signature series 9, 1970) book cover, written partly by Beckett, best sums up what this text is about:

> to do with the collapse of some such refuge as that last attempted in *Ping* and with the ensuing situation of the refugee. Ruin, exposure, wilderness, mindlessness, past and future denied and affirmed, are the categories, formally distinguishable, through which the writing winds, first in one disorder, then in another. (Quoted here from Knowlson (1997: 564))

This brief synopsis clearly encapsulates the thematics of the text, illustrating the paradoxes contained in the writing and the 'wilful' disorder which manifests itself through theme and structure. And, once again, we wonder whether *Lessness* is a metalinguistic text which is fundamentally about itself, language and expression. The limitations imposed by traditional fiction would have prevented Beckett creating a work such as *Lessness*. He needed a style that would accommodate the formlessness of experience. Hence, there is the paradox that Beckett actually 'shapes' formlessness. Form therefore complements meaning, as the 'apparent formlessness' of *Lessness* successfully reflects the chaos of man's existence.

The difficulty of dying, and the struggle with continuing, in a land dominated by sand is conveyed through a language that appears to be falling into ruin. The manipulation of language, form and syntax produces a narrative which transcends conventional fiction, as there exists no plot development, no recognizable characters and a landscape that appears apocalyptic, thereby reflecting the narrative that conveys it. In other words, we are witnessing the degeneration of man and artistic conventional form simultaneously. 'Lessness' is fundamentally dominating man's existence and facilitating Beckett's linguistic contraction.

It is evident from the opening lines that the manipulation of syntax produces a narrative which at first appears incomprehensible. Similar to *Enough*, *Lessness* is a comma-less text which undoubtedly adds to its complexity while

simultaneously facilitating its innovation, thereby creating a text that is stylistically transcendent. The third person narrative allows the text, and indeed
the other *Fizzles*, to be different from earlier short prose fiction, due to the fact
that the narrators are no longer concerned with determining identity, thereby
placing greater emphasis on the necessity to convey 'how it is' and the difficulty of artistic expression. As Pattie states, 'For the Unnamable, stories were
untrustworthy, because they could not describe the self; in these late works,
Beckett seems to find the same problem, but this time in words themselves'
(2000: 87).

Art is for Beckett 'the apotheosis of solitude' (Beckett 1965: 64), and *Lessness*
abandons the motif of the couple and instead explores the solitary figure.
Existing in, what can only be described as, an apocalyptic landscape, he is the
predecessor of the figure in 'For to end yet again'. He exudes little sign of life,
appearing almost statuesque: 'Little body ash grey locked rigid heart beating
face to endlessness' (Beckett 1999i: 47). He is existing within the void – 'earth
sky as one all sides endlessness' (ibid.) – as nothingness dominates the landscape. Everything appears to be static except for when he endeavours to take
a step forwards. Perhaps he is on a 'journey' searching for a new refuge, the
two pale blue eyes providing the only glimpse of colour against the greyness
of the landscape. The predominance of the colour grey illustrates that this
text is neither black nor white but instead a fusion of opposites, for example,
time past and time present, degeneration and continuing, and images of
horizontals and verticals, thereby adding to the complexity of the narrative.
Everything that is recognizable is therefore 'all gone from mind' (ibid.), as
we enter Beckett's fiction which is dominated by 'disorder'. It is the 'figment'
of Beckett's imagination, which creates the beauty among this decay and produces a style that encapsulates it. As Finney points out, *Lessness* 'is an image
of the artist's consciousness examining its own condition' (1972: 19). This text
is an examination of man's condition and the chaos which surrounds him.
Man is dominated by disorder and therefore Beckett uses a language which
appears disordered in an attempt to demonstrate this reality. *Lessness* presents
the universal condition of humanity, as we are all essentially alone, existing in
a world that is falling into ruin, trapped in a body that fails to function effectively, and staring out perhaps towards 'endlessness', if death does not provide
a termination. However, no matter how horrific the scene Beckett presents, his
language counterbalances the dismay with its poetic beauty.

One hundred and twenty sentences fused together in apparent formlessness
constitute *Lessness*. The 24 paragraphs vary in length adding to the 'shapelessness' of the narrative, and each of the sentences in the first 12 paragraphs is
repeated 'randomly' in the second 12, thereby heightening the text's complexity. As Pilling says 'In *Enough* the repetition of all the possible hypotheses in
a given permutation is only one paragraph long, but *Ping* and *Lessness* are in
permutative form throughout' (1976: 29). Repetition itself can be viewed as

a form of reductionism, as the artist can avoid implementing new words, as previously stated words are reiterated, resulting in 'lessness' and the ultimate in experimentation with language. This repetition also draws attention to the limitations of language itself. It is therefore not surprising that some readers turn away from Beckett's later prose, viewing it as too difficult and unwilling to embrace his evolving style. And yet within these shorter fictions exists a language so rich in beauty that they demand to be read. No one can deny the poetic quality of the final line of *Lessness*: 'Figment dawn dispeller of figments and the other called dusk' (Beckett 1999i: 51). Therefore, despite the horrific scene depicted in *Lessness*, through his use of language and form, Beckett once again achieves artistic 'moreness'.

Beckett's ambivalent attitude towards language is clearly illustrated in *Worstward Ho*, published in 1983. This text, which is perhaps the prose equivalent to *Catastrophe*, illustrates the tragedy of language, as Beckett ironically uses words to convey the 'ineptitude' of language, attempting to use the 'worst word' to illustrate the futility of words and the worsening state of humanity. The decline of language runs parallel with the deterioration of the human condition. The extreme manipulation of language, and Beckett's employment of neologisms, results in a narrative which at times appears to be beyond comprehension, as Beckett invents words that are not recognizable and yet succeed in conveying meaning. As Calder says 'The style, constantly juxtaposing everything that belongs to pure imagination, whether possible or not, with its opposite, becomes a new language' (2001: 102). Beckett is pushing language to its limit in this text, challenging it at every stage, and forcing it to express even though it is disintegrating before him. This new idiom allows Beckett to confront and demolish the possibilities of language itself. As Vivian Mercier says, 'Nowhere is Beckett more totally the artist than in his absorbed exploration of the possibilities of a medium' (1977: 182). The increasing poeticization of the writing demands that *Worstward Ho* be read aloud in order for one to appreciate Beckett's innovative wordplay and the beauty of his style. This work possibly transcends anything which has gone before it in terms of linguistic and artistic innovation, and, as Knowlson (1997: 677) correctly points out, *Worstward Ho*, alongside *Ill Seen Ill Said*, will probably be ranked as one of Beckett's greatest works.

It plays on the title of Webster and Dekker's play *Westward Hoe* (1607) and Charles Kingsley's novel *Westward Ho!* (1855), and not surprisingly it took Beckett 7 months to complete the initial draft. The title, of course, suggests that everything 'evolves' into something more terrible; it is a sequence of decline. The text is a representation of decay in every sense, as in it we witness the degeneration of language coupled with the deterioration of man's existence, and we recognize that Beckett achieves a new language that allows him to express, 'With worsening words' (Beckett 1999a: 27), the worsening situation of man and artist. However, although the words appear to disintegrate

into meaninglessness, they ultimately 'evolve' into a language which is artistically transcendent. The acceptance of failure noted in his conversations with
Georges Duthuit[5] is elaborated upon in this text, as Beckett not only accepts
failure but also desires to 'fail better': 'All of old. Nothing else ever. Ever tried.
Ever failed. No matter. Try again. Fail again. Fail better' (Beckett 1999a: 7).
These words encapsulate the fundamental theme of *Worstward Ho* and, perhaps, Beckett's attitude to his work in general, as he strives to illustrate the
'worst' in language and life simultaneously. 'Disimprovement' therefore dominates this text, as everything appears subject to degeneration and decline on
a verbal, physical and mental level.

The desire to create, coupled with the impossibility of successful artistic
expression, is illustrated in the following sequence:

> First the body. No. First the place. No. First both. Now either. Now the other.
> Sick of the either try the other. Sick of it back sick of the either. So on.
> Somehow on. Till sick of both. Throw up and go. Where neither. Till sick of
> there. Throw up and back. The body again. Where none. The place again.
> Where none. Try again. Fail again. Better again. Or better worse. Fail worse
> again. Still worse again. Till sick for good. Throw up for good. Go for good.
> Where neither for good. Good and all. (Beckett 1999a: 8)

Language seems to challenge itself, and it appears as if an internal battle is
taking place among the words, as each word seems to vie for position, and each
subsequently 'fails'. The sickness, which is referred to six times, is perhaps a
motif for language, illustrating that words are not healthy and will eventually
die; and until that moment when they finally run out they will continue to
'Somehow ooze on' (Beckett 1999a: 38). Viewing language as a sickness helps
one to comprehend how words are fundamentally failing and must ultimately
expire. Here language is nearly successful in actually cancelling itself out,
illustrating that *Worstward Ho* is, primarily, a metalinguistic text.

As everything gravitates towards a worsening state, words and new combin-
ations of words highlight the disorder of language and life. Beckett essentially
writes himself out of accepted modes of expression while continuing to ensure
that his theme is 'Ununsaid' (Beckett 1999a: 32), hence said. The creation of
the word 'ununsaid' illustrates Beckett's ability to convey meaning through
words which have no 'meaning'. Therefore, paradoxically, Beckett creates new
words in an attempt, perhaps, to destroy language, increasingly endeavouring to implement lessness.[6] Commas are unnecessary here in these short terse
sentences, adding to the telegrammatic quality of the narrative. However, the
spaces between each of the paragraphs result in a structure that appears similar to *How It Is*, and we recognize the intrusion of silence which surely must
dominate when language deteriorates beyond repair ('Blanks for when words
gone' (Beckett 1999a: 40)). The process of creation is undermined by the act

of deconstruction. Language is Beckett's primary mode of expression and, yet, in this text he consciously endeavours to destroy this medium. Through deteriorating language Beckett achieves, perhaps, the best form of expression, as form fundamentally reflects his theme. Reductionism, ('Meremost minimum' (Beckett 1999a: 9)), therefore facilitates stylistic innovation, as Beckett perhaps wishes to 'Know no more. See no more. Say no more' (Beckett 1999a: 18), ultimately seeking a deliverance from language. The mistrust of language, which has plagued Beckett throughout his working life, ironically results in works that are linguistically revolutionary despite their apparent 'Gnawing to be gone' (Beckett 1999a: 41).

The final sequence of the text encapsulates Beckett's desire to end, coupled with the unrelenting need to go on, which is evident throughout his work. Everything has been discarded, including the old man and child, the skull and the old woman, and all we are left with is three pins and one pinhole. Everything had been reduced to this one image which exists 'At bounds of boundless void' (Beckett 1999a: 46–47), illustrating how Beckett structures 'nothingness'. And despite the call for 'enough' the stoic quality of the language prompts it to end with the word 'on', and we recognize that in spite of erosion it might somehow continue. As Pattie confirms, 'the contradiction between the futility and necessity of expression is now contained in the two-word formulation nohow on' (2000: 97). It may be suggested that this two-word formulation best captures the essence of Beckett's writing, both structurally and thematically.

Worstward Ho provides an insight into the journey of life and Beckett's innovation in literary expression. As Beckett manipulates language in an attempt perhaps to destroy it, he ironically succeeds in creating a new language that accommodates his new style. Therefore as Beckett's language 'worsens' it paradoxically transcends anything which has gone before, in terms of linguistic innovation. And the linguistic/artistic contraction, evident in the shorter prose fictions and the shorter drama, thus allows Beckett to further explore the silence of the Real, facilitating the world of 'shades' that dominates his final texts.

Chapter 12

Voices, Ghosts, Silence
Into Nothingness

Nothing is more real than nothing

Malone Dies

Beckett's determination to depict the void and illustrate 'nothingness' is evidently achieved in his later writings. This world of 'shades'[1] illustrates Beckett's increasing determination to escape the burden of language, as everything appears subject to decay, and we witness the tragedy and death of language itself. These later works convey the 'screams' located amidst the silence, as the voices display a burning need to be gone. Beckett's final writings capture the evanescence of life and language, as the supreme aesthetic moment is, perhaps, attained in the illustration of 'nothing'.

Ghost Trio, a television play written during 1975, allowed Beckett to further push back the boundaries of drama, as he used this medium to successfully capture the ghostly aura which dominates the work. The evanescent quality of the drama prompts it to appear almost 'otherworldly' as Beckett has successfully captured, on screen, the 'spirit' world, and has thus given form to 'nothingness'. The feeling of 'goneness' dominates this work, and it appears all the more poignant due to the fact that in it we recognize ourselves and the future that awaits us, when everyone we have loved is gone and the unavoidable confrontation with 'I' alone takes precedence.

Initially entitled 'Tryst', *Ghost Trio* dramatizes the act of waiting, based around a meeting that never takes place, and we again acknowledge Beckett's subjects of time, isolation and death. Unlike *Eh Joe*, the protagonist in this play is perhaps not plagued with voices in his mind, as the voice appears to be external, but is instead tormented by his isolation, as the woman he awaits fails to arrive. The title suggests that there are three ghosts, and perhaps we can conclude that the woman, the boy and the protagonist himself are in fact dead. Again Beckett forces us to confront a situation which appears rather disturbing, as he suggests that even in death one is not guaranteed peace, and the isolation which plagues us during life continues to haunt us during death.

Of course, the trio could also refer to the three stages in the play itself. Death, which Beckett often illustrates as a process, is approached differently in the later texts and we recognize that he is endeavouring to represent the final stage of that process, culminating inevitably in silence.

Divided into three sections labelled Pre-action, Action and Re-action, the drama appears to encapsulate the notion of 'goneness' and the desire to end. The room itself, where the protagonist holds his vigil, is bare; stripped of non-essentials, it is a symbolic representation of the existence the man now endures. It possesses a ghostly quality: 'The light: faint, omnipresent. No visible source. As if all luminous. Faintly luminous. No shadow. [*Pause*] No shadow. Colour: none. All grey. Shades of grey' (Beckett 1990: 408). Again we witness Beckett's familiar aversion to colour. The luminosity of the room, coupled with the non-existent shadows, suggests that the room is unworldly. Described as the 'Sole sign of life' (Beckett 1990: 409), the man appears to display little sign of life, as his bowed image, seated upon the stool, is an image of dejection and despair, and he appears to exude a deep longing to be gone. His movements are minimal, suggesting that his 'life' force is disintegrating, and as he awaits his 'lost love', we recognize that he is perhaps resigned to the fact that she will not come. The small cassette, which he clutches, contains the music from Largo of Beethoven's 5th Piano Trio, often referred to as *The Ghost*, therefore adding to the deathly mood of the drama. Knowlson says that this piece of music 'retained for Beckett something of *Macbeth*'s doom-laden atmosphere and involvement in the spirit world' (1997: 622). The music is not just an accompaniment to the words; it functions as a primary component of the drama. And in the final part of the performance, labelled Re-action, the music dominates, as the voice (V) has been removed, thus giving precedence to the non-linguistic medium. Again we are reminded that Beckett viewed music as transcendent, constituting perhaps the supreme art form, because of its ability to come closest to silence. In his letter to Axel Kaun, Beckett speaks of 'a whisper of that final music or that silence that underlies All' (Beckett 1983: 172). Clearly music and silence are equated here, as Beckett does not differentiate between the two; however, even without music, the poetic quality of Beckett's words serves to highlight the musicality of the language, illustrating that through words Beckett strives for the supreme art form which will take him one step closer to silence.

The female voice that we hear appears omniscient, as she details the movements of the protagonist, suggesting that this is a ritual to which he adheres each evening. The voice, labelled (V), is nameless and lacking in identity; she functions as a type of narrator who appears removed from the situation that she comments upon. She is almost clinical in her approach, appearing similar to the narrator in *Imagination Dead Imagine*. Knowlson (1997: 621) describes the voice as flat and unearthly, and its faintness suggests that it is gravitating towards silence. Perhaps the voice is growing weak because it is subject to reciting the same details each evening, and has become dejected from the lack of new material, appearing similar to any actor involved in the endless repetition of old lines. It is possible that Beckett is again drawing our attention to the futility of language and the difficulty of the creative process. As the voice asks us to 'tune accordingly' (Beckett 1990: 408), we are reminded that this drama is written specifically for television, highlighting the fact that Beckett used many different mediums in his endeavour to illustrate how it is to be alive, and how difficult it is to demonstrate this reality and capture the essence and evanescence of our existence.

Haunted by the voice within his mind ('v: He will now think he hears her' (Beckett 1990: 410)), the protagonist searches for her, opening the door and the window; however, his search is futile as there is no one there. As he stands irresolute, we witness Beckett's ability in producing drama that is profoundly moving, as his use of silences often speaks louder than words. The emotion that Beckett conveys, especially in the later works, is often not commented upon. It was, of course, Beckett's desire to play on our emotions as well as appeal to our intellect. Beckett's ability to capture the evanescence of life and depict the 'nothingness', which surrounds us, illustrates the complexity of his creative process and also his desire to represent the final stage in that process, where silence is attained and sustained. The growing use of silence, which dominates the later works, illustrates his desire to escape the burden of language. The words, 'I shall state silences more competently than ever a better man spangled the butterflies of vertigo' (Beckett 1993b: 138), illustrate Beckett's desire to capture the formlessness of experience through an artistic medium which has, itself, no form, and yet, paradoxically, is intrinsically crafted. To state silences is to capture 'nothingness'. In his early novel, *Dream of Fair to Middling Women*, Beckett clearly illustrates his belief that silences would be paramount in his work, and located within the silences would be the essential experience and comprehension of the work:

> The experience of my reader shall be between the phrases, in the silence, communicated by the intervals, not the terms, of the statement, between the flowers that cannot coexist, the antithetical (nothing so simple as antithetical) seasons of words, his experience shall be the menace, the miracle, the memory, of an unspeakable trajectory. (ibid.)

The view of the corridor in *Ghost Trio*, described as 'Long narrow (0.70m.) grey rectangle between grey walls, empty, far end in darkness' (Beckett 1990: 412), provides little hope for the protagonist, as it illustrates the 'vacuum' which surrounds him. The corridor is perhaps a representation of the passage between his present state and the next stage in the 'death' process. It offers a connection to another 'place', perhaps another state of emptiness, where he will continue to be alone, plagued by the memory of her image and voice. The mirror, which reflects nothing, therefore confirms that he is a ghost; however, it also serves to reflect the reality of life, capturing the void of existence. As the small boy arrives ('Dressed in black oilskin with hood glistening with rain. White face raised to invisible F' (Beckett 1990: 413)), we recognize that he lacks substantiality, thereby adding to his ghostly aura, as he appears more detached than the boy in *Godot*. Knowlson comments on the appearance and the disappearance of the boy, detailing how Beckett's German version of the drama was very different from other productions. He points out 'the narrowness of the corridor extending behind the boy and the way in which he is filmed on it make it seem as if he is emerging from a coffin' (Brater 1986: 199). It is evident, therefore, that Beckett conceived of the boy as dead. And, similar to the boy in *Godot*, he too functions as a messenger. Words are not required, as the negative shake of the head confirms that the protagonist will not be reunited with the woman this night. The silence that follows the end of the Largo dominates the final moments of the play; and as we witness the 'Face seen clearly for second time' (Beckett 1990: 414), we recognize the face of loss. The substantiality of the figure becomes reduced as the camera slowly fades and we presume that the protagonist, surrounded by silence, will continue to wait. Beckett's world of 'shades' is undoubtedly a profound one, where silence and isolation appear dominant, and ending is a process which must be endured.

Beckett's following play . . . *but the clouds* . . ., written in 1976, again dramatizes life as a 'walking shadow'. The title, taken from the last lines of W. B. Yeats' poem *The Tower*, captures the evanescence of existence, as once more we are presented with voices, isolation and loss, and we recognize that this drama points forward to the later plays *Ohio Impromptu* and *Nacht und Träume*.

The circular set of this television play conveys a sense of the never-ending, thereby suggesting that the protagonist will continue begging each evening for her to appear to him. A feeling of restlessness is apparent, and unlike the man in *Ghost Trio*, this protagonist must walk the roads by day, returning only when night falls. The voice we hear is his own, as he provides the commentary on his actions and hence, the dialogue is interspersed with images of him coming and going, as he enters and returns from the shadows. Beckett successfully captures the tragedy of existence for those who are forced to live on after those they have loved have died, as the desire to be gone often haunts them.

Night is his worst time ('When I thought of her it was always night' (Beckett 1990: 419)), when he can no longer walk the roads and is forced to travel the tracks of his mind. The shadows intensify the feeling of isolation and loss which plague him, as there appears to be 'no escape from the hours and the days. Neither from tomorrow nor from yesterday' (Beckett 1965: 13), as he cannot shun the burning desire to see her again. The dark hat and greatcoat, which he wears during the day, are discarded, as he dons the light robe and skullcap at night in preparation for her arrival.

Locked away in his little sanctum, in the dark, he sits upon an invisible stool, bowed over an invisible table, contemplating the image of her face and begging her to appear. Everything, including objects, has been discarded so that the protagonist, an image of dejection, becomes paramount. The repetition of his movements suggests that this is a routine to which he adheres each evening, and we recognize that he is imprisoned in the process of ending, as he awaits his own demise and an end to the ending. Although the protagonist comments on his daily walks, Beckett does not show him during daylight hours, due to the fact that night time dominates his existence and everything else is of little importance in relation to his feeling of loss and his desire to be gone. The darkness, which dominates Beckett's later plays, is representative of the hopelessness which plagues his protagonists, as daylight fails to bring a sense of renewal or relief, and therefore they exist devoid of the desire to live. Hence, they too are similar to the ghosts that appear to them, and we are reminded of the words from *A Piece of Monologue*: 'Thirty thousand nights of ghosts beyond. Beyond that black beyond. Ghost light. Ghost nights. Ghost rooms. Ghost graves. Ghost . . . he all but said ghost loved ones' (Beckett 1990: 429).

The protagonist is subjected to a mental torture from which there is no escape, as he endures a continuing 'begging of the mind' (Beckett 1990: 420), and the relief of silence is denied him. The intensity of feeling, which the play captures, is conveyed through a language that is stripped of non-essentials, and again we witness Beckett's linguistic expertise, as everything is pared down and the minimalist approach conveys his artistic proficiency. The appearance of the protagonist's lost 'love' demonstrates Beckett's pre-occupation with dramatic image, as the woman's face is 'reduced as far as possible to eyes and mouth' (Beckett 1990: 417), thereby appearing similar to *Not I*, and illustrating his reductionism, as the body is discarded in favour of an image which is so reduced that it appears almost foreign in its representation. The eyes and mouth perhaps hold the most significance for the protagonist, as they are the windows to the soul and the orifice through which communication is possible. Ironically she fails to speak to him, appearing to be beyond verbalization, but 'uttering inaudibly' (Beckett 1990: 421), she mouths the words, '. . . clouds . . . but the clouds . . . of the sky . . .' (ibid.). Clouds must have appealed to Beckett as their wispy, insubstantial, ethereal nature perhaps encapsulated his view of existence. Maybe the woman is urging the protagonist to accept that she has gone. However, his desire for recognition will not allow her to rest in peace, as he begs her to look at him or speak to him. The words, 'With those unseeing eyes I so begged when alive to look at me' (Beckett 1990: 420), suggests perhaps that his love was unrequited, and we recognize the poignancy of the drama, as even after death he continues to want her despite the possibility that she failed to truly see him when they were together.

As the drama ends with the image of the protagonist waiting in the sanctum fading into darkness, we acknowledge that his 'begging of the mind' will continue until he too can journey 'among the deepening shades'. Beckett's distress at the death of his friends over the years has been well documented.[2] It is probable that these heart-felt occasions fuelled his desire to capture in words, and silences, the poignant image of loss, and his fascination with what lay beyond this life, undoubtedly, influenced Beckett's writing. Beckett successfully captures the feeling of emptiness which plagues the protagonist in . . . *but the clouds.* . . . As the Unnamable declares, 'all is a question of voices' (Beckett 1994: 348), and the voices which Beckett conveys in these later works do not have that strong desire to go on, which their earlier counterparts possessed, but instead display a greater feeling of despondency and an ever increasing desire for silence. The voices are related to the dispersal of the personality but they also possess a haunting quality. As everything around them degenerates, including the words they speak, these voices, subjected to the burden of language, require an ending that must surely be located amidst the silence.

The Lost Ones, which Beckett began writing in French in 1965 and which lay unfinished for 5 years,[3] illustrates a different style of writing and creates an alternative hermeneutics of 'existence'. The haunting quality which the text possesses is similar to that found in *Imagination Dead Imagine*, and we again witness, as Pilling says, the 'impassive detachment of the speaker' (Knowlson and Pilling 1979: 162), who describes the hellish environment, in which these lost ones exist, with little emotion. Beckett's fascination with closed spaces[4] is again conveyed through this narrative and, unlike *Imagination Dead Imagine* where only two people are confined to the rotunda, the lost ones' cylinder is populated by roughly 200 inhabitants, thereby creating a sense of claustrophobia, as space is visibly restricted, and the zones into which the cylinder is divided are reminiscent of Dante's vision of hell.

This text conveys many themes and critics have developed numerous interpretations. However, one theory which has not been fully explored is the possibility that the narrative is a direct comment on Beckett's creative process. As Levy (1980: 96) says, in this text we witness a tribe of naked bodies pursuing a barren existence. This pursuance of a barren existence, or 'nothingness', reflects Beckett's own determination to illustrate the void and convey real silence. He is therefore similar to the searchers, continually looking for that which is perhaps beyond reach: a style that will illustrate 'nothing' or a 'nothingness' that will illustrate style. The title itself possesses a haunting quality as we imagine a world populated by lost souls and acknowledge the sense of hopelessness which the text conveys. Here we witness an 'Abode where lost bodies roam each searching for its lost one. Vast enough for search to be in vain' (Beckett 1999i: 55). Their search is therefore inefficacious, as they will never find what they are looking for and yet, similar to all of Beckett's characters, they go on, searching for that which does not perhaps exist and recalling Beckett's words from his essay on Proust: 'We are alone. We cannot know and we cannot be known' (1965: 66). The French title (*Le Dépeupleur*) encompasses the notion of degeneration and decline, and we wonder whether the human race will eventually 'shrink and dwindle' (Beckett 1990: 43) until there is nobody left and silence dominates. A world with no population, littered with books that can no longer be read, would be the ultimate representation of the futility of language and the definitive illustration of the silent word.

The extremes of temperature produce a fluctuating environment, as the temperature oscillates between hot and cold. The light, 'Its dimness. Its yellowness. Its omnipresence' (Beckett 1999i: 55), creates a hellish and ghostly atmosphere. Within this habitat the lost ones are prone to decay as their skin ultimately shrivels, and 'The bodies brush together with a rustle of dry leaves' (ibid.). However, apart from this occasional rustle of dried flesh, it is apparent that silence dominates this world:

> Floor and wall are of solid rubber or suchlike. Dash against them foot or fist or head and the sound is scarcely heard. Imagine then the silence of the steps. The only sounds worthy of the name result from the manipulation of the ladders or the thud of bodies striking against one another or of one against itself as when in sudden fury it beats its breast. Thus flesh and bone subsist. The ladders. These are the only objects. (Beckett 1999i: 55–56)

Despite the feeling of turbulence, the silence produces the wraithlike aura in this narrative, as we recognize the disturbing reality that these 200 inhabit-ants of this closed space search each day in a world dominated by silence but lacking in peace. The environment is devoid of objects apart from the ladders which are used by the climbers to seek out niches. They are ultimately alone – 'Man and wife are strangers' (Beckett 1999i: 67) – because the light which is 'uniformly luminous' (Beckett 1999i: 69), similar to that in *Ghost Trio* and *Ping*, makes recognition difficult, as the eyes become burnt from the glare. Perhaps they search for an ending, taking refuge at times in the niches, which provide a temporary respite, but unaware that to end completely is perhaps an impos-sibility. The climbers' code, which they adhere to most of the time, is used as a means of instilling order in an environment that appears chaotic. It may also be suggested that the climber's code is a metaphor for Beckett's writing style, as the form of precision he applies to his texts, and the stringent directions he applies to his drama, possess the accuracy of a mathematician. Beckett searched for a style that would capture the 'amorphousness' of existence, and the 'lost ones' may therefore be viewed, on one level, as the texts, which Beckett believed, did not successfully capture the experience of Nothing.

The vanquished are similar to Dante's Belacqua, as they acknowledge the futility of searching and remain resolute in their desire to do nothing. They accept the hopelessness of existence, representing the ultimate image of dejec-tion, and they are perhaps to be envied in their willingness to believe that con-tinuing is ineffectual. The inhabitants of this world are empty, and there exists neither desire to discover self nor any determination to acknowledge 'I'. This lack of identity suggests that they are similar to lost souls or perhaps ghosts as, unlike other Beckett characters, they do not search for meaning. They 'exist' without fully living and we recognize that they represent the final stage in the life process where the body is degenerating, the spirit is weak, and to end is to be released. The image of the vanquished woman (the north)[5] encapsulates the feeling of hopelessness that this text evokes. This woman, like many of Beckett's later characters, is nameless. She functions solely as a point of reference by which all other lost ones can locate their position 'because of her greater fixity' (Beckett 1999i: 76). Beckett has reduced humanity to a point of worthlessness, or perhaps he has illustrated the reality of existence. Similar to many characters, this vanquished woman embraces herself, assuming the foetal position. Devoid of companionship she becomes her own other. She is of little interest to the rest of the population, except for the occasions when her head is lifted by a passer-by, who studies her eyes out of curiosity and then moves on. Again we recognize the dominance of failure and the impossibility of communication. 'Unknowability' prevails.

The silent dark – 'whence suddenly such silence as to drown all the faint breathings put together' (Beckett 1999i: 79) – which encompasses the conclusion of this text denies any possibility of improvement, leaving the reader with a feeling of dejection, as he/she acknowledges that the narrative is perhaps a representation of life. The conclusion does not represent an ending, and as the narrator declares, 'All has not been told and never shall be' (Beckett 1999i: 74), we question whether Beckett finds it impossible to end absolutely, as the impossibility of saying/writing the last word is suggested; hence, the tale of life is never fully told. To write oneself out of language and to illustrate Nothing would, in theory, be the death of the artist, as once this supreme aesthetic moment is achieved, it can never be surpassed. However, Beckett's creative process suggests that he was working towards this 'end', and the 'degeneration of language' facilitated his desire to convey Nothing and encapsulate the silence which, paradoxically, would produce an artistic transcendence.

The Unnamable declares, 'I believe in silence' (Beckett 1994: 410), and the poetic quality of *Still*, a short prose fiction written in 1972–1973, possesses a tranquillity that Beckett's other writings strive to attain. The clinical tone employed in *The Lost Ones* has been discarded in favour of a narrative that conveys an emotional quality in encapsulating the protagonist's desire to be still. The discarding of paragraphs, and the syntactical fluctuation evident in the narrative, produces a text that, when read aloud, ironically conveys a sense of peace and silence; and the ability to illustrate 'silence' through words confirms Beckett's artistic expertise. What is not said, paradoxically, takes precedence over that which is clearly defined, as a sense of peace is conveyed through the idea of stillness rather than through the sometimes stuttering syntax that illustrates the reality that to be still is perhaps an impossibility.

The image which the text conveys is of a man seated in a 'small upright wicker chair with armrests' (Beckett 1999d: 19); the chair of course emerges again later as a rocker in *Rockaby* and as an old spindlebacked in *Ill Seen Ill Said*.[6] The narrative, due to its attention to detail, creates an image, which appears similar to a painting, as Beckett conveys his picture through language, thus creating a linguistic 'still life'. There is no physical description of the man, due to the fact that his appearance is of little importance, and we recognize how Beckett has discarded everything that he deems to be non-essential in the creation of 'stillness'. The opening lines are remarkably close to the terminology used in *Rockaby*. The lack of movement is apparent and a sense of tiredness evident, as the protagonist appears unable now to turn his head and witness the sun going down. It is poignant that he prefers the sun setting rather than the sunrise, welcoming the darkness and the death of the day. Perhaps it reassures him that time is passing, and he takes comfort in the knowledge that soon he too can be 'still'. Although he lacks physical movement, his mind is not at rest, and as his 'Eyes stare out unseeing' (ibid.), we know that he cannot succumb to nothingness. Therefore, although the protagonist appears tranquil he is, like the majority of Beckett's characters, not at peace; and yet the narrative conveys a sense of acceptance, suggesting that this man is 'content' to await death: short of suicide there is of course no alternative. Although his mind declines to be calm, the sound patterns, evident in the text, restore the sense of tranquillity, through the soothing rhythm of the words. However, this tranquillity is in fact the desired state rather than the actuality in the text, as Beckett's words deny the possibility of stillness even though the word 'still' is mentioned 24 times.

At first sight everything appears quite still; however, on 'close inspection not still at all but trembling all over' (Beckett 1999d: 19). We see that the protagonist is indeed aged, and is perhaps suffering from the degenerative effects of Parkinson's disease, which Beckett's mother also endured. Beckett again captures the tragedy of the human condition, as we recognize that *Still*, is 'not still at all' (Beckett 1999d: 20), but is instead an illustration of the tragedy of existence which stresses the inescapability of our own solitude. And so he sits, staring out of the window at some one thing, such as a tree or a bush, which similar to him, is alone; or at nothing but the failing light. The slowness of his movements are almost imperceptible, and as he endeavours to move his arm towards his head, 'it hesitates and hangs half open trembling in mid air' (Beckett 1999d: 21), before, 'All quite still again then head in hand' (ibid.). Everything around him appears calm and externally he too seems at rest, but his trembling is perhaps the physical manifestation of his mind which cannot be subdued. The language, which is so compelling, describes the torment and the impossibility of being still, while simultaneously conveying the silence which dominates his existence. And as the text concludes we question whether this is the closest we will ever get to silence.

However, Beckett's following texts entitled 'Sounds' and 'Still 3' (published in *Essays In Criticism* 1978), further probe the issues raised in the initial text. The texts may be viewed as a trilogy and should perhaps be read in this context, although they can of course, be appreciated as individual works. The closing sentence of *Still* anticipates the theme of the following text 'Sounds', which illustrates the protagonist listening for sounds that ironically he hopes not to hear: 'Sounds' is therefore, paradoxically, about silence. The protagonist in 'Sounds' desires soundlessness, because by eradicating sound he can believe that he has effectively been 'dreamt away' (Beckett 1978: 155). The desire to be gone, therefore, again manifests itself in this text. The concept of stillness is again explored here, as the opening lines describe a night in which nothing appears to move and where sounds are few. Everything appears to be in decline, as even the nightbirds no longer pass by. The opening of 'Sounds' anticipates the general tone of the text, and we recognize that this work conveys the possibility that it is 'almost' devoid of life. However, similar to the fact that total stillness cannot be attained in *Still*, the total absence of sound cannot be achieved here, due to the fact that the protagonist still lives. It is for this reason that he longs to be 'dreamt away' to a place where sounds are no longer heard. As Pilling says, by abolishing sound the protagonist 'will be able to convince himself that he has effectively ceased to exist' (1978: 151).

It is interesting how he leaves the chair and ventures up to the tree, where he switches off his light and embraces it with his 'head against the bark as if a human' (Beckett 1978: 155). His actions illustrate his isolation, as he has no other to embrace; but primarily they convey his overwhelming need to embrace the silence, before he returns to his chair and remains 'quite still as before' (ibid.). However, despite the stillness of the night it is impossible for him to achieve inner peace, as outwardly he may appear at rest but inwardly he is in turmoil. His mind is unable to be still and silence can therefore not be attained while he continues to think about sounds. The act of listening forces the mind to function, thereby denying the possibility of mental silence even though the environment in which he exists is practically devoid of sound. Beckett denies the possibility of a complete silence or stillness, as the inability to achieve mental quietude is coupled with the incapability of achieving physical silence. It is possible that Beckett longed to be 'dreamt away where no such thing no more than ghosts make nothing to listen for no such thing as a sound' (Beckett 1978: 156): this final sentence encapsulates the silence which dominates 'Sounds' and is perhaps the closest Beckett comes to capturing silence.

'Still 3' returns again to the protagonist 'Back in the chair at the window before the window head in hand as shown dead still listening again in vain' (ibid.). Pilling states:

> The very brief 'Still 3' returns us to the whicker-chair of *Still* and shows Beckett following the premises of *Still* and 'Sounds' through to their

conclusions. All activity has ceased, all inquiry has been abandoned, all categories have been destroyed. (1978: 152)

At first the mind appears more at peace as 'dim questions fade' (Beckett
1978: 156) and the protagonist is no longer aware if it is night or day: he
appears to have attained the darkness he craved in *Still*, as it is 'always the
same dark now' (ibid.). However, the second half of this brief text illustrates
that his mind is just as disturbed as it is in the previous text, and again we
recognize how Beckett establishes an image, which appears positive, and
then destroys it through a language that refuses to be still. The inability to
prevent thought denies the possibility of the mind becoming tranquil, and
hence the 'stillness' which is evident in *Still* and 'Sounds' no longer exists in
this final text: as Beckett illustrates the impossibility of achieving a stillness,
either physically, mentally or artistically, which is not momentary. The dead
faces, which the protagonist imagines, are not comforting, as these ghosts of
the mind prevent peace. He no longer ventures out of the chair, appearing
static in his position before the window. The physical trembling that is evident
in *Still* appears to have ceased, as now he contends with a trembling of the
mind. He is a still life, existing without moving in a 'soundless place' (Beckett
1978: 157), where silence fails to provide relief because the mind declines to
be calm. As Mary Bryden affirms:

> The aspiration towards a profundity of silence is a recurrent one in Beckett's
> oeuvre, although its realisation can only be partial. The most that can be
> achieved is the kind of lingering and silent stillness which pervades Beckett's
> late prose writing in particular. (1998b: 175)

It is perhaps an impossibility to encapsulate real silence through the use of
words, and yet we acknowledge that Beckett's creative process captures the
evanescence of life and language, as his desire to escape the burden of language produces texts that ultimately chart the process towards absence. As
everything appears to fade, Beckett's artistic contraction encapsulates the
experience of existence, and the 'decay', which manifests itself through theme
and form, ensures that Beckett's writing has undoubtedly left a 'stain upon the
silence' (Bair 1978: 681).[7]

Conclusion

to be an artist is to fail, as no other dare fail
Proust and Three Dialogues with Georges Duthuit

As this study draws to a 'conclusion' it becomes clear that it resembles one of Beckett's characters, as it gravitates towards an ending and yet finds it difficult to finish. How does one conclude about works which have (themselves) no end point? The difficulty undoubtedly stems from the fact that Beckett's work cannot be easily summed up, or a label placed upon it stating this is 'how it is'.

This study has investigated Beckett's representations of the body and mind, his views on existence, including life and death, the implications of 'that double-headed monster of damnation and salvation – Time' (Beckett 1965: 11), and how everything is pre-disposed to failure because all things are subject to deterioration. We have seen how Beckett illustrates life as a tragic condition, a condition that cannot be alleviated until it is eradicated, and even then we are not assured that we will not be subject to an even more tragic state. The fact that we are born 'astride of a grave' (Beckett 1990: 83) is perhaps to be welcomed, as we take comfort in the knowledge that our suffering will be 'brief' in the context of time and space.

There is no doubt that Beckett had many philosophical influences which found their way into his work (Geulincx, Descartes, Schopenhauer and Heidegger, to name but a few),[1] and it is true that the work is an illustration of how it is to be alive. However, the work is more than just a representation of the harshness of existence; it is more than an illustration of the deleterious influence of time; it is more than a portrayal of man's inhumanity to man; and it is more than just a depiction of stoicism. Beckett's work is, of course, a combination of all these things, and more, which formulate his 'philosophical message', but it goes beyond a fundamental study of the nature of existence, as the aesthetic beauty of the work brings us back to Beckett as artist. In his conversation with Georges Duthuit, on the subject of Bram Van Velde, Beckett states:

> I know that all that is required now, in order to bring even this horrible matter to an acceptable conclusion, is to make of this submission, this admission,

this fidelity to failure, a new occasion, a new term of relation, and of the act
which, unable to act, obliged to act, he makes, an expressive act, even if only
of itself, of its impossibility, of its obligation. (Beckett 1965: 125)

The obligation to express, coupled with the impossibility of successful artistic expression, dominated Beckett's view of his own work, and he
acknowledged that language was subject to failure. As has been illustrated,
Beckett endeavoured to find the form that would accommodate the chaos
of existence and language simultaneously: a form that would, in essence,
have no form. Hence, the structure and style of the work became as fundamental as the message it conveyed, as Beckett endeavoured to break conventional form in an attempt to capture the shapelessness of being. The
form was therefore as fundamental as the theme, as the style of the work
encompassed its thematics. Without the artistic innovation the 'philosophical' message would perhaps become redundant. Jacques Derrida believes
that it is fundamentally more important to consider the style of Beckett's
work as opposed to the thematics. In his essay, 'This Strange Institution
Called Literature', he says:

> The composition, the rhetoric, the construction and the rhythm of his works,
> even the ones that seem the most 'decomposed,' that's what 'remains' finally
> the most 'interesting,' that's the work, that's the signature, this remainder
> which remains when the thematics is exhausted (Attridge (1990: 61) quoted
> here from Abbott (1996: 62))

Beckett's creative process is evidently complex; as he dispensed with everything he deemed to be superfluous, the works became intrinsically crafted,
each endeavouring to convey 'lessness' and each a triumph in artistic creation. As Beckett dispensed with conventional plots and characterization, he
created new genres and original dramatic experiences. His use of neologisms,
and periodic abandonment of punctuation, takes language to its extremes,
to the point where it becomes, to use Shimon Levy's term, self-referential,
commenting on itself and its own inadequacies. Beckett crosses the boundaries of conventional literature and drama in terms of style and form.
Therefore it is possible that Beckett was stylistically more innovative than
thematically, as we acknowledge that throughout his work the theme generally remains the same, while the form continually evolves. Of course, one
may argue that the world, and man's condition in it, is immutable, thereby
illustrating the reasons for Beckett's thematics remaining unaltered. Hence,
we acknowledge the paradoxical nature of the writing, as we recognize a
style that was continually evolving in its pursuit to illustrate a thematic that
remained unchanged.

Beckett's theme and form have each been explored throughout the course of this study, and the objective has not been to decide which is fundamentally more important. The principal aim has been to investigate the representations of decay found throughout the works, and it is here that Beckett's theme and form become equated, as both are dominated by the undeniable presence of 'decay'. As the Unnamable says:

> the words continue, the wrong words, until the order arrives, to stop every-thing or to continue everything, no, superfluous, everything will continue automatically, until the order arrives, to stop everything. Perhaps they are somewhere there, the words that count, in what has just been said, the words it behoved to say, they need not be more than a few. (Beckett 1994: 373)

This appears to be Beckett's comment on his own creative process, illustrating that he was very much aware of his objective to discard everything, which he deemed unnecessary, and recognizing that he would write towards 'lessness'. The works are essentially gravitating towards failure, increasingly becoming representations of the human consciousness endeavouring to depict the diffi-culty of existence through ever-decreasing words, resulting in an artistic con-traction and straining towards evanescence and extinction.

Beckett wrote because he had the imperative to create, but he recognized the futility of language and acknowledged that 'to be an artist is to fail, as no other dare fail' (Beckett 1965: 125). Therefore, he made 'failure' his world, presenting characters that are far from perfection, in worlds that are sterile and hopeless. He taught us to 'abandon hope' and accept the impossibility of improvement and then endeavour to pass the time while we await death. Beckett illustrates this failure of life through words which are themselves failing, as they struggle to convey meaning while attempting to return to the 'nothingness' from which they came. We recognize that despite the 'impossibility' of successful artistic expression, and even though they are pre-disposed to failure, Beckett's words, similar to the characters, go on; and so we witness the spirit of stoicism located in the words themselves, as they continue to try and fail better.

Beckett criticism is often concerned with labelling Beckett. Hence, terms such as artist and philosopher, modernist and postmodernist are used in order to pro-vide a clear definition of what Beckett is, or what period his writing belongs to. Cronin's biography labels Beckett 'The Last Modernist',[2] and Lodge states that he 'has a strong claim to be considered the first postmodernist writer' (1977: 221). However, Beckett's writing appears to transcend definition. Therefore, perhaps we should not become obsessed with placing a label on him because, as Beckett warns, 'The danger is in the neatness of identifications' (1983: 19). Instead we should appreciate that Beckett's writing conveys 'how it is' through new forms, and illustrates, through language, the 'philosophy' of decay.

Notes

Introduction

[1] Driver explains that he reconstructed Beckett's remarks from notes he made following their conversation.

Chapter 1

[1] See, for example, Alvarez (1992: 97), Ackerley and Gontarski (2006: 174).
[2] *Molloy, Malone Dies, The Unnamable*. Written in French between May 1947 and January 1950. Although, as Ackerley and Gontarski (2006: 586) point out, Beckett resisted the term 'trilogy' in relation to these three texts.
[3] René Descartes' phrase 'I think therefore I am' would be replaced in Beckett's world with 'I suffer therefore I am'.
[4] See Knowlson (1997: 438–439, 464, 511, 530–531, 533, 535, 541).
[5] For the classic statement of the oral phase sub-divisions see Abraham (1988: 450–453).

Chapter 2

[1] The Bible suggests that the average life expectancy is 70 years: 'The days of our years are threescore years and ten' (Ps. 90.10). Extracts from the Authorized Version of the Bible (The King James Bible).
[2] In his essay on Proust Beckett suggests that the individual is a succession of individuals and that we have no fixed identity. See Beckett (1965: 19).
[3] Driver explains that he reconstructed Beckett's remarks from notes he made following their conversation.
[4] See Knowlson (1997: 616).
[5] It has been suggested that the Twelve are in fact (megalithic?) stones. See Ackerley and Gontarski (2006: 270).
[6] Bishop Berkeley's famous phrase *'esse est percipi'* ('To be is to be perceived'), which Beckett made the subject of *Film* written in 1963. See Beckett (1990: 321–334). Knowlson details Beckett's trip to New York in 1964 to film *Film*, and

explains how it is about the perceived and the perceiver. See Knowlson (1997: 520–525).

7   See (Mk 15.22).

Chapter 3

1   See Knowlson (1997: 649–651).
2   Beckett implements Democritus' idiom in *Malone Dies*. See Beckett (1994: 193). The idea that everything gravitates towards 'Nothingness' is explored throughout Beckett's work.
3   Beckett further explores the idea of silence in his texts *Still*, 'Sounds' and 'Still 3'.
4   See Beckett (1999c: 54).

Chapter 4

1   See Knowlson (1997: 616).
2   'For to end yet again' is the first story in the British and French editions but the last narrative in the American edition. For further information see Ackerley and Gontarski (2006: 204).
3   Ackerley and Gontarski state that the French text ('*Se voir*') 'is sometimes cited by its opening words as '*Endroit clos*', translated variably as 'Closed place' or 'Closed space'. SB used both, but finally preferred 'place,' as in the Grove Press version. In *For to End Yet Again and Other Fizzles* (1976), John Calder cited 'Closed place' in the list of contents, but 'Closed space' within the text. Ackerley and Gontarski (2006: 99).

Chapter 5

1   See Beckett (1965: 32–34).
2   Following his discussions with Beckett about *Company*, Knowlson says, 'it was clear throughout our discussions, not only that real-life incidents had been shaped and transformed to fit the fiction but that the scepticism that, as a young man, he had brought to his criticism of the role of memory in Proust (involuntary as well as voluntary) had been reinforced by the distance that separated him from his own past. Memory emerges here as very much like invention' (1997: 652–653).

Chapter 6

1   Diamond develops this theory further in her essay 'Feminist readings of Beckett'. See Oppenheim (2004: 53–59).

² Knowlson states that 'It all' was the play's alternative title. See Knowlson and Pilling (1979: 220).

Chapter 7

¹ See Knowlson (1997: 538–539).
² For a comprehensive study of schizophrenia and other mental disorders see R. D. Laing, *The Divided Self: An Existential Study in Sanity and Madness* (London: Penguin Books, 1990).
³ See Beckett (1990: 365–367).
⁴ R. D. Laing states that, 'Despite his longing to be loved for his "real self" the schizophrenic is terrified of love' (1990: 163).
⁵ Beckett says, in his essay on Proust, 'We cannot know and we cannot be known' (1965: 66); suggesting, therefore, that universal identity is questionable. No one can ever fully know anyone if we are all predisposed to change.
⁶ Caravaggio's famous painting of the 'Beheading of St John the Baptist' provided Beckett with the inspiration to write *Not I*. Knowlson provides further details of the genesis of this drama. See (1997: 588–590).
⁷ Wilfred Ruprecht Bion (1897–1979) treated Beckett at the Tavistock Clinic from 1934–1935. At this time Beckett was suffering immensely with night terrors and palpitations. See Ackerley and Gontarski (2006: 59–61) also Knowlson (1997: 175–182).
⁸ Beckett himself claimed to have memories of the womb. See Knowlson (1997: 2).
⁹ Arnold Geulincx's axiom is located in *Murphy* Beckett (1993a: 101). Knowlson states that Beckett referred scholars to Geulincx's statement about worth and will as being one of the keys to an understanding of *Murphy*. See (1997: 218–219). Also, Ackerley (1998: 148–149).
¹⁰ Endon's name also encompasses the Beckett character's desire for an end which is counteracted with his need to go on – 'end on' – and also denotes the paradox of 'ending on' or 'Dying on', as it is described in *A Piece of Monologue* (Beckett 1990: 426).
¹¹ See Beckett (1976: 98–109).
¹² See Beckett (1976: 169–196).
¹³ See Beckett (1976: 163–167).

Chapter 8

¹ Beckett used these words in a letter to Alan Schneider, dated 19 November 1963, after learning about the death of Schneider's father. And in a conversation with Patrick Bowles on 10 November 1955, Beckett acknowledged the importance of spirit. See Knowlson (2006:110).
² Knowlson pointed out in his discussion entitled 'Albrecht Dürer seen through Samuel Beckett's eyes' (which formed part of the Beckett and the visual arts

round table discussion held on 9 April 2006 at the National Gallery of Ireland)
that Beckett greatly admired the work of Albrecht Dürer, and, as a child, had a
reproduction of the *Praying Hands* in his bedroom at Cooldrinagh. He also commented on how Beckett took many notes on Dürer's life and work and explored
Beckett's reaction to many of Dürer's paintings. This discussion, along with the
other talks from this event, has been published in *Samuel Beckett: A Passion for
Paintings*. See Croke (2006: 86–88). This book is invaluable to anyone interested
in Beckett's relationship with art.

3 Beckett told the cameraman, Jim Lewis, that the cloth alluded to the veil
Veronica used. See Knowlson (1997: 682).

4 Pilling's critique of the *Texts for Nothing* is invaluable to anyone interested in this
text. See Knowlson and Pilling (1979: 41–59.) Also Ackerley and Gontarski
(2006: 561–568).

5 See Beckett (1999f: 13).

Chapter 9

1 Beckett used these words in a conversation with Knowlson while attempting to
define his debt to Joyce. See Knowlson (1997: 352).

2 Calder says 'As with music, Beckett yields up his treasures little by little, and
familiarity enhances the understanding and the appreciation' (2001: 89).

Chapter 10

1 Beckett speaks of the music or the silence that underlies All. See Beckett
(1983: 172).

2 Ackerley and Gontarski say that 'The meditation on love lost is as poignant and
erotic as the lyric scene in the punt that haunts the aged Krapp' (2006: 651).

3 For a comprehensive study of Beckett's relationship with music see Bryden
(1998a).

4 Esslin suggests in his essay, 'Telling It How It Is: Beckett and the Mass Media' that
Fox alludes to Vox, meaning 'the voice'. See Smith (1991: 212).

5 Fritz Mauthner (1849–1923) wrote *Contributions toward a Critique of Language*.
'By subsuming all knowledge under language, then denying its efficacy, Mauthner illustrates how language may interdict itself' (Ackerley and Gontarski
2006: 359).

6 Czech playwright who was imprisoned in 1979 for 4 years for supporting human
rights and his part in the 'Velvet Revolution'. See Ackerley and Gontarski
(2006: 248).

7 Alberto Giacometti (1901–1966) a Swiss sculptor, who lived in Paris and, at times,
socialized with Beckett. See Knowlson (1997: 370–371). He sculpted the tree for
the 1961 Odéon Théâtre production of *En attendant Godot*. Beckett undoubtedly
found the art of sculpting interesting, as it involved the gradual chipping away of
material, gravitating towards 'lessness'.

Chapter 11

1 For a comprehensive study of Beckett's 'literature of the unword' see Locatelli (1990).
2 See Beckett (1999i: 37).
3 Beckett explores 'breathing' in 'Sounds'. See Beckett (1978: 156).
4 See Beckett (1999i: 28–29).
5 See Beckett (1965: 125).
6 See Beckett (1999a: 39).

Chapter 12

1 'Shades' was Beckett's title for a television program on BBC2, *The Lively Arts* (17 April 1977), consisting of *Not I*, *Ghost Trio* and . . . *but the clouds*. . . . See Ackerley and Gontarski (2006: 521).
2 See, for example, Knowlson (1997: 464, 548–549).
3 See Knowlson (1997: 535–536).
4 Paul Davies gives an interesting critique of this text, suggesting how it relates to the other Rotunda texts. See Davies (1994: 153–158).
5 See Beckett (1999i: 76).
6 It has been suggested that the setting of *Still*, 'Sounds' and 'Still 3' is the summerhouse, which is also mentioned in *Company* – Beckett (1996a: 53) – and 'As the Story Was Told' (Beckett 1999g: 7). See Ackerley and Gontarski (2006: 547–548).
7 Beckett said, 'I could not have gone through the awful wretched mess of life without having left a stain upon the silence'.

Conclusion

1 For more on Beckett and the philosophers see Fletcher (1967: 121–137).
2 Hugh Kenner famously dubbed Beckett 'the Last Modernist'. See Birkett and Ince (2000: 23).

Bibliography

Works by Samuel Beckett

(1999h), *All Strange Away*. Beckett Short No. 3 London: John Calder.

(1999g), 'As the Story Was Told' in *As The Story Was Told*. Beckett Short No. 9 London: John Calder.

(1999d), 'Closed place' in *For to End Yet Again*. Beckett Short No. 6 London: John Calder.

(1996a), *Company*. London: John Calder.

(1983), *Disjecta: Miscellaneous Writings and a Dramatic Fragment*. ed. with a foreword by Ruby Cohn. London: John Calder.

(1993b), *Dream of Fair to Middling Women*. London; Paris: Calder Publications.

(1999i), *Enough* in *Six Residua*. Beckett Short No. 5 London: John Calder.

(1999c), *First Love*. Beckett Short No. 8 London: John Calder.

(1999d), 'For to end yet again' in *For to End Yet Again*. Beckett Short No. 6 London: John Calder.

(1996b), *How It Is*. London: John Calder.

(1999d), 'I gave up before birth' in *For to End Yet Again*. Beckett Short No. 6 London: John Calder.

(1982), *Ill Seen Ill Said*. London: John Calder.

(1999i), *Imagination Dead Imagine* in *Six Residua*. Beckett Short No. 5 London: John Calder.

(1999i), *Lessness* in *Six Residua*. Beckett Short No. 5 London: John Calder.

(1994), *Molloy, Malone Dies, The Unnamable*. London; Montreuil; New York: Calder Publications.

(1993a), *Murphy*. Montreuil; London: Calder Publications.

(1999i), *Ping* in *Six Residua*. Beckett Short No. 5 London: John Calder.

(1965), *Proust and Three Dialogues with Georges Duthuit*. London: John Calder.

(1978), 'Sounds'. *Essays in Criticism* Vol. 28, No. 2, 155–156.

(1999d), *Still* in *For to End Yet Again*. Beckett Short No. 6 London: John Calder.

(1978), 'Still 3' in *Essays in Criticism* Vol. 28, No. 2, 156–157.

(1999j), *Tailpiece* in *Selected Poems*. Beckett Short No. 12 London: John Calder.

(1999f), *Texts for Nothing*. Beckett Short No. 1 London: John Calder.

(1990), *The Complete Dramatic Works*. London: Faber and Faber.

(1999e), *The End* in *Three Novellas*. Beckett Short No. 10 London: John Calder.

(1999e), 'The Expelled' in *Three Novellas*. Beckett Short No. 10 London: John Calder.

(1999i), *The Lost Ones* in *Six Residua*. Beckett Short No. 5 London: John Calder.

(1999b), *The Old Tune*. Beckett Short No. 7 London: John Calder
(1976), *Watt*. London: John Calder.
(1999a), *Worstward Ho*. Beckett Short No. 4 London: John Calder.

Secondary Sources

Abbott, H. P. (1996), *Beckett Writing Beckett: The Author in the Autograph*. Ithaca, NY;
    London: Cornell University Press.
Abraham, K. (1988), *Selected Papers on Psychoanalysis*. (new edn). London: Karnac.
Acheson, J. and Arthur, K. (eds), (1987), *Beckett's Later Fiction and Drama: Texts for
    Company*. Basingstoke: Macmillan.
Ackerley, C. J. (1998), *Demented Particulars: The Annotated Murphy*. Florida: Journal
    of Beckett Studies Books.
Ackerley, C. J. and Gontarski, S. E. (eds), (2006), *The Faber Companion to Samuel
    Beckett: A Reader's Guide to His Works, Life, and Thought*. London: Faber and
    Faber.
Alvarez, A. (1992), *Beckett*. (second edn) edited by Frank Kermode. London:
    Fontana Press.
Asmus, W. D. (1977), 'Rehearsal notes for the German premier of Beckett's *That
    Time* and *Footfalls* at the Schiller-Theatre Werkstatt, Berlin (directed by Beckett)'
    in *Journal of Beckett Studies* 2, 82–95.
Attridge, D. (ed.), (1990), *Acts of Literature*. New York: Routledge.
Bair, D. (1978), *Samuel Beckett: A Biography*. New York: Harcourt Brace Jovanovich.
Birkett, J. and Ince, K. (eds), (2000), *Samuel Beckett*. London; New York: Longman.
Brater, E. (1987), *Beyond Minimalism: Beckett's Late Style in the Theatre*. New York:
    Oxford University Press.
—(1977), 'Fragment and Beckett's form in *That time* and *Footfalls*' in *Journal of
    Beckett Studies* 2, 70–81.
—(1989), *Why Beckett*. London: Thames and Hudson.
Brater, E. (ed.), (1986), *Beckett at 80: Beckett in Context*. New York: Oxford University
    Press.
Brienza, S. (1982), '*Imagination dead imagine*: the microcosm of the mind' in *Journal
    of Beckett Studies* 8, 59–74.
Bryden, M. (1998b), *Samuel Beckett and the Idea of God*. Basingstoke: Macmillan
    Press.
—(1993), *Women in Samuel Beckett's Prose and Drama: Her Own Other*. Lanham, MD:
    Barnes and Noble; Basingstoke: Macmillan.
Bryden, M. (ed.), (1998a), *Samuel Beckett and Music*. Oxford: Clarendon Press.
Calder, J. (2001), *The Philosophy of Samuel Beckett*. London: Calder Publications; New
    Jersey: Riverrun Press.
Cardy, M. and Connon, D. (eds), (2000), *Aspects of Twentieth-century Theatre in French*.
    Oxford: PeterLang.
Cormier, R. and Pallister, J. L. (1979), *Waiting for Death: The Philosophical Significance
    of Beckett's 'En attendant Godot'*. Alabama: The University of Alabama Press.
Croke, F. (ed.), (2006), *Samuel Beckett: A Passion for Paintings*. Dublin: National
    Gallery of Ireland.

Cronin, A. (1997), *Samuel Beckett: The Last Modernist.* London: Flamingo.

Davies, P. (1994), *The Ideal Real: Beckett's Fiction and Imagination.* London; Toronto: Associated University Press.

Davis, R. J. and Butler, L. St J. (eds), (1988), *'Make Sense Who May': Essays on Samuel Beckett's Later Works.* Gerrards Cross: Colin Smythe.

Driver, T. F. (1961), 'Beckett by the Madeleine', *Columbia University Forum,* IV, 21–25.

Esslin, M. (ed.), (1965), *Samuel Beckett: A Collection of Critical Essays.* Englewood Cliffs, NJ: Prentice-Hall.

Feder, L. (1980), *Madness in Literature.* New Jersey: Princeton University Press.

Felstein, I. (1973), *Living to be a Hundred: A Study of Old Age.* Newton Abbot: David and Charles.

Finney, B. (1972), *Since 'How It Is': A Study of Samuel Beckett's Later Fiction.* London: Covent Garden Press.

Fletcher, J. (2003), *About Beckett: The Playwright and the Work.* London: Faber and Faber.

—(2000), *Samuel Beckett: Waiting for Godot, Endgame, Krapp's Last Tape.* London: Faber.

—(1967), *Samuel Beckett's Art.* London: Chatto & Windus.

Foucault, M. (1989), *Madness and Civilization: A History of Insanity in the Age of Reason.* Translated from the French by Richard Howard. London: Tavistock/ Routledge.

Graver, L. and Federman, R. (eds), (1979), *Samuel Beckett: The Critical Heritage.* London, Henley and Boston: Routledge and Kegan Paul.

Harmon, Maurice (ed.), (1998), *No Author Better Served: The Correspondence of Samuel Beckett and Alan Schneider.* Cambridge: Harvard University Press.

Hayman, Ronald (1970), *Samuel Beckett: Contemporary Playwrights.* London: Heinemann.

Hesla, D. H. (1971), *The Shape of Chaos: An Interpretation of the Art of Samuel Beckett.* Minneapolis: University of Minnesota Press; London: Oxford University Press.

Ionesco, E. (1962), *Rhinoceros. The Chairs. The Lesson.* London: Penguin Books.

Jung, C. G. (1998), *The Essential Jung: Selected Writings.* Introduced by Anthony Storr. London: Fontana Press.

Kenner, H. (1973), *A Reader's Guide to Samuel Beckett.* London: Thames and Hudson.

Knowlson, J. (1997), *Damned To Fame: The Life of Samuel Beckett.* London: Bloomsbury.

Knowlson, J. and Knowlson, E. (2006), *Beckett Remembering Remembering Beckett: Uncollected Interviews with Samuel Beckett and Memories of Those Who Knew Him.* London: Bloomsbury.

Knowlson, J. and Pilling, J. (1979), *Frescoes of the Skull: The Later Prose and Drama of Samuel Beckett.* London: John Calder.

Laing, R. D. (1990), *The Divided Self: An Existential Study in Sanity and Madness.* London: Penguin Books.

Levy, E. P. (1980), *Beckett and the Voice of Species: A Study of the Prose Fiction.* Dublin: Gill and Macmillan.

Levy, S. (1990), *Samuel Beckett's Self-referential Drama: The Three 'I's.* London: The Macmillan Press.

Locatelli, C. (1990), *Unwording the World: Samuel Beckett's Prose Works after the Nobel Prize*. Philadelphia: University of Pennsylvania Press.

Lodge, D. (1977), *The Modes of Modern Writing: Metaphor, Metonymy, and the Typology of Modern Literature*. London: Edward Arnold.

Lyons, C. R. (1983), *Samuel Beckett*. London: Macmillan.

MacGowran, J. (1973), 'MacGowran on Beckett', *Theatre Quarterly* 11, 15–22.

McMullan, A. (1993), *Theatre on Trial: Samuel Beckett's Later Drama*. New York; London: Routledge.

Mercier, V. (1977), *Beckett/Beckett*. Oxford: Oxford University Press.

Murray, C. (ed.), (2006), *Samuel Beckett: 100 Years*. Dublin: New Island.

Oppenheim, L. (1994), *Directing Beckett*. Ann Arbor: University of Michigan Press.

Oppenheim, L. (ed.), (2004), *Palgrave Advances in Samuel Beckett Studies*. Basingstoke: Palgrave Macmillan.

—(1999), *Samuel Beckett and the Arts: Music, Visual Arts, and Non-print Media*. New York, London: Garland Publishing, Inc.

Pattie, D. (2000), *The Complete Critical Guide to Samuel Beckett*. London: Routledge.

Pilling, J. (1997), *Beckett before Godot*. Cambridge: Cambridge University Press.

—(1976), *Samuel Beckett*. London: Routledge and Kegan Paul.

—(1978), 'The significance of Beckett's *Still*' in *Essays in Criticism* Vol. 28., No. 2, 143–153.

Pilling, J. (ed.), (1994), *The Cambridge Companion to Beckett*. Cambridge: Cambridge University Press.

Pilling, J. and Bryden, M. (eds), (1992), *'The Ideal Core of the Onion': Reading Beckett Archives*. Reading: Beckett International Foundation.

Pountney, R. (1988), *Theatre of Shadows: Samuel Beckett's Drama 1956–1976: From 'All That Fall' to 'Footfalls' with Commentaries on the Latest Plays*. Gerrards Cross: Colin Smythe.

Richetti, J. (ed.), (1994), *The Columbia History of the British Novel*. New York; Chichester: Columbia University Press.

Ricks, C. (1993), *Beckett's Dying Words*. Oxford: Oxford University Press.

Robinson, M. (1969), *The Long Sonata of the Dead: A study of Samuel Beckett*. London: Rupert Hart-Davis.

Shakespeare, W. (1967), *Macbeth*. Edited by G. K. Hunter. London: Penguin Books.

Smith, J. H. (ed.), (1991), *The World Of Samuel Beckett*. Baltimore; London: The Johns Hopkins University Press.

The Authorised Version of the Bible (King James Bible). Cambridge: Cambridge University Press.

Woodworth, R. (1963), *Contemporary Schools of Psychology*. London: Methuen.

Worth, K. (ed.), (1975), *Beckett the Shape Changer: A Symposium*. London; Boston: Routledge and Kegan Paul.

Index

Printed in Great Britain
by Amazon.co.uk, Ltd.,
Marston Gate.